Intermediate Chinese

Edited by
Erin Quirk and Tanying Dong

:: LIVING LANGUAGE®

Content in this program has been modified and enhanced from *Starting Out in Chinese* and *Complete Course Chinese: The Basics*, both published in 2008.

Published in the United States by Living Language, an imprint of Random House, Inc.

www.livinglanguage.com

Editor: Erin Quirk
Production Editor: Ciara Robinson
Production Manager: Tom Marshall
Interior Design: Sophie Chin
Illustrations: Sophie Chin

First Edition

Library of Congress Cataloging-in-Publication Data

Intermediate Chinese / edited by Erin Quirk and Tanying Dong. — 1st ed.
p. cm.
ISBN 978-0-307-97166-1
1. Chinese language—Textbooks for foreign speakers—English. 2. Chinese language—Grammar.
3. Chinese language—Spoken Chinese. I. Quirk, Erin. II. Dong, Tanying.
PL1129.E5I686 2011
495.1'82421—dc23
                    2011021871

This book is available at special discounts for bulk purchases for sales promotions or premiums. Special editions, including personalized covers, excerpts of existing books, and corporate imprints, can be created in large quantities for special needs. For more information, write to Special Markets/ Premium Sales, 1745 Broadway, MD 3-1, New York, New York 10019 or e-mail specialmarkets@ randomhouse.com.

PRINTED IN THE UNITED STATES OF AMERICA

10 9 8 7 6 5 4 3

Acknowledgments

Thanks to the Living Language team: Amanda D'Acierno, Christopher Warnasch, Suzanne McQuade, Laura Riggio, Erin Quirk, Amanda Munoz, Fabrizio LaRocca, Siobhan O'Hare, Sophie Chin, Sue Daulton, Alison Skrabek, Carolyn Roth, Ciara Robinson, and Tom Marshall.

How to Use This Course 9

UNIT 1: Talking about Yourself and Your Family 13

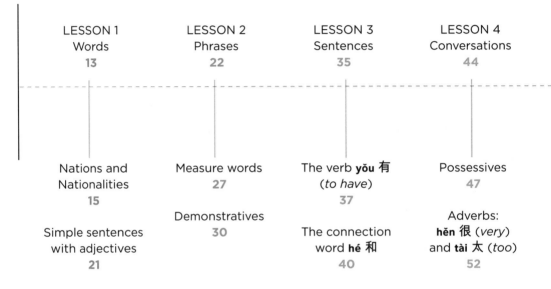

LESSON 1	LESSON 2	LESSON 3	LESSON 4
Words	Phrases	Sentences	Conversations
13	22	35	44

Nations and Nationalities
15

Simple sentences with adjectives
21

Measure words
27

Demonstratives
30

The verb **yǒu** 有 (*to have*)
37

The connection word **hé** 和
40

Possessives
47

Adverbs: **hěn** 很 (*very*) and **tài** 太 (*too*)
52

COURSE

UNIT 2: Everyday Life **70**

LESSON 5
Words
70

LESSON 6
Phrases
82

LESSON 7
Sentences
95

LESSON 8
Conversations
106

Days of the Week
72

Expressing months
and dates
75

Using Verbs
83

Měi 每 (*every/each*)
90

Xǐhuan/bù xǐhuan
喜欢/不喜欢
(*to like/not like*)
97

Zài 在 and **zhe** 着
100

Superlatives
with **zuì** 最
109

Question word
shénme (*what*)
114

OUTLINE

UNIT 3: Going Shopping **129**

LESSON 9
Words
129

LESSON 10
Phrases
139

LESSON 11
Sentences
152

LESSON 12
Conversations
163

Measure words
for clothing and
accessories
131

Colors
135

Negation with
méiyǒu 没有
141

Asking *how much*
and *how many*
145

This one and
that one
154

Money expressions
158

Numbers 21-1000
166

Quantity
expressions and
the number *two*
(**èr** 二 and **liǎng** 两)
169

UNIT 4: Doctors and Health **187**

LESSON 13
Words
187

LESSON 14
Phrases
197

LESSON 15
Sentences
209

LESSON 16
Conversations
219

Negation with **bù**
不 and **bùshì** 不是
before adjectives
and adverbs
189

Commands
192

Expressing a
completed action
with **le** 了
199

Asking *how long?*
204

Asking *how?*
211

Negating completed
actions: **méiyǒu** 没有
214

Asking *where?*
222

Asking questions
about completed
actions with **yǒu
méiyǒu** 有没有
226

OUTLINE

UNIT 5: On the Phone and Making Appointments 244

LESSON 17	LESSON 18	LESSON 19	LESSON 20
Words	Phrases	Sentences	Conversations
244	257	267	278

Telling time
246

More on time
expressions
259

More on telling time
270

Use of **guò** 过
283

Use of time
expressions
and **huì** 会
251

Use of **shéi** 谁
(who)
263

Shénme shíhou
什么时候 (when)
274

Lái 来 (to come)
and **qù** 去 (to go)
289

Pronunciation and Pīnyīn Guide 308
Grammar Summary 313
Glossary 339

How to Use This Course

Huānyíng! 欢迎! *Welcome!* Welcome to *Living Language Intermediate Chinese*!

Before we begin, let's take a quick look at what you'll see in this course.

CONTENT

Intermediate Chinese is a continuation of *Essential Chinese*. It will review, expand on, and add to the foundation that you received in *Essential Chinese*. In other words, this course contains:

• An in-depth review of important vocabulary and grammar from *Essential Chinese*.

• An expanded and more advanced look at some key vocabulary and grammar from *Essential Chinese*.

• An introduction to idiomatic language and more challenging Chinese grammar.

UNITS

There are five units in this course. Each unit has four lessons arranged in a "building block" structure: the first lesson will present essential *words*, the second will introduce longer *phrases*, the third will teach *sentences*, and the fourth will show how everything works together in everyday *conversations*.

At the beginning of each unit is an introduction highlighting what you'll learn in that unit. At the end of each unit you'll find the Unit Essentials, which reviews the key information from that unit, and a self-graded Unit Quiz, which tests what you've learned.

LESSONS

There are four lessons per unit for a total of 20 lessons in the course. Each lesson has the following components:

- **Introduction** outlining what you will cover in the lesson.

- **Word Builder 1** (first lesson of the unit) presenting key words and phrases.

- **Phrase Builder 1** (second lesson of the unit) introducing longer phrases and expressions.

- **Sentence Builder 1** (third lesson of the unit) teaching sentences.

- **Conversation 1** (fourth lesson of the unit) for a natural dialogue that brings together important vocabulary and grammar from the unit.

- **Word/Phrase/Sentence/Conversation Practice 1** practicing what you learned in Word Builder 1, Phrase Builder 1, Sentence Builder 1, or Conversation 1.

- **Grammar Builder 1** guiding you through important Chinese grammar that you need to know.

- **Work Out 1** for a comprehensive practice of what you saw in Grammar Builder 1.

- **Word Builder 2/Phrase Builder 2/Sentence Builder 2/Conversation 2** for more key words, phrases, or sentences, or a second dialogue.

- **Word/Phrase/Sentence/Conversation Practice 2** practicing what you learned in Word Builder 2, Phrase Builder 2, Sentence Builder 2, or Conversation 2.

- **Grammar Builder 2** for more information on Chinese grammar.

- **Work Out 2** for a comprehensive practice of what you saw in Grammar Builder 2.

- **Drive It Home** ingraining an important point of Chinese grammar for the long term.

- **Tip** or **Culture Note** for a helpful language tip or useful cultural information related to the lesson or unit.

- **How Did You Do?** outlining what you learned in the lesson.

- **Word Recall** reviewing important vocabulary and grammar from any of the previous lessons in *Intermediate* or *Essential Chinese*.

- **Take It Further** sections appear throughout the lessons, providing extra information about new vocabulary, expanding on certain grammar points, or introducing additional words and phrases.

UNIT ESSENTIALS

You will see the **Unit Essentials** at the end of every unit. Vocabulary Essentials present the English translations of key vocabulary that you've learned, so they give you a chance to test yourself on the most important words and phrases that you've learned. Grammar Essentials summarize the key grammar that you've learned and act as a "cheat sheet" that will remind you of the key structures you've learned. Character Essentials give you a chance to test your knowledge of Chinese characters by reading two dialogues in characters only.

UNIT QUIZ

After each Unit Essentials, you'll see a **Unit Quiz**. The quizzes are self-graded so it's easy for you to test your progress and see if you should go back and review.

PROGRESS BAR

You will see a **Progress Bar** on each page that has course material. It indicates your current position within the unit and lets you know how much progress you're making. Each line in the bar represents a Grammar Builder section.

AUDIO

Look for the symbol ▶ to help guide you through the audio as you're reading the book. It will tell you which track to listen to for each section that has audio. When you see the symbol, select the indicated track and start listening. If you don't see the symbol, then there isn't any audio for that section. You'll also see Ⓘ, which will tell you where that track ends.

You can listen to the audio on its own, when you're on the go, to brush up on your pronunciation or review what you've learned in the book.

PRONUNCIATION GUIDE, GRAMMAR SUMMARY, GLOSSARY

At the back of this book you will find a **Pronunciation and Pīnyīn Guide**, **Grammar Summary**, and **Glossary**. The Pronunciation and Pīnyīn Guide provides information on Chinese pronunciation and the pīnyīn transliteration system. The Grammar Summary contains an overview of key Chinese grammar, some of which is covered in *Essential* and *Intermediate Chinese,* and some of which you won't formally learn until *Advanced Chinese.* The Glossary (Chinese–English and English–Chinese) includes vocabulary that's covered throughout this course, as well as vocabulary introduced in *Essential* and *Advanced Chinese.*

FREE ONLINE TOOLS

Go to **www.livinglanguage.com/languagelab** to access your free online tools. The tools are organized around the units in this course, with audiovisual flashcards, and interactive games and quizzes for each unit. These tools will help you to review and practice the vocabulary and grammar that you've seen in the units, as well as provide some bonus words and phrases related to the unit's topic.

Unit 1: Talking about Yourself and Your Family

Tán zìjǐ hé jiārén

谈自己和家人

In Unit 1, you'll review and learn a lot of vocabulary that will help you to talk about your family and describe where you live in Chinese. We'll also cover some more basics of Chinese grammar.

Lesson 1: Words

In this lesson you'll learn:

☐ Key vocabulary related to people and the family.

☐ How to talk about nationalities.

☐ More family terms.

☐ How to form simple sentences with hěn 很.

Word Builder 1

▶ 1A Word Builder 1 (CD 4, Track 1)

jiā	家	*family, home*
bàba	爸爸	*father*
māma	妈妈	*mother*
érzi	儿子	*son*

nǚ'ér	女儿	*daughter*
gēge	哥哥	*older brother*
jiějie	姐姐	*older sister*
dìdi	弟弟	*younger brother*
mèimei	妹妹	*younger sister*
xiōngdìjiěmèi	兄弟姐妹	*sibling*
yéye	爷爷	*grandfather (paternal side)*
nǎinai	奶奶	*grandmother (paternal side)*
wàigōng	外公	*grandfather (maternal side)*
wàipó	外婆	*grandmother (maternal side)*
péngyou	朋友	*friend*
línjū	邻居	*neighbor*
nánrén	男人	*man*
nǚrén	女人	*woman*
nǚháiér, nǚhái	女孩儿, 女孩	*girl*
nánháiér, nánhái	男孩儿, 男孩	*boy*

⏸

✎ Word Practice 1

Fill in the blank with the missing part of the pīnyīn words. The Chinese characters are provided for additional help and practice.

1. ér _____

儿子

2. xiōngdì _____

兄弟姐妹

3. _____ gōng

外公

4. _____ nai

奶奶

5. péng _____

朋友

6. nǚ_____'ér

女孩儿

ANSWER KEY

1. zi 子 (*son*); 2. jiěmèi 姐妹 (*siblings*); 3. wài 外 (*maternal grandfather*); 4. nǎi 奶 (*paternal grandmother*); 5. you 友 (*friend*); 6. hái 孩 (*girl*)

Grammar Builder 1
NATIONS AND NATIONALITIES

Let's look at the Chinese names for countries.

▶ 1B Grammar Builder 1 (CD 4, Track 2)

Měiguó	美国	*America*
Zhōngguó	中国	*China*
Yīngguó	英国	*Britain*
Fǎguó	法国	*France*
Xībānyá	西班牙	*Spain*
Déguó	德国	*Germany*
Yìdàlì	意大利	*Italy*
Rìběn	日本	*Japan*
Àozhōu	澳洲	*Australia*

And here is some key vocabulary for talking about nationalities.

Nǎ guórén?	哪国人？	*What nationality?*
Měiguórén	美国人	*American*
Zhōngguórén	中国人	*Chinese*
Yīngguórén	英国人	*British*
Fǎguórén	法国人	*French*
Xībānyárén	西班牙人	*Spanish*
Déguórén	德国人	*German*
Yìdàlìrén	意大利人	*Italian*
Rìběnrén	日本人	*Japanese*
Àozhōurén	澳洲人	*Australian*
Běijīngrén	北京人	*Pekingese*
Shànghǎirén	上海人	*Shanghaiese*
Xiānggǎngrén	香港人	*Hongkongese*
Nánjīngrén	南京人	*Nanjingese*
Guǎngdōngrén	广东人	*Cantonese*

As you can probably guess, nationality is expressed in Chinese by adding rén 人 (*person*) after a country name, so that the combined form literally means a person born in a specific country. It's also very common in Chinese to add rén 人 after a city or other place name to indicate where a person is from.

Tā shì Zhōngguórén.
他是中国人。
He is Chinese.

Wǒmen shì Měiguórén.
我们是美国人。
We are American.

Tā shì Běijīngrén.

她是北京人。

She is from Beijing.

✎ Work Out 1

Translate the following sentences into English.

1. Wǒmen shì Měiguórén. 我们是美国人。 _____

   _____

2. Tāmen shì Fǎguórén. 他们是法国人。 _____

   _____

3. Tā shì Zhōngguórén. 她是中国人。 _____

   _____

4. Wǒ bú shì Rìběnrén. 我不是日本人。 _____

   _____

5. Tāmen shì Guǎngdōngrén. 他们是广东人。 _____

   _____

ANSWER KEY

1. *We are American.* 2. *They are French.* 3. *She is Chinese.* 4. *I am not Japanese.* 5. *They are Cantonese.*

Take It Further
TITLES OF ADDRESS

In Chinese, the common titles of address are: xiānsheng 先生, tàitai/fūren 太太/夫人 and xiǎojiě 小姐. For example, use xiānsheng 先生 to address Mr. Wang. Use xiǎojiě 小姐 to address Miss Wang. Finally, use tàitai 太太 or fūren 夫人to address Mrs. Wang. Note that tàitai 太太 is commonly used in Hong Kong and Taiwan. Fūren is commonly used in Mainland China and is more formal and respectful than tàitai 太太.

Also note that the placement of a person's last name before his or her title is the opposite of what is familiar to English speakers. For example, if you want to address Mr. Wang in Chinese, you need to say Wáng xiānsheng 王先生. Full names in Chinese are also placed in a different order than in the English tradition. In Chinese, the last name is put before the first name. In other words, if someone's first name is Yi and last name is Wang, then the correct order in Chinese would be Wang Yi.

There are also a few things to keep in mind when addressing family members in Chinese. For example, there are two ways to refer to or address your grandparents, depending on whether they are your mother's or father's parents. Your father's father must be addressed as yéye 爷爷, and your mother's father is wàigōng 外公. Since these words define separate genealogical relationships, they cannot be used interchangeably. Similarly, you probably noticed that there are different words for *brother* and *sister*, depending on age.

If you look closely at the word for *sibling* in Chinese (xiōngdìjiěmèi 兄弟姐妹), you'll see that it is composed of four syllables, which is written in Chinese with four different characters. They are: xiōng 兄 (*older brother*), dì 弟 (*younger brother*), jiě 姐 (*older sister*), and mèi 妹 (*younger sister*). So, xiōngdìjiěmèi 兄弟姐妹 is a descriptive word that actually includes all possible relationships between brothers and sisters.

Word Builder 2

▶ 1C Word Builder 2 (CD 4, Track 3)

bóbo	伯伯	uncle (father's older brother)
bómǔ	伯母	aunt (father's older brother's wife)
shūshu	叔叔	uncle (father's younger brother)
shěnshen	婶婶	aunt (father's younger brother's wife)
gūgu	姑姑	aunt (father's sister)
gūfu	姑夫	uncle (father's sister's husband)
jiùjiu	舅舅	uncle (mother's brother)
jiùmǔ/jiùmā	舅母/舅妈	aunt (mother's brother's wife)
yímǔ/yímā	姨母/姨妈	aunt (mother's sister)
yífu	姨夫	uncle (mother's sister's husband)
tánggē	堂哥	cousin (father's brother's son, older than you)
tángdì	堂弟	cousin (father's brother's son, younger than you)
tángjiě	堂姐	cousin (father's brother's daughter, older than you)
tángmèi	堂妹	cousin (father's brother's daughter, younger than you)
biǎogē	表哥	cousin (mother's sibling's or father's sister's son, older than you)
biǎodì	表弟	cousin (mother's sibling's or father's sister's son, younger than you)

| biǎojiě | 表姐 | cousin (mother's sibling's or father's sister's daughter, older than you) |
| biǎomèi | 表妹 | cousin (mother's sibling's or father's sister's daughter, younger than you) |

💡 Tip!

All of those family terms probably seem very complicated. After all, there are eight words for *cousin*! But there is an easy way to remember which one to use. In general, you will notice that words used in Chinese for addressing family members all have two syllables. Just remember to use the prefix táng 堂 when addressing cousins from your father's side and use the prefix biǎo 表 when addressing cousins from your mother's side. In all cases, the syllable that follows is dependent on the age and gender of the cousin you want to address. For example, if your father's brother's daughter, Nancy, is one year older than you, then you would use the suffix jiě 姐 and refer to her as your tángjiě 堂姐. If your mother's brother's son, David, is younger than you, then you would use the suffix dì 弟 and address him as biǎodì 表弟.

✏️ Word Practice 2

Translate the following English phrases into Chinese.

1. *Father's older brother* _____

2. *Mother's sister* _____

3. *Mother's brother* _____

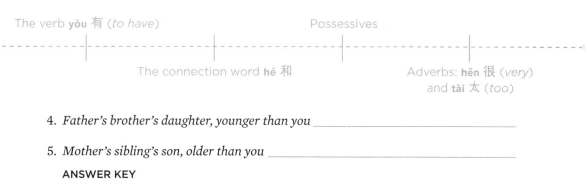
4. *Father's brother's daughter, younger than you* _____

5. *Mother's sibling's son, older than you* _____

ANSWER KEY
1. bóbo 伯伯; 2. yímǔ 姨母 or yímā 姨妈; 3. jiùjiu 舅舅; 4. tángmèi 堂妹; 5. biǎogē 表哥

Grammar Builder 2
SIMPLE SENTENCES WITH ADJECTIVES

▶ 1D Grammar Builder 2 (CD 4, Track 4)

In English, if you want to link a noun and an adjective, you use a form of *to be*: *The girl is short*, *The mountains are tall*, etc. In Chinese, though, normally shì 是 (*to be*) is not placed between a noun and an adjective describing that noun. Instead, the adverb hěn 很 (*very*) is used:

Tā hěn gāo.
他/她很高。
He/She is very tall.

Tāmen hěn cōngmíng.
他们很聪明。
They are very intelligent.

Nàge rén hěn qiángzhuàng.
那个人很强壮。
That person is very strong.

Zhège chéngshì hěn piàoliang.
这个城市很漂亮。
This city is very beautiful.

In colloquial Chinese, it's very common to add a degree adverb such as hěn 很 (*very*) or tǐng 挺 (*quite, very*) before the adjective. Keep in mind that hěn 很 is stronger than tǐng 挺, which adds little meaning to the sentence.

Ⅱ

✎ Work Out 2

Each of the following short sentences in Chinese tells you something about its subject, but not all of them are grammatically correct. Read each sentence, and determine whether it's correct or not. If it's incorrect, correct the error.

1. Biǎogē gāo. 表哥高。 _____

2. Yéye shì gāo. 爷爷是高。 _____

3. Tā shì dìdi. 他是弟弟。 _____

4. Shūshu shì lǎoshī. 叔叔是老师。 _____

5. Tángjiě shì xuésheng. 堂姐是学生。 _____

ANSWER KEY
1. incorrect (Biǎogē hěn gāo. 表哥很高。); 2. incorrect (Yéye hěn gāo. 爷爷很高。); 3. correct;
4. correct; 5. correct

✎ Drive It Home

Let's practice using hěn 很 in simple sentences with adjectives. Use tāmen 他们 as a subject, and form sentences with the adjectives gāo 高 (*tall*), cōngmíng 聪明 (*intelligent*), qiángzhuàng 强壮 (*strong*), and piàoliang 漂亮(*beautiful*).

_____

_____

ANSWER KEY

Tāmen hěn gāo. 他们很高。 Tāmen hěn cōngmíng. 他们很聪明。 Tāmen hěn qiángzhuàng. 他们很强
壮。 Tāmen hěn piàoliang. 他们很漂亮。

How Did You Do?

Let's see how you did in this lesson. You should know:

☐ Key vocabulary related to people and the family.
(Still unsure? Go back to 13.)

☐ How to talk about nationalities.
(Still unsure? Go back to 15.)

☐ More family terms.
(Still unsure? Go back to 19.)

☐ How to form simple sentences with hěn 很.
(Still unsure? Go back to 21.)

✎ Word Recall

Match the English word in the left column with its appropriate translation in the right column.

1. *What nationality?*   a. tángmèi 堂妹

2. *friend*   b. wàipó 外婆

3. *grandmother (paternal side)*   c. Nǎ guórén? 哪国人？

4. *America*   d. péngyou 朋友

5. *uncle (father's younger brother)*   e. jiùjiu 舅舅

6. *China*   f. xiōngdìjiěmèi 兄弟姐妹

7. *cousin (father's brother's daughter,*   g. shūshu 叔叔
   younger than you)

8. *cousin (mother's sibling's or father's* h. Měiguó 美国
   sister's daughter, older than you)

9. *uncle (mother's brother)*　　　　i. shēnshen 婶婶

10. *sibling*　　　　j. nǎinai 奶奶

11. *aunt (father's younger brother's wife)*　　k. Zhōngguó 中国

12. *grandmother (maternal side)*　　l. biǎojiě 表姐

ANSWER KEY
1. c; 2. d; 3. j; 4. h; 5. g; 6. k; 7. a; 8. l; 9. e; 10. f; 11. i; 12. b

Lesson 2: Phrases

In this lesson, we'll focus on:

☐ Numbers and measure words.

☐ More common vocabulary for talking about the home.

☐ Using zhè 这 (*this*) and nà 那 (*that*).

Phrase Builder 1

Study the following phrases, which use measure words between the number yī (*one*) and the noun. Notice that yī (*one*) changes tone depending on what follows it. We will learn more about this below. For now, just note that we show the changes here for expository purposes, but eslewhere yī (*one*) will be written in its canonical form. This is a standard of writing, but the pronunciation is as shown below.

▶ 2A Phrase Builder 1 (CD 4, Track 5)

yí ge rén	一个人	*one/a person*
liǎng ge rén	两个人	*two people*
yì tiáo gǒu	一条狗	*one/a dog*

sān tiáo gǒu	三条狗	*three dogs*
yì zhī bǐ	一只笔	*one/a pen*
sì zhī bǐ	四只笔	*four pens*
yì zhāng zhǐ	一张纸	*one/a sheet of paper*
yì běn shū	一本书	*one/a book*
yí ge jiějie	一个姐姐	*one/an older sister*
yí ge gēge	一个哥哥	*one/an older brother*
yì tiáo lù	一条路	*one/a road*
yì zhī bēizi	一只杯子	*one/a cup, one/a glass*
yì zhāng chuáng	一张床	*one/a bed*
yì běn zìdiǎn	一本字典	*one/a (character) dictionary*

💡 Tip!

Notice that yī changes to the second tone before a syllable in the fourth tone and to the fourth tone before a syllable in the first, second or third tone.

yí ge rén
一个人
one/a person

yì tiáo gǒu
一条狗
one/a dog

Ge 个 is in the fourth tone (gè), but it is most often written without any tone at all.

✎ Phrase Practice 1

Fill in the blanks with the missing measure words. The Chinese characters are provided for additional help and practice.

1. Liǎng _____ mèimei.

   两个妹妹。

2. Qī _____ shū.

   七本书。

3. Sān_____ gǒu.

   三条狗。

4. Wǔ _____ bēizi.

   五只杯子。

5. Liù _____ chuáng.

   六张床。

ANSWER KEY

1. ge; 2. běn; 3. tiáo; 4. zhī; 5. zhāng

Take It Further: Asking Someone's Name

Chinese has two verbs that can be used to give your name. The verb xìng 姓 is used to give last names, and the verb jiào 叫 is usually used to give full names. Remember that the order of full names in Chinese is last name followed by first name. The verb jiào 叫 can also be used to give first names when the conversation is among people who have a close relationship with each other.

Qǐngwèn nín guìxìng?

请问您贵姓?

May I ask your (fml.) last name?

Wǒ xìng Huáng.

我姓黄。

My last name is Huang.

Wǒ jiào Huáng Xìn.

我叫黄信。

My name is Huang Xin.

Grammar Builder 1
MEASURE WORDS

In *Essential Chinese* you were introduced to measure words, which are needed when a noun is counted with a number, or when a demonstrative (*this* or *that*) is used. The measure word is placed between the demonstrative or number and the noun itself. There are different measure words for different types of nouns, some of which you learned in *Essential Chinese*.

▶ 2B Grammar Builder 1 (CD 4, Track 6)

MEASURE WORD	USED WITH	EXAMPLES
ge 个	*people*	yī ge rén 一个人 (*one person*) sān ge nǚrén 三个女人 (*three women*)
tiáo 条	*objects that are long and thin, also some animals*	yī tiáo xiàn 一条线 (*one/a string*) wǔ tiáo yú 五条鱼 (*five fish*) sì tiáo gǒu 四条狗 (*four dogs*)

MEASURE WORD	USED WITH	EXAMPLES
zhī 只	objects that are pointed and thin, utensils, and some animals	yī zhī wǎn 一只碗 (one/a bowl) liǎng zhī jī 两只鸡 (two chickens)
zhāng 张	objects that have a flat surface	qī zhāng zhuōzi 七张桌子 (seven tables) jiǔ zhāng zhǐ 九张纸 (nine pieces of paper)
běn 本	books	sān běn shū 三本书 (three books)

Notice in the above examples, and also in the phrase list, expressions with yī 一 (one) are translated as one/a. Don't forget that Chinese doesn't have articles, so a noun on its own can be translated with the or a depending on context. Use yī 一 plus a measure word only when you want to emphasize that there is one of something. Don't use it everywhere you'd use an indefinite article in English.

✎ Work Out 1

Translate each of the following nouns, and then find the right measure word. Form phrases with the number wǔ 五 (five).

1. book _____

2. dog _____

3. pen _____

4. bed _____

5. people _____

6. string _____

7. *cup* _____

8. *chicken* _____

ANSWER KEY

1. wǔ běn shū 五本书; 2. wǔ tiáo gǒu 五条狗; 3. wǔ zhī bǐ 五只笔; 4. wǔ zhāng chuáng 五张床; 5. wǔ ge rén 五个人; 6. wǔ tiáo xiàn 五条线; 7. wǔ zhī bēizi 五只杯子; 8. wǔ zhī jī 五只鸡

Phrase Builder 2

Here are some phrases that will help you describe where you live.

▶ 2C Phrase Builder 2 (CD 4, Track 7)

zhège gōngyù	这个公寓	*this apartment*
zhège fángzi	这个房子	*this house*
piàoliang de fángzi	漂亮的房子	*a beautiful house*
nàge fángjiān	那个房间	*that room*
nàge dà fángjiān	那个大房间	*that big room*
nàge wòfáng	那个卧房	*that bedroom*
nàge xiǎo wòfáng	那个小卧房	*that small bedroom*
zhège chúfáng	这个厨房	*this kitchen*
gānjìng de chúfáng	干净的厨房	*a clean kitchen*
nàge wèishēngjiān	那个卫生间	*that bathroom*
hěn zāng de wèishēngjiān	很脏的卫生间	*a very dirty bathroom*
zhè zhāng shāfā	这张沙发	*this sofa*
zhè zhāng zhuōzi	这张桌子	*this table*
zhè bǎ yǐzi	这把椅子	*this chair*
zhè zhāng chuáng	这张床	*this bed*
zhè zhāng zhàopiàn	这张照片	*this photograph*
nà tái diànnǎo	那台电脑	*that computer*
zhè tái diànshì	这台电视	*this television*

✎ Phrase Practice 2

Match the English phrase in the left column with its appropriate translation in the right column.

1. *this sofa*

2. *a clean kitchen*

3. *that bedroom*

4. *this apartment*

5. *that room*

a. zhège gōngyù 这个公寓

b. nàge fángjiān 那个房间

c. gānjìng de chúfáng 干净的厨房

d. nàge wòfáng 那个卧房

e. zhè zhāng shāfā 这张沙发

ANSWER KEY
1. e; 2. c; 3. d; 4. a; 5. b

Grammar Builder 2
DEMONSTRATIVES

Zhè 这 (*this*) and nà 那 (*that*) are demonstratives in Chinese. When they are followed by a noun, a measure word is needed in between zhè 这/nà 那 and the noun.

▶ 2D Grammar Builder 2 (CD 4, Track 8)

zhège rén	这个人	*this person*
nàge rén	那个人	*that person*
zhè tiáo gǒu	这条狗	*this dog*
nà zhī bǐ	那只笔	*that pen*

Nàge rén hěn piàoliang.
那个人很漂亮。
That person (is) very beautiful.

Nà tiáo gǒu hěn dà.
那条狗很大。
That dog (is) very big.

Zhège wèishēngjiān hěn zāng!
这个卫生间很脏!
This bathroom (is) very dirty!

Zhège wòfáng hěn xiǎo!
这个卧房很小!
This bedroom (is) very small!

For the plural forms of zhè 这 and nà 那, a collective measure word xiē 些 can be added after zhè 这 or nà 那: zhèxiē 这些 (*these*) and nàxiē 那些 (*those*). Xiē 些 is invariable—it can be used with any noun. For example:

| zhèxiē rén | 这些人 | *these people* |
| nàxiē bēizi | 那些杯子 | *those cups* |

Zhèxiē nǚhái hěn kě'ài.
这些女孩很可爱。
These girls (are) adorable.

Nàxiē chē hěn kuài.
那些车很快。
Those cars (are) very fast.

Nàxiē fángzi hěn dà.
那些房子很大。
Those houses (are) very big.

⏸

✎ Work Out 2

Translate the following sentences into Chinese. Remember to use hěn 很 (very) between the noun and the adjective, as is customary in Chinese.

1. *That dog is big.* _____

_____

2. *This house is beautiful.* _____

_____

3. *That sofa is new.* _____

_____

4. *These photographs are beautiful.* _____

_____

5. *This bed is small.* _____

_____

6. *That chair is small.* _____

_____

7. *This kitchen is big.* _____

_____

ANSWER KEY
1. Nà tiáo gǒu hěn dà. 那条狗很大。 2. Zhège fángzi hěn piàoliang. 这个房子很漂亮。 3. Zhè zhāng shāfā hěn xīn. 这张沙发很新。 4. Zhèxiē zhàopiàn hěn piàoliang. 这些照片很漂亮。 5. Zhè zhāng chuáng hěn xiǎo. 这张床很小。 6. Nà bǎ yǐzi hěn xiǎo. 那把张椅子很小。 7. Zhège chúfáng hěn dà. 这个厨房很大。

🌐 Culture Note

Another useful room name to know is kètīng 客厅 (*living room*), which literally means *guest room*. Fàntīng 饭厅 is a room where people eat. It literally means *rice room* and is commonly translated as *dining room* in English. Also note that wèishēngjiān 卫生间 can mean *restroom*, *toilet*, or *bathroom*.

✎ Drive It Home

Form phrases using a measure word and the given nouns. For each measure word-noun pair, form phrases with the words for *this*, *that*, and a number you choose. For example, with the measure word zhāng 张, the nouns are zhuōzi 桌子, zhǐ 纸, and shāfā 沙发. You would write out: zhè zhāng zhuōzi 这张桌子, nà zhāng zhuōzi 那张桌子, sì zhāng zhuōzi 四张桌子, and then do the same with zhǐ 纸 and shāfā 沙发。If you use the number one, write the tone changes for practice. Remember that elsewhere in this book, we will follow writing conventions and write yī (*one*) with its original tone.

1. zhī 只: wǎn 碗, jī 鸡, bǐ 笔 _____

   _____

2. tiáo 条: xiàn 线, yú 鱼, gǒu 狗 _____

   _____

3. ge 个: fángjiān 房间, rén 人, xuésheng 学生 _____

   _____

ANSWER KEY
(For convenience sake, the number one is used here. You can use any number.)
1. zhè zhī wǎn 这只碗, nà zhī wǎn 那只碗, yì zhī wǎn 一只碗; zhè zhī jī 这只鸡, nà zhī jī 那只鸡, yì zhī jī 一只鸡; zhè zhī bǐ 这只笔, nà zhī bǐ 那只笔, yì zhī bǐ 一只笔 2. zhè tiáo xiàn 这条线, nà tiáo xiàn 那条线, yì tiáo xiàn 一条线; zhè tiáo yú 这条鱼, nà tiáo yú 那条鱼, yì tiáo yú 一条鱼; zhè tiáo gǒu 这条狗, nà tiáo gǒu 那条狗, yì tiáo gǒu 一条狗 3. zhège fángjiān 这个房间, nàge fángjiān 那个房间, yí ge fángjiān 一个房间; zhège rén 这个人, nàge rén 那个人, yí ge rén 一个人; zhège xuésheng 这个学生, nàge xuésheng 那个学生, yí ge xuésheng 一个学生

How Did You Do?

We've reached the end of Lesson 2. We focused on:

☐ Numbers and measure words.
(Still unsure? Go back to 25.)

☐ More common vocabulary for talking about the home.
(Still unsure? Go back to 29.)

☐ Using zhè (*this*) and nà (*that*).
(Still unsure? Go back to 30.)

✎ Word Recall

Match the English word in the left column with its appropriate translation in the right column.

1. *bowl*   a. zāng 脏

2. *kitchen*   b. wǎn 碗

3. *measure word for objects that are*   c. wèishēngjiān 卫生间
   long and thin, also some animals

4. *sofa*   d. gǒu 狗

5. *clean*   e. chúfáng 厨房

6. *dirty*   f. chuáng 床

7. *bathroom*   g. gānjìng 干净

8. *dog*   h. lù 路

9. *room*   i. fángjiān 房间

10. *house*   j. shāfā 沙发

11. *road*   k. tiáo 条

12. *bed*   l. fángzi 房子

ANSWER KEY
1. b; 2. e; 3. k; 4. j; 5. g; 6. a; 7. c; 8. d; 9. i; 10. l; 11. h; 12. f

Lesson 3: Sentences

By the end of this lesson, you should know:

☐ How to use the verb yǒu 有 (*to have*).

☐ How to use the connection word hé 和 (*and*).

Sentence Builder 1

▶ 3A Sentence Builder 1 (CD 4, Track 9)

Wǒ yǒu sān ge dìdi.	我有三个弟弟。	*I have three younger brothers.*
Wǒ yǒu yī zhī bǐ.	我有一只笔。	*I have one pen.*
Tā yǒu yī ge fángzi.	他有一个房子。	*He has one house.*
Tā yǒu yī ge dà fángzi.	他有一个大房子。	*He has one big house.*
Nín yǒu zhuōzi ma?	您有桌子吗？	*Do you (fml.) have a table/desk?*
Nǐ yǒu gēge ma?	你有哥哥吗？	*Do you have an older brother?*
Zhège fángzi yǒu sān ge wòfáng.	这个房子有三个卧房。	*This house has three bedrooms.*
Nàge fángzi yǒu yī ge hěn dà de chúfáng.	那个房子有一个很大的厨房。	*That house has one very big kitchen.*

⑪

✎ Sentence Practice 1

Let's practice those sentences that you just learned. Fill in the blanks with the missing words or phrases, using the translations as a guide.

1. Wǒ _____ yī _____ bǐ.

   我有一只笔。

   (*I have one pen.*)

2. Nǐ _____ gēge _____?

   你有哥哥吗?

   (*Do you have an older brother?*)

3. Tā yǒu _____ ge dà _____.

   他有一个大房子。

   (*He has one big house.*)

4. Zhè _____ fángzi yǒu sān ge _____.

   这个房子有三个卧房。

   (*This house has three bedrooms.*)

5. Nín _____ zhuōzi ma?

   您有桌子吗?

   (*Do you (fml.) have a table/desk?*)

6. Wǒ yǒu _____ ge _____.

   我有三个弟弟。

   (*I have three younger brothers.*)

   ANSWER KEY
   1. yǒu, zhī; 2. yǒu, ma; 3. yī, fángzi; 4. ge, wòfáng; 5. yǒu; 6. sān, dìdi

Grammar Builder 1
YǑU 有 (*TO HAVE*)

You first came across the verb yǒu 有 in Lesson Two of *Essential Chinese*. It has a few different uses in Chinese, but as you know one of its most common functions is to indicate possession, like the English verb *to have*. Typically, yǒu 有 is placed immediately after the subject of a sentence, and it's followed by an object, along with its measure word if necessary.

▶ 3B Grammar Builder 1 (CD 4, Track 10)

Wǒ yǒu fángzi.
我有房子。
I have a house.

Tāmen yǒu liǎng ge fángzi.
他们有两个房子。
They have two houses.

Wǒmen yǒu sān ge mèimei.
我们有三个妹妹。
We have three younger sisters.

To ask a question with yǒu 有, you can use the question particle ma 吗 at the end of the sentence.

Nǐ yǒu fángzi ma?
你有房子吗?
Do you have a house?

�(II)

✎ Work Out 1

Translate the following sentences into English:

1. Wǒ yǒu zhuōzi. 我有桌子。

2. Nǐ yǒu fángzi ma? 你有房子吗?

3. Měiguórén yǒu gǒu. 美国人有狗。

4. Tā yǒu gēge ma? 她有哥哥吗?

5. Nǐmen yǒu shū ma? 你们有书吗?

6. Nǐ yǒu tàitai ma? 你有太太吗?

7. Tā yǒu sān ge lǎoshī. 他有三个老师。

ANSWER KEY

1. *I have a table.* 2. *Do you have a house?* 3. *Americans have dogs.* 4. *Does she have an older brother?* 5. *Do you (pl.) have books?* 6. *Do you have a wife?* 7. *He has three teachers.*

Sentence Builder 2

▶ 3C Sentence Builder 2 (CD 4, Track 11)

Wǒ yǒu bǐ hé zhǐ.	我有笔和纸。	*I have a pen and paper.*
Wǒ yǒu yī zhī māo hé yī zhī gǒu.	我有一只猫和一条狗。	*I have one cat and one dog.*
Wǒ yǒu diànshì hé diànnǎo.	我有电视和电脑。	*I have a TV and computer.*
Nǐ yǒu shōuyīnjī hé diànnǎo ma?	你有收音机和电脑吗?	*Do you have a radio and computer?*
Wǒmen yǒu sūdǎ shuǐ hé jiǔ.	我们有苏打水和酒。	*We have soda and wine.*
Wǒ hé tā shì Zhōngguórén.	我和他/她是中国人。	*She and I are Chinese.*
Nǐ yǒu zhè piàn xīn de jīguāng chàngpiàn ma?	你有这片新的激光唱片吗?	*Do you have the new CD?*
Tā yǒu yī liàng piàoliang de chē.	他有一辆漂亮的车。	*He has a beautiful car.*
Tāmen yǒu hěn hǎo de píjiǔ.	他们有很好的啤酒。	*They have very good beer.*

⏸

✎ Sentence Practice 2

Fill in the blanks with the missing words or phrases, using the translations as a guide.

1. Wǒ _____ diànshì _____ diànnǎo.

我有电视和电脑。

(*I have a TV and computer.*)

2. Tā yǒu yī _____ piàoliang _____ chē.

他有一辆漂亮的车。

(*He has a beautiful car.*)

3. Wǒ _____ tā shì _____.

我和她是中国人。

(*She and I are Chinese.*)

4. Wǒmen yǒu _____ jiǔ.

我们有苏打水和酒。

(*We have soda and wine.*)

5. Nǐ yǒu _____ hé diànnǎo _____?

你有收音机和电脑吗?

(*Do you have a radio and computer?*)

6. _____ yǒu _____ de píjiǔ.

他们有很好的啤酒。

(*They have very good beer.*)

ANSWER KEY

1. yǒu, hé; 2. liàng, de; 3. hé, Zhōngguórén; 4. sūdǎ shuǐ, hé; 5. shōuyīnjī, ma; 6. Tāmen, hěn hǎo

Grammar Builder 2
THE CONNECTION WORD HÉ 和

▶ 3D Grammar Builder 2 (CD 4, Track 12)

Hé 和 (*and*) can be used to connect two nouns or two phrases. For example, *an apple and an orange* can be expressed as píngguǒ hé júzi 苹果和橘子. But note that not every *and* in English can be translated as hé 和. Sometimes the English *and* has a sense of *then*, as in *please sign and return this document*. For now, however, we'll just focus on hé 和, which is the *and* that simply combines two things.

Wǒmen yǒu shū hé zìdiǎn.

我们有书和字典。

We have a book and dictionary.

Nà shì yī ge nánrén hé yī ge nǚrén.

那是一个男人和一个女人。

That is a man and a woman.

✎ Work Out 2

Translate the following sentences into English:

1. Nǐ hé tā shì péngyou. 你和她是朋友。 _____

   _____

2. Wǒ hé Wáng Xiānsheng shì línjū. 我和王先生是邻居。 _____

   _____

3. Wáng Xiānsheng hé Wáng Xiǎojiě yǒu bǐ. 王先生和王小姐有笔。 _____

   _____

4. Nǐ hé Wáng Tàitai shì péngyou ma? 你和王太太是朋友吗？ _____

   _____

5. Wǒ yǒu zhuōzi hé shū. 我有桌子和书。 _____

   _____

6. Wǒmen yǒu yī zhī māo hé sì tiáo gǒu. 我们有一只猫和四条狗。 _____

_____

7. Nǐ yǒu lǜshī ma? 你有律师吗? _____

_____

8. Lǎoshī yǒu fángzi ma? 老师有房子吗? _____

_____

ANSWER KEY

1. _You and she are friends._ 2. _Mr. Wang and I are neighbors._ 3. _Mr. Wang and Miss Wang have pens._ 4. _Are you and Mrs. Wang friends?_ 5. _I have a table and a book._ 6. _We have a cat and four dogs._ 7. _Do you have a lawyer?_ 8. _Does the teacher have a house?_

🔊 Drive It Home

Make sentences using yǒu 有, a noun phrase and subjects. For each noun phrase, form a sentence with each of the subjects in parentheses. For example, with yī zhī bǐ 一只笔 (wǒ 我, lǎoshī 老师, Wáng Tàitai 王太太), you would write: Wǒ yǒu yī zhī bǐ 我有一只笔, lǎoshī yǒu yī zhī bǐ 老师有一只笔, Wáng Tàitai yǒu yī zhī bǐ 王太太有一只笔.

1. sān tiáo gǒu 三条狗 (tā 他, Lǐ Xiānsheng 李先生, wǒ de mèimei 我的妹妹) _____

_____

2. yī ge dà chúfáng 一个大厨房 (nǐmen 你们, Huáng Lǎoshī 黄老师, Zhāng Xiǎojiě 张小姐) _____

_____

3. liǎng ge péngyou 两个朋友 (nàge xuésheng 那个学生, wǒ de yéye 我的爷爷, tāmen 他们) _____

_____

4. yī liàng piàoliang de chē 一辆漂亮的车 (wǒmen 我们, wǒ de yímā 我的姨妈, Lín

Tàitai 林太太)_____

ANSWER KEY

1. Tā yǒu sān tiáo gǒu. 他有三条狗。Lǐ Xiānsheng yǒu sān tiáo gǒu. 李先生有三条狗。Wǒ de mèimei yǒu sān tiáo gǒu. 我的妹妹有三条狗。 2. Nǐmen yǒu yī ge dà chúfáng. 你们有一个大厨房。Huáng Lǎoshī yǒu yī ge dà chúfáng. 黄老师有一个大厨房。Zhāng Xiǎojiě yǒu yī ge dà chúfáng. 张小姐有一个大厨房。 3. Nàge xuésheng yǒu liǎng ge péngyou. 那个学生有两个朋友。Wǒ de yéye yǒu liǎng ge péngyou. 我的爷爷有两个朋友。Tāmen yǒu liǎng ge péngyou. 他们有两个朋友。 4. Wǒmen yǒu yī liàng piàoliang de chē. 我们有一辆漂亮的车。Wǒ de yímā yǒu yī liàng piàoliang de chē. 我的姨妈有一辆漂亮的车。Lín Tàitai yǒu yī liàng piàoliang de chē. 林太太有一辆漂亮的车。

How Did You Do?

By now, you should know:

☐ How to use the verb yǒu 有 (*have*). (Still unsure? Go back to 37.)

☐ How to use the connection word hé 和 (*and*). (Still unsure? Go back to 40.)

✎ Word Recall

Match the English word in the left column with its appropriate translation in the right column.

1. *soda*

2. *dictionary*

3. *and*

4. *slice, flake; measure word for tile, tablets, other thin and flat objects.*

5. *cat*

6. *radio*

7. *beautiful*

a. shōuyīnjī 收音机

b. piàoliang 漂亮

c. sūdǎ shuǐ 苏打水

d. hé 和

e. piàn 片

f. māo 猫

g. zìdiǎn 字典

ANSWER KEY

1. c; 2. g; 3. d; 4. e; 5. f; 6. a; 7. b

Lesson 4: Conversations

By the end of this lesson, you should know:

☐ How to express possession.

☐ How to use hěn 很 (*very*) and tài 太 (*too*).

🔊 Conversation 1

Wang Hai and his classmate Jess are talking about their families.

▶ 4A Conversation 1 (CD 4, Track 13-Chinese, Track 14-Chinese and English)

Hǎi:	Jiéxī, zǎo ān!
海:	洁希, 早安!
Jiéxī:	Wáng Hǎi, zǎo ān!
洁希:	王海, 早安!
Hǎi:	Jiéxī, nǐ yǒu xiōngdìjiěmèi ma?
海:	洁希, 你有兄弟姐妹吗?
Jiéxī:	Méiyǒu, wǒ de jiā zhǐyǒu sān kǒu rén. Wǒ, bàba hé māma. Wáng Hǎi, nǐ jiā yǒu jǐ kǒu rén?
洁希:	没有, 我的家只有三口人。 我、爸爸和妈妈。 王海, 你家有几口人?
Hǎi:	Wǒ jiā yǒu wǔ kǒu rén. Bàba, māma, jiějie, dìdi hé wǒ.
海:	我家有五口人。 爸爸、妈妈、姐姐、弟弟和我。
Jiéxī:	Ā, nǐ de jiā zhēn rènào.
洁希:	啊, 你的家真热闹。
Hǎi:	Wǒmen háiyǒu yī tiáo xiǎogǒu hé liǎng zhī māo.
海:	我们还有一条小狗和两只猫。
Jiéxī:	Wǒ jiā méiyǒu gǒu, yě méiyǒu māo, zhǐyǒu sān tiáo yú.
洁希:	我家没有狗, 也没有猫, 只有三条鱼。

Hai:	*Good morning, Jess!*
Jess:	*Good morning, Wang Hai!*
Hai:	*Jess, do you have any siblings?*
Jess:	*No. My family has only three people, (my) father, (my) mother and myself. Wang Hai, how many people are there in your family?*
Hai:	*My family has five people: (my) father, (my) mother, (my) older sister, (my) younger brother and myself.*
Jess:	*Oh, your home must be really busy.*
Hai:	*We also have a puppy and two cats.*
Jess:	*My family doesn't have a dog or cat. We only have three fish.*

Take It Further

When you talk about a number of family members, the measure word kǒu 口 (*lit.,
mouth*) is used instead of ge 个.

Also, note how the adverb yě 也 (*also*) is used in this example from the dialogue:
Wǒ jiā méiyǒu gǒu, yě méiyǒu māo. 我家没有狗, 也没有猫。 This sentence
was translated as *my family doesn't have a dog or cat.* However, the translation
is literally *my family doesn't have a dog, also not a cat.* The adverb yě 也 (*also*) is
placed before the verb, as in these other examples:

Tā shì shíbā suì. Wǒ yě shì shíbā suì.
他是十八岁。我也是十八岁。
He is eighteen years old. I'm also eighteen years old.

Wǒ shì lǎoshī. Tāmen yě shì lǎoshī.
我是老师。他们也是老师。
I am a teacher. They're teachers too.

In the sentence translated as *We also have a puppy and two cats,* Chinese uses
háiyǒu 还有, but not yě 也. Háiyǒu 还有 means *in addition* here.

Unit 1 Lesson 4: Conversations

✎ Conversation Practice 1

Fill in the blanks with the missing words in pīnyīn. The Chinese characters are provided for additional help and practice. Refer to the conversation with Hai and Jess.

1. Hǎi de jiā yǒu _____ kǒu rén.

   海的家有五口人。

2. Jiéxī méi yǒu _____.

   洁希没有兄弟姐妹。

3. Hǎiyǒu yī ge jiějie hé yī ge _____.

   海有一个姐姐和一个弟弟。

4. Jiéxī yǒu sān tiáo _____.

   洁希有三条鱼。

5. Hǎide jiā yǒu _____ zhī māo.

   海的家有两只猫。

ANSWER KEY
1. wǔ; 2. xiōngdìjiěmèi; 3. dìdi; 4. yú; 5. liǎng

Grammar Builder 1
POSSESSIVES

Back in Lesson Five of Essential Chinese you learned the possessive particle de 的. This dialogue gave you several more good examples of how it is used. Don't forget that the possessive particle de 的 is added to a pronoun to form the possessive, as shown in the following chart:

▶ 4B Grammar Builder 1 (CD 4, Track 15)

wǒ de	我的	*my/mine*
nǐ de	你的	*your/yours*
nín de (*fml.*)	您的 (*fml.*)	*your/yours*
tā de	他的/她的	*his, her, its/his, hers, its*
wǒmen de	我们的	*our/ours*
nǐmen de (*pl.*)	你们的 (*pl.*)	*your/yours*
tāmen de	他们的	*their/theirs*

Wǒmen de lǎoshī shì Měiguórén.
我们的老师是美国人。
Our teacher is American.

Tāmen de fángzi hěn piàoliang.
他们的房子很漂亮。
Their house is beautiful.

Tā de gǒu dà, wǒ de gǒu xiǎo.
她的狗大, 我的狗小。
Her dog is big, and my dog is small.

Note that English has possessive adjectives (*my house, your car*) and possessive pronouns (*mine, yours*). In Chinese, the same forms are used for both types of possessives.

Zhè shì wǒ de bǐ.
这是我的笔。
This is my pen.

Zhè zhī bǐ shì wǒ de.
这只笔是我的。
This pen is mine.

As you've already learned, the particle de 的 is also used with nouns and names to indicate possession. Here are a few more examples:

Zhè shì lǎoshī de bǐ.
这是老师的笔。
This is the teacher's pen.

Zhè shì Jiéxī de bǐ.
这是洁希的笔。
This is Jess's pen.

Xiàng de bízi hěn cháng.
象的鼻子很长。
The elephant's trunk is very long.

(II)

Sometimes, the possessive particle can be omitted when it indicates a close personal relationship. For example, the expression wǒ de māma 我的妈妈 (*my mother*) can be also expressed as wǒ māma 我妈妈.

✎ Work Out 1

Indicate whether the following statements are *true* (shì 是) or *false* (fēi 非) in Chinese:

1. Jiéxī yǒu yī ge gēge. 洁希有一个哥哥。

2. Hǎi yǒu yī ge mèimei. 海有一个妹妹。

3. Hǎi de jiā yǒu sì kǒu rén. 海的家有四口人。

4. Jiéxī de māma yǒu yī ge dìdi. 洁希的妈妈有一个弟弟。

5. Hǎi méiyǒu bàba, yě méiyǒu māma. 海没有爸爸, 也没有妈妈。

6. Jiéxī de jiā yǒu sān tiáo yú. 洁希的家有三条鱼。

7. Jiéxī de jiā yǒu sān kǒu rén. 洁希的家有三口人。

8. Hǎi yǒu yī tiáo xiǎogǒu. 海有一条小狗。

ANSWER KEY
1. fēi 非 (*false*); 2. fēi 非 (*false*); 3. fēi 非 (*false*); 4. fēi 非 (*false*); 5. fēi 非 (*false*); 6. shì 是 (*true*); 7. shì 是 (*true*); 8. shì 是 (*true*)

ᴄᴄ Conversation 2

▶ 4C Conversation 2 (CD 4, Track 16-Chinese, Track 17-Chinese and English)

Wang Hai has invited Jess to his home. Listen to their conversation.

Hǎi: Qǐng zuò!

海: 请坐!

Jiéxī: Wáng Hǎi, nǐ de jiā hěn piàoliang! Yǒu jǐ ge wòfáng?

洁希: 王海, 你的家很漂亮! 有几个卧房?

Hǎi: Wǒmen de gōngyù tài xiǎo le, zhǐyǒu sān ge wòfáng hé yī ge yùshì.

         Wǒ hé dìdi yòng yī ge fángjiān.

海: 我们的公寓太小了, 只有三个卧房和一个浴室。 我和弟弟
         用一个房间。

Jiéxī: Nà shì nǐmen de zhàopiàn ma?

洁希: 那是你们的照片吗?

Hǎi: Shì, nà shì wǒmen de zhàopiàn.

海: 是, 那是我们的照片。

Jiéxī: Zhè shì nǐ de jiějie ma?

洁希: 这是你的姐姐吗?

Hǎi: Bùshì, zhè shì wǒ māma.

海: 不是, 这是我妈妈。

Jiéxī: Duìbùqǐ.

洁希: 对不起。

Hǎi: Búyàojǐn. Wǒ māma shì lǎoshī.

海: 不要紧。 我妈妈是老师。

Jiéxī: Tā hěn niánqīng.

洁希: 她很年轻。

Hai: *Please sit down.*

Jess: *Your home is very pretty! How many bedrooms do you have?*

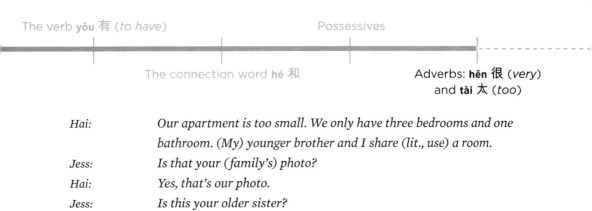

Hai:	*Our apartment is too small. We only have three bedrooms and one bathroom. (My) younger brother and I share (lit., use) a room.*
Jess:	*Is that your (family's) photo?*
Hai:	*Yes, that's our photo.*
Jess:	*Is this your older sister?*
Hai:	*No. This is my mother.*
Jess:	*(I'm) sorry.*
Hai:	*That's alright. My mother is a teacher.*
Jess:	*She looks very young.*

Take It Further
QĬNG 请 (*PLEASE*)

Notice that when Hai asked Jess to please sit down, he said: Qǐng zuò! 请坐!
When you ask someone to do something, the word qǐng 请 (*please*) is used to
preface your request in order to be polite.

Qǐng hē chá.
请喝茶。
Please have some tea. (lit., Please drink tea.)

Qǐng jìnlái.
请进来。
Please come in.

✎ Conversation Practice 2

Fill in the blanks with the missing words in pīnyīn. The Chinese characters are
provided for additional help and practice. Refer to the second conversation with
Hai and Jess.

1. Hǎi de gōngyù yǒu sān ge _____.

   海的公寓有三个卧房。

2. Hǎi hé tā de _____ yòng yī ge fángjiān.

   海和他的弟弟用一个房间。

3. Zhàopiàn lǐ shì Hǎi de _____.

   照片里是海的妈妈。

4. Hǎi de māma shì _____.

   海的妈妈是老师。

5. Hǎi de māma hěn _____.

   海的妈妈很年轻。

ANSWER KEY
1. wòfáng; 2. dìdi; 3. māma; 4. lǎoshī; 5. niánqīng

Grammar Builder 2
ADVERBS: HĚN 很 (*VERY*) AND TÀI 太 (*TOO*)

▶ 4D Grammar Builder 2 (CD 4, Track 18)

Adverbs are words or phrases that indicate how, how much, or how often something is done. They modify adjectives and verbs, but not nouns. Some English adverbs are *very, well, often, quickly, slowly, beautifully,* and so on.

In Chinese, adjectives do not change form when they are used as adverbs. In other words, there's no ending *-ly*. So, kuài 快 can be translated as an adjective (*fast, quick*) or as an adverb (*fast, quickly*), and so can màn 慢 (*slow, slowly*). The difference is how these words are used, to modify nouns (as adjectives) or verbs (as adverbs). Take a look at these examples:

Nà liàng chē hěn kuài.

那辆车很快。

That car is very fast.

Tā kāichē kāi de hěn kuài.

他开车开得很快。

He drives very fast.

Note the use of the particle de 得 between the verb and the adverb in the last example. You will learn more about this adverbial construction a bit later.

Also note the use of the adverb hěn 很 (*very*) between the noun chē 车 (*car*) and the adjective kuài 快 (*fast*) in the first example. As you know, it is common in Chinese to add a degree adverb like hěn 很 or tài 太 (*too, exceedingly*) before an adjective to help link that adjective with the subject.

Wáng xiǎojie hěn piàoliang.

王小姐很漂亮。

Miss Wang is very pretty.

Měiguórén hěn gāo.

美国人很高。

Americans are very tall.

Zhè zhī bǐ tài guì.

这只笔太贵。

This pen is too expensive.

Nín tài kèqi.

您太客气。

You're too polite.

✎ Work Out 2

Insert tài 太 or hěn 很 into the following sentences, using the English cues. Then translate each sentence.

1. Zhège kètīng dà. 这个客厅大。 (very) _____

2. Nǐ de dìdi niánqīng. 你的弟弟年轻。 (too) _____

3. Wáng Xiānsheng de fángzi xiǎo. 王先生的房子小。 (very) _____

4. Tā de línjū de chē guì. 他的邻居的车贵。 (very) _____

5. Nà tiáo gǒu hǎo. 那条狗好。 (very) _____

6. Wǒ de fángzi dà. 我的房子大。 (very) _____

7. Zhè zhī māo xiǎo. 这只猫小。 (too) _____

ANSWER KEY

1. Zhège kètīng hěn dà. 这个客厅很大。 (*This living room/guest room is very big.*) 2. Nǐ de dìdi tài niánqīng. 你的弟弟太年轻。 (*Your younger brother is too young.*) 3. Wáng xiānsheng de fángzi hěn xiǎo. 王先生的房子很小。 (*Mr. Wang's house is very small.*) 4. Tā de línjū de chē hěn guì. 他的邻居的车很贵。 (*His neighbor's car is very expensive.*) 5. Nà tiáo gǒu hěn hǎo. 那条狗很好。 (*That dog is very good.*) 6. Wǒ de fángzi hěn dà. 我的房子很大。 (*My house is very big.*) 7. Zhè zhī māo tài xiǎo. 这只猫太小。 (*This cat is too small.*)

✎ Drive It Home

Let's practice possession. You'll see an object followed by a possessor, and you should link the two to form a possessive phrase.

1. bǐ 笔, lǎoshī 老师 _____

2. fángzi 房子, tángdì 堂弟 _____

3. zìxíngchē 自行车, Běijīngrén 北京人 _____

4. wǎn 碗, yéye 爷爷 _____

ANSWER KEY

1. lǎoshī de bǐ 老师的笔; 2. tángdì de fángzi 堂弟的房子; 3. Běijīngrén de zìxíngchē 北京人的自行车;
4. yéye de wǎn 爷爷的碗

Now let's turn to hěn 很. This time, you'll see a subject, and then an adjective.
Form sentences linking the two together.

1. lǎoshī de chē, kuài

老师的车, 快

_____

_____

2. jiā de chúfáng, gānjìng

家的厨房, 干净

_____

_____

3. péngyou de shāfā, xiǎo

朋友的沙发, 小

_____

_____

4. Déguó de píjiǔ, hǎo

德国的啤酒, 好

_____

_____

ANSWER KEY

1. Lǎoshī de chē hěn kuài. 老师的车很快。 2. Jiā de chúfáng hěn gānjìng. 家的厨房很干净。
3. Péngyou de shāfā hěn xiǎo. 朋友的沙发很小。 4. Déguó de píjiǔ hěn hǎo. 德国的啤酒很好。

How Did You Do?

By now, you should know:

☐ How to express possession. (Still unsure? Go back to 47.)

☐ How to use hěn 很 (very) and tài 太 (too). (Still unsure? Go back to 52.)

✎ Word Recall

Match the English word in the left column with its appropriate translation in the right column.

1. _elephant_   a. guì 贵

2. _photograph_   b. kǒu 口

3. _lively, busy, bustling_   c. qǐng zuò 请坐

4. _young, youthful_   d. yě 也

5. _also, in addition_   e. yùshì 浴室

6. _expensive_   f. xiàng 象

7. *mouth; measure word for number of people in the household*

    g. háiyǒu 还有

8. *please sit, have a seat*

    h. bízi 鼻子

9. *polite*

    i. zhàopiàn 照片

10. *also*

    j. niánqīng 年轻

11. *bathroom (in a private home)*

    k. kèqi 客气

12. *nose, trunk*

    l. rènào 热闹

ANSWER KEY

1. f; 2. i; 3. l; 4. j; 5. g; 6. a; 7. b; 8. c; 9. k; 10. d; 11. e; 12. h

Don't forget to practice and reinforce what you've learned by visiting **www.livinglanguage.com/ languagelab** for flashcards, games, and quizzes.

Unit 1 Essentials

Vocabulary Essentials

Test your knowledge of the key material in this unit by filling in the blanks in the following charts. Once you've completed these pages, you'll have tested your retention, and you'll have your own reference for the most essential vocabulary. This is also a great time to practice a few Chinese characters. Fill in the middle column with the characters that you remember. Or, if you only remember the pīnyīn, go back through the unit to find the character.

FAMILY

PĪNYĪN	CHARACTER	
		father
		mother
		son
		daughter
		older brother
		older sister
		younger brother
		younger sister
		grandfather (paternal side)
		grandmother (paternal side)
		grandfather (maternal side)
		grandmother (maternal side)
		uncle (father's older brother)
		aunt (father's older brother's wife)
		uncle (father's younger brother)

PĪNYĪN	CHARACTER	
		aunt (father's younger brother's wife)
		aunt (father's sister)
		uncle (father's sister's husband)
		uncle (mother's brother)
		aunt (mother's brother's wife)
		aunt (mother's sister)
		uncle (mother's sister's husband)
		cousin (father's brother's son, older than you)
		cousin (father's brother's son, younger than you)
		cousin (father's brother's daughter, older than you)
		cousin (father's brother's daughter, younger than you)
		cousin (mother's sibling's or father's sister's son, older than you)
		cousin (mother's sibling's or father's sister's son, younger than you)
		cousin (mother's sibling's or father's sister's daughter, older than you)
		cousin (mother's sibling's or father's sister's daughter, younger than you)

NATIONALITIES

PĪNYĪN	CHARACTER	
		American
		Chinese
		British
		French
		Spanish
		German
		Italian
		Japanese
		Australian
		Pekingese
		Shanghaiese
		Hongkongese
		Nanjingese
		Cantonese

If you're having a hard time remembering this vocabulary, don't forget to check out the flashcards, games and quizzes for this unit online. Go to **www.livinglanguage.com/languagelab** for a great way to help you practice what you've learned.

Grammar Essentials

Here is a reference for the key grammar that was covered in Unit 1. Make sure you understand the summary and can use all of the grammar it covers.

MEASURE WORDS

MEASURE WORD	USED WITH	EXAMPLES
ge 个	people	yī ge rén 一个人 (one/a person) sān ge nǚrén 三个女人 (three women)
tiáo 条	objects that are long and thin, also some animals	yī tiáo xiàn 一条线 (one/a string) wǔ tiáo yú 五条鱼 (five fish) sì tiáo gǒu 四条狗 (four dogs)
zhī 只	objects that are pointed and thin, utensils, and some animals	yī zhī wǎn 一只碗 (one/a bowl) liǎng zhī jī 两只鸡 (two chickens)
zhāng 张	objects that have a flat surface	qī zhāng zhuōzi 七张桌子 (seven tables) jiǔ zhāng zhǐ 九张纸 (nine pieces of paper)
běn 本	books	sān běn shū 三本书 (three books)

POSSESSIVES

PĪNYĪN	CHARACTER	
wǒ de	我的	*my/mine*
nǐ de	你的	*your/yours*
nín de (fml.)	您的 *(fml.)*	*your/yours*
tā de	他的	*his, her, its/his, hers, its*
wǒmen de	我们的	*our/ours*
nǐmen de (pl.)	你们的 *(pl.)*	*your/yours*
tāmen de	他们的	*their/theirs*

DEMONSTRATIVES

PĪNYĪN	CHARACTER	
zhège rén	这个人	*this person*
nàge rén	那个人	*that person*
zhè tiáo gǒu	这条狗	*this dog*
nà zhī bǐ	那只笔	*that pen*

Intermediate Chinese

Character Essentials

To practice the Chinese characters you learned in Unit 1, Conversations 1 and 2 are repeated here without pīnyīn or English translations. Translate as many characters as you can. Check your answers by listening to the conversations from your audio. Don't wory if you can't remember all of the characters. Just try to remember as many as you can.

Conversation 1

4A Conversation 1 (CD 4, Track 13-Chinese, Track 14-Chinese and English)

海: 洁希, 早安!

_____

_____

洁希: 王海, 早安!

_____

_____

海: 洁希, 你有兄弟姐妹吗?

_____

_____

洁希: 没有, 我的家只有三口人。 我,、爸爸和妈妈。 王海, 你家有几口人?

_____

_____

海:　　　　我家有五口人。爸爸、妈妈、姐姐、弟弟和我。

洁希:　　　啊, 你的家真热闹。

海:　　　　我们还有一条小狗和两只猫。

洁希:　　　我家没有狗, 也没有猫, 只有三条鱼。

Conversation 2

4C Conversation 2 (CD 4, Track 16-Chinese, Track 17-Chinese and English)

海:　　　　请坐!

洁希: 王海, 你的家很漂亮！ 有几个卧房?

海: 我们的公寓太小了, 只有三个卧房和一个浴室。 我和弟弟
用一个房间。

洁希: 那是你们的照片吗?

海: 是, 那是我们的照片。

洁希: 这是你的姐姐吗?

海: 不是, 这是我妈妈。

洁希:　　　对不起。

_____

_____

海:　　　　不要紧。 我妈妈是老师。

_____

_____

洁希:　　　她很年轻。

_____

_____

⑪

Unit 1 Quiz

A. Translate the following sentences into Chinese.

1. *He is intelligent.* _____

_____

2. *He is tall.* _____

_____

3. *I am American.* _____

_____

4. *You are Chinese.* _____

_____

B. Fill in the blanks with the correct measure words.

1. yī _____ zhǐ

一张纸

2. liǎng _____ rén

两个人

3. yī _____ zìdiǎn

一本字典

4. sì _____ diànnǎo

四台电脑

5. shí _____ jiǔ

十瓶酒

6. sān _____ gǒu

三条狗

C. Translate these demonstrative phrases into Chinese.

1. *that sofa* _____

2. *this bedroom* _____

3. *that cat* _____

4. *this bed* _____

5. *this apartment* _____

D. Translate these sentences into Chinese.

1. *That house has four bedrooms.* _____

_____

2. *The teacher has twenty students.* _____

_____

3. *Mr. Wang's car is very big.* _____

_____

4. *That kitchen is very clean.* _____

_____

5. *She and I are Chinese.* _____

_____

ANSWER KEY

A. 1. Tā hěn cōngmíng. 他很聪明。 2. Tā hěn gāo. 他很高。 3. Wǒ shì Měiguórén. 我是美国人。 4. Nǐ shì Zhōngguórén. 你是中国人。

B. 1. zhāng 张; 2. ge 个; 3. běn 本; 4. tái 台; 5. píng 瓶; 6. tiáo 条

C. 1. nà zhāng shāfā 那张沙发; 2. zhège wòfáng 这个卧房; 3. nà zhī māo 那只猫; 4. zhè zhāng chuáng 这张床; 5. zhège gōngyù 这个公寓

D. 1. Nàge fángzi yǒu sì ge wòfáng. 那个房子有四个卧房。 2. Lǎoshī yǒu èrshí ge xuésheng. 老师有二十个学生。 3. Wáng Xiānsheng de chē hěn dà. 王先生的车很大。 4. Nàge chúfáng hěn gānjìng. 那个厨房很干净。 5. Tā hé wǒ shì Zhōngguórén. 她和我是中国人。

How Did You Do?

Give yourself a point for every correct answer, then use the following key to tell whether you're ready to move on:

0-7 points: It's probably a good idea to go back through the lesson again. You may be moving too quickly, or there may be too much "down time" between your contact with Chinese. Remember that it's better to spend 30 minutes with Chinese three or four times a week than it is to spend two or three hours just once a week. Find a pace that's comfortable for you, and spread your contact hours out as much as you can.

8-12 points: You would benefit from a review before moving on. Go back and spend a little more time on the specific points that gave you trouble. Re-read the Grammar Builder sections that were difficult, and do the Work Outs one more time. Don't forget about the online supplemental practice material, either. Go to **www.livinglanguage.com/languagelab** for games and quizzes that will reinforce the material from this unit.

13-17 points: Good job! There are just a few points that you might consider reviewing before moving on. If you haven't worked with the games and quizzes on **www.livinglanguage.com/languagelab**, please give them a try.

18-20 points: Great! You're ready to move on to the next unit.

 points

Unit 2: Everyday Life

Rìcháng shēnghuó

日常生活

In Unit 2, you'll review some basic vocabulary for talking about your daily routine, and you'll learn a lot of new vocabulary as well, especially common verbs. You'll also take another look at expressing likes and dislikes.

Lesson 5: Words

In this lesson you'll learn:

☐ How to use days of the week.

☐ How to express dates and seasons.

Word Builder 1

Here is a review of the days of the week in Chinese, along with some other useful vocabulary for talking about the week.

▶ 5A Word Builder 1 (CD 4, Track 19)

lǐbài yī/xīngqī yī	礼拜一/星期一	Monday
lǐbài èr/xīngqī èr	礼拜二/星期二	Tuesday
lǐbài sān/xīngqī sān	礼拜三/星期三	Wednesday
lǐbài sì/xīngqī sì	礼拜四/星期四	Thursday
lǐbài wǔ/xīngqī wǔ	礼拜五/星期五	Friday

Xǐhuan/bù xǐhuan 喜欢/不喜欢
(to like/not like)

Superlatives with **zuì** 最

Zài 在 and **zhe** 著

Question word
shénme (*what*)

líbài liù/xīngqī liù	礼拜六/星期六	*Saturday*
líbài tiān/xīngqī tiān	礼拜天/星期天	*Sunday*
jīntiān	今天	*today*
zhōumò	周末	*weekend*
gōngzuòrì	工作日	*weekday (lit., workday)*
zǎoshang	早上	*morning*
xiàwǔ	下午	*afternoon*
wǎn/wǎnshang	晚/晚上	*evening*
wǎnshang	晚上	*night*

✎ Word Practice 1

Translate the following English phrases into Chinese (use either word for week).

1. *Monday morning* _____

2. *Saturday afternoon* _____

3. *Tuesday evening* _____

4. *Sunday night* _____

5. *Friday afternoon* _____

ANSWER KEY
1. xīngqī/líbài yī zǎoshang 星期/礼拜一早上; 2. xīngqī/líbài liù xiàwǔ 星期/礼拜六下午; 3. xīngqī/líbài èr wǎn/wǎngshang 星期/礼拜二晚/晚上; 4. xīngqī/líbài tiān wǎnshang 星期/礼拜天晚上; 5. xīngqī/líbài wǔ xiàwǔ 星期/礼拜五下午

Grammar Builder 1
DAYS OF THE WEEK

As you can see in the Word Builder, there are two ways to express the days of the week in Chinese. You have a choice of combining either the word lǐbài 礼拜 or xīngqī 星期 (both of which mean *week*) with a number from yī 一 (*one*) to liù 六 (*six*) to indicate one of the first six days of the week. Both of these forms are correct, but xīngqī 星期 is more formal and is often used in written language. In each case, note that the number used to indicate the day of the week is placed immediately after lǐbài 礼拜 or xīngqī 星期.

Given this pattern, you might think that lǐbài qī 礼拜七 or xīngqī qī 星期七 would be the logical way of saying *Sunday*. However, these two forms don't exist in Chinese. Instead, the word tiān 天 (which literally means *day*) is placed after lǐbài 礼拜 or xīngqī 星期 to express the seventh day of the week.

⏸ 5B Grammar Builder 1 (CD 4, Track 20)

Jīntiān shì lǐbài jǐ?
今天是礼拜几?
What day is today?

Jīntiān shì lǐbài èr.
今天是礼拜二。
Today is Tuesday.

⏸

Xǐhuan/bù xǐhuan 喜欢/不喜欢
(to like/not like)

Superlatives with zuì 最

Zài 在 and zhe 着

Question word
shénme (what)

✎ Work Out 1

Multiple choice: Choose the correct translation in Chinese.

1. *Monday*

   a. xīngqī yī 星期一

   b. xīngqī tiān 星期天

   c. xīngqī sān 星期三

2. *Sunday*

   a. xīngqī yī 星期一

   b. xīngqī qī 星期七

   c. xīngqī tiān 星期天

3. *Wednesday*

   a. xīngqī liù 星期六

   b. xīngqī qī 星期七

   c. xīngqī sān 星期三

4. *Tuesday*

   a. lǐbài wǔ 礼拜五

   b. xīngqī èr 星期二

   c. xīngqī liù 星期六

5. *Friday*

   a. lǐbài wǔ 礼拜五

   b. xīngqī liù 星期六

   c. xīngqī yī 星期一

6. *Saturday*

   a lǐbài wǔ 礼拜五

   b. lǐbài sān 礼拜三

   c. xīngqī liù 星期六

7. *Thursday*

   a. lǐbài yī 礼拜一

   b. lǐbài sān 礼拜三

   c. lǐbài sì 礼拜四

8. *weekend*

   a. gōngzuòrì 工作日

   b. xīngqī tiān 星期天

   c. zhōumò 周末

ANSWER KEY
1. a; 2. c; 3. c; 4. b; 5. a; 6. c; 7. c; 8. c

Word Builder 2

▶ 5C Word Builder 2 (CD 4, Track 21)

Here are some useful words related to the months and seasons.

nián	年	*year*
yī yuè	一月	*January*
èr yuè	二月	*February*
sān yuè	三月	*March*
sì yuè	四月	*April*
wǔ yuè	五月	*May*
liù yuè	六月	*June*

Xīhuan/bù xīhuan 喜欢/不喜欢
(to like/not like)

Superlatives with **zuì** 最

Zài 在 and **zhe** 着

Question word
shénme (what)

qī yuè	七月	July
bā yuè	八月	August
jiǔ yuè	九月	September
shí yuè	十月	October
shíyī yuè	十一月	November
shí'èr yuè	十二月	December
jìjié	季节	season
chūntiān	春天	spring
xiàtiān	夏天	summer
qiūtiān	秋天	autumn
dōngtiān	冬天	winter

Grammar Builder 2:
EXPRESSING MONTHS AND DATES

As you can see, it's very easy to learn the months of the year in Chinese. All you need to do is place the word yuè 月 (*month*) immediately after a number from yī 一 (*one*) to shí'èr 十二 (*twelve*). For instance, October is the tenth month of the year, so it would be shí 十 (*ten*) + yuè 月 (*month*) = shí yuè 十月 (*October*).

It's also very easy to express dates in Chinese. All you need to do is put a number from yī 一 (*one*) to sānshíyī 三十一 (*thirty-one*) —you've only learned up through 20 so far, but we'll come back to the others—right before the word hào 号 (which literally means *number*). So, the first day of the month is yī hào 一号 (*lit., number one*) while the thirty-first day of the month is sānshíyī hào 三十一号 (*lit., number thirty-one*).

To give a specific day and month, say the name of the month first and then the day. For example, July 4th would be expressed as qī yuè sì hào 七月四号, where qī yuè 七月 is the seventh month of the year (*July*), and sì hào 四号 is the fourth day of the month.

5D Grammar Builder 2 (CD 4, Track 22)

Jīntiān shì jǐ yuè jǐ hào?
今天是几月几号?
What is the date today?

Jīntiān shì sān yuè èrshí hào.
今天是三月二十号。
Today is March 20th.

Jīntiān shì bā yuè sān hào.
今天是八月三号。
Today is August 3rd.

Work Out 2

Multiple choice: Choose the correct translation in Chinese.

1. *November*

a. shí yuè 十月

b. shíyī yuè 十一月

c. sān yuè 三月

Xǐhuan/bù xǐhuan 喜欢/不喜欢
(to like/not like)

Superlatives with **zuì** 最

Zài 在 and **zhe** 着

Question word
shénme (*what*)

2. *March*

   a. shí yuè 十月

   b. shí'èr yuè 十二月

   c. sān yuè 三月

3. *July*

   a. qī yuè 七月

   b. shí yuè 十月

   c. sì yuè 四月

4. *December*

   a. shí yuè 十月

   b. shí'èr yuè 十二月

   c. sān yuè 三月

5. *August*

   a. shí yuè 十月

   b. bā yuè 八月

   c. yī yuè 一月

6. *January*

   a. yī yuè 一月

   b. shí'èr yuè 十二月

   c. sān yuè 三月

7. *May*

   a. yī yuè 一月

   b. shí yuè 十月

   c. wǔ yuè 五月

8. *June*

   a. liù yuè 六月

   b. shí'èr yuè 十二月

   c. sān yuè 三月

9. *September*

   a. yī yuè 一月

   b. shí'èr yuè 十二月

   c. jiǔ yuè 九月

10. *the fourth day of the month*

   a. shí hào 十号

   b. sì hào 四号

   c. yī hào 一号

ANSWER KEY

1. b; 2. c; 3. a; 4. b; 5. b; 6.a; 7. c; 8. a; 9. c; 10. b.

⊕ Culture Note

In the past, the Chinese used a lunar calendar called nónglì 农历, which literally means agriculture calendar. The first month of the lunar calendar is known as yī yuè 一月 or zhēngyuè 正月 (*lit., exact month*). The first ten days of each lunar month are expressed using the prefix chū 初 followed by a number from one to ten: chūyī 初一 (*1st day*), chū'èr 初二 (*2nd day*), chūsān 初三 (*3rd day*), chūsì 初四

Xǐhuan/bù xǐhuan 喜欢/不喜欢
(to like/not like)

Superlatives with zuì 最

Zài 在 and zhe 着

Question word
shénme (what)

(4th day), chūwǔ 初五 (5th day), chūliù 初六 (6th day), chūqī 初七 (7th day), chūbā
初八 (8th day), chūjiǔ 初九 (9th day), and chūshí 初十 (10th day).

Nowadays, the lunar calendar is still used to mark important Chinese festivals, such as the Lunar New Year, which is the first day of the first month in the lunar calendar. This date falls sometime between January and February, and the exact date varies each year according to the western calendar. This is because the lunar calendar and the western calendar mark time in substantially different ways. While the western calendar divides the year up neatly into twelve months regardless of the lunar cycle, the lunar calendar divides the year into twelve months based on the phases of the moon, with an additional 13th month added to the year in a Leap Year.

✎ Drive It Home

Write the following dates in pīnyīn.

1. *December 23rd* _____

2. *June 2nd* _____

3. *August 30th* _____

4. *April 6th* _____

5. *September 20th* _____

6. *January 1st* _____

ANSWER KEY
1. shí'èr yuè èrshísān hào 十二月二十三号; 2. liù yuè èr hào 六月二号; 3. bā yuè sānshí hào 八月三十号; 4. sì yuè liù hào 四月六号; 5. jiǔ yuè èrshí hào 九月二十号; 6. yī yuè yī hào 一月一号

How Did You Do?

By now, you should know:

- ☐ How to use days of the week.
  (Still unsure? Go back to 72.)
- ☐ How to express dates and seasons.
  (Still unsure? Go back to 75.)

✎ Word Recall

Fill in the blanks of the pīnyīn words and phrases. You may need to refer to the characters for cues.

1. zhōu _____

   周末

2. wǔ _____ èrshíyī _____

   五月二十一号

3. xīng _____ sì _____ shang

   星期四晚上

4. chūn _____

   春天

5. qī yuè _____ hào

   七月十九号

6. gōng _____ rì

   工作日

Xǐhuan/bù xǐhuan 喜欢/不喜欢
(to like/not like)

Superlatives with **zuì** 最

Zài 在 and **zhe** 着

Question word
shénme (what)

7. _____ èr zǎoshang

礼拜二早上

8. lǐbàitiān _____ wǔ

礼拜天傍晚

9. jīn _____

今天

10. _____ yuè èrshí _____ hào

十月二十六号

11. _____ tiān

夏天

12. xīngqī _____ xià _____

星期三下午

13. _____ jié

季节

14. _____ yuè _____ hào

十一月十一号

15. _____ tiān

冬天

ANSWER KEY
1. mò 末; 2. yuè 月, hào 号; 3. qī 期, wǎn 晚; 4. tiān 天; 5. shíjiǔ 十九; 6. zuò 作; 7. lǐbài 礼拜; 8. bàng 傍;
9. tiān 天; 10. shí 十, liù 六; 11. xià 夏; 12. sān 三, wǔ 午; 13. jì 季; 14. shíyī 十一, shíyī 十一; 15. dōng 冬

Lesson 6: Phrases

In this lesson, you'll learn:

☐ Some common verbs and how to use them.

☐ Expressions of time that will help you talk about your daily routine.

Phrase Builder 1

▶ 6A Phrase Builder 1 (CD 4, Track 23)

wǒ chīfàn	我吃饭	I eat (a meal)
tā yóuyǒng	她游泳	she swims
nǐ kāichē	你开车	you drive (a car)
tāmen tiàowǔ	他们跳舞	they dance (a dance)
tā chànggē	他唱歌	he sings (a song)
tā zuòfàn	她做饭	she cooks (a meal)
shàngxué	上学	to go to school
shàngbān	上班	to go to work
kànshū	看书	to read a book
wǒ shuìjiào	我睡觉	I sleep/I go to bed
lái	来	to come
lái Měiguó	来美国	to come to the U.S.
qù	去	to go
qù yínháng	去银行	to go to the bank
hē shuǐ	喝水	to drink water

Xǐhuan/bù xǐhuan 喜欢/不喜欢
(to like/not like)

Superlatives with zuì 最

Zài 在 and zhe 着

Question word
shénme (what)

✎ Phrase Practice 1

Translate the phrases from English into pīnyīn.

1. *to go to school* _____

2. *you drive (a car)* _____

3. *to read a book* _____

4. *he sings (a song)* _____

5. *she cooks (a meal)* _____

6. *to go to the bank* _____

ANSWER KEY
1. shàngxué 上学; 2. nǐ kāichē 你开车; 3. kànshū 看书; 4. tā chànggē 他唱歌; 5. tā zuòfàn 她做饭;
6. qù yínháng 去银行

Grammar Builder 1
USING VERBS

Let's review what you've learned about Chinese verbs. You've learned a few verbs so far, the most common of which are shì 是 (*to be*) and yǒu 有 (*to have*). You know that Chinese verbs don't conjugate, meaning that they don't change forms depending on when the action takes place or to agree with their subject. So depending on the context, shì 是 (*to be*) can be translated as *am, is, are, was,* or *were,* and yǒu 有 (*to have*) can be translated as *have, has,* or *had.*

Now let's move on to other verbs. If you look at the verbs listed in the Phrase Builder above, you will see some "simple" verbs like lái 来 (*to come*) and qù 去 (*to go*), which are made up of only one syllable. Since every character in Chinese is one syllable, such verbs are only written with one character. Some other examples of one-syllable verbs include jiàn 见 (*to see*), zǒu 走 (*to leave/to walk*), jiào 叫 (*to call*), and xìng 姓 (*to be called a last name*).

▶ 6B Grammar Builder 1 (CD 4, Track 24)

Wǒ xué Zhōngwén.

我学中文。

I study Chinese.

Wǒ jiào Jiéxī.

我叫洁希。

I'm called Jess. My first name is Jess.

Wǒ de péngyou lái Měiguó.

我的朋友来美国。

My friend is coming to America.

There are also a lot of verbs in Chinese that are made up of two characters, and therefore two syllables, although they fall into a few different categories. Two of these categories are regular two-syllable verbs and verb-object verbs. These types of verbs look alike—they both have two syllables—but they behave slightly differently.

Let's start with verb-object verbs. Verb-object verbs are two-syllable verbs that combine a verb with an object in order to help clarify the nature or purpose of an action. The verb chīfàn 吃饭, for example, is made of the verb chī 吃 (*to eat*) and the object fàn 饭 (*meal, food; lit., cooked rice*), which helps to qualify the act of eating by expressing what's being eaten. It is important to note, however, that the meaning of this verb is not limited to eating rice. In fact, it refers to the act of eating food or a meal in general.

Note that, as in the case of other verb-object verbs listed above, such as kāichē 开车 (*drive*), tiàowǔ 跳舞 (*dance*), chànggē 唱歌 (*sing*), and zuòfàn 做饭 (*cook*), the object (such as chē 车—*car*; wǔ 舞—*a dance*; gē 歌—*song*; fàn 饭—*meal, food* in the above examples) always takes the position of the second syllable. You should also

Xǐhuan/bù xǐhuan 喜欢/不喜欢
(to like/not like)

Superlatives with zuì 最

Zài 在 and zhe 着

Question word
shénme (*what*)

keep in mind that the object contained within these verbs is usually not translated literally into English, although its meaning is usually implicit in the translation.

Wáng tàitai xǐhuan tiàowǔ hé chànggē.
王太太喜欢跳舞和唱歌。
Mrs. Wang likes dancing and singing.

Wǒ zuòfàn.
我做饭。
I cook.

Tā kāichē qù Niǔyuē.
他开车去纽约。
He drives to New York.

Two-syllable verbs are just that—verbs made up of two syllables, like rènshi 认识 (*to know [a person], to meet*), míngbai 明白 (*to understand*) or jiǎnchá 检查 (*to examine, to check*). The difference in use between regular two-syllable verbs and verb-object verbs is that when a suffix or adverb is used, a verb-object verb can be split into two parts (the verb and the object), while a two-syllable verb cannot. For example:

Wǒ tiàole liǎng nián de wǔ. **OR** Wǒ tiàowǔ tiàole liǎng nián.
我跳了两年的舞。 **OR** 我跳舞跳了两年。
I have danced for two years.

Wǒ jiǎnchá le.
我检查了。
I checked.

The particle le 了 is a suffix that indicates a completed action and is often used to express the past. You will learn more about it later.

As you know, to negate a verb in Chinese, whether it's a one-syllable verb or a two-syllable compound verb phrase, the negative particle bù 不 is added before the verb.

Wǒ bù qù nà jiā cānguǎn.
我不去那家餐馆。
I don't go to that restaurant.

Tā bù kāichē qù Niǔyuē.
他不开车去纽约。
He/She doesn't (won't) drive to New York.

Wǒ bù zuòfàn.
我不做饭。
I don't cook.

Wǒ bù rènshi tā.
我不认识他。
I don't know him.

⑪

✎ Work Out 1

Multiple choice: Fill in the blank with the right verb.

1. Wǒ 我 _____ *(sleep)*.

   a. zuòfàn 做饭

   b. shuìjiào 睡觉

   c. tiàowǔ 跳舞

Xǐhuan/bù xǐhuan 喜欢/不喜欢
(to like/not like)

Superlatives with zuì 最

Zài 在 and zhe 着

Question word
shénme (what)

2. Wǒmen 我们 _____ (eat).

   a.zuòfàn 做饭

   b.shuìjiào 睡觉

   c.chīfàn 吃饭

3. Nǐ 你 _____ (go to work).

   a.shàngbān 上班

   b.shuìjiào 睡觉

   c.chīfàn 吃饭

4. Tā 他 _____ (dance).

   a.shàngbān 上班

   b.tiàowǔ 跳舞

   c.chīfàn 吃饭

5. Wáng Xiānsheng hé Wáng Tàitai 王先生和王太太_____ (sing).

   a.chànggē 唱歌

   b.shuìjiào 睡觉

   c.chīfàn 吃饭

6. Wǒ de línjū 我的邻居_____ (cook).

   a.zuòfàn 做饭

   b.tiàowǔ 跳舞

   c.chīfàn 吃饭

7. Xuésheng 学生_____ (go to school).

   a.chànggē 唱歌

b. shuìjiào 睡觉

c. shàngxué 上学

8. Wǒ bù 我不 _____ (*drive*).

a. shàngxué 上学

b. kāichē 开车

c. chànggē 唱歌

ANSWER KEY
1. b; 2. c; 3. a; 4. b; 5. a; 6. a; 7. c; 8. b.

Phrase Builder 2

▶ 6C Phrase Builder 2 (CD 4, Track 25)

měi tiān	每天	*every day*
měi tiān zǎoshang	每天早上	*every morning*
měi tiān xiàwǔ	每天下午	*every afternoon*
měi tiān wǎn/wǎnshang	每天晚/晚上	*every evening*
měi tiān wǎnshang	每天晚上	*every night*
měi nián	每年	*every year*
měi ge lǐbài/xīngqī	每个礼拜/星期	*every week*
měi ge yuè	每个月	*every month*
měi ge zhōumò	每个周末	*every weekend*
měi ge lǐbài sān	每个礼拜三	*every Wednesday*
měi nián sìyuè	每年四月	*every April*
měi nián xiàtiān	每年夏天	*every summer*
měi ge xiǎoshí/měi ge zhōngtóu	每个小时/每个钟头	*every hour*
měi ge rén	每个人	*everyone*
yīqiè	一切	*everything*

Xǐhuan/bù xǐhuan 喜欢/不喜欢
(to like/not like)

Superlatives with **zuì** 最

Zài 在 and **zhe** 着

Question word
shénme (*what*)

měi tái diànnǎo	每台电脑	*every computer*
měi zhāng zhuōzi	每张桌子	*every table*

✏️ Phrase Practice 2

Fill in the blanks in the pīnyīn words and phrases. The characters are provided for additional help and practice.

1. měi _____ xiàwǔ

   每天下午

2. _____ nián

   每年

3. měi ge _____ mò

   每个周末

4. měi _____ rén

   每个人

5. yī _____

   一切

6. měi ge _____ shí

   每个小时

ANSWER KEY

1. tiān; 2. měi; 3. zhōu; 4. ge; 5. qiè; 6. xiǎo

Grammar Builder 2
MĚI 每 (*EVERY/EACH*)

When měi每 (*every/each*) is combined with a noun, a measure word is often inserted between měi每 and the noun. This is shown above by such expressions as měi ge yuè 每个月 (*every month*) and měi zhāng zhuōzi每张桌子 (*every table*), where ge个 and zhāng张 are the appropriate measure words for yuè月 and zhuōzi桌子 respectively. However, you will also see that there are some exceptions to this rule: měi tiān每天 (*every day*), měi nián每年 (*every year*), měi fēn每分 (*every minute*), and měi miǎo 每秒 (*every second*). In the above cases, měi每 is linked directly to the noun. This is because tiān天 (*day*), nián年 (*year*), fēn分 (*minute*), and miǎo秒 (*second*) function grammatically as both nouns and measure words in these expressions.

▶ 6D Grammar Builder 2 (CD 4, Track 26)

Wǒ měi tiān shàngbān.
我每天上班。
I go to work everyday.

Wǒmen měi nián xiàtiān dōu shàng shān.
我们每年夏天都上山。
We go to the mountains every summer.

Tā měi tiān zǎoshang dōu zài zhèlǐ chī zǎocān.
她每天早上都在这里吃早餐。
She eats breakfast here every morning.

Tāmen měi ge lǐbài wǔ wǎnshang dōu qù tiàowǔ.
他们每个礼拜五晚上都去跳舞。
They go to dance every Friday night.

Xǐhuan/bù xǐhuan 喜欢/不喜欢
(to like/not like)

Superlatives with **zuì** 最

Zài 在 and **zhe** 着

Question word
shénme (*what*)

Tāmen měi ge zhōumò qù kàn diànyǐng.

他们每个周末去看电影。

They go to a movie every weekend.

Note that an adverb dōu都 (*all*) is added in some of the above examples. In colloquial Chinese, dōu都 is added to indicate that an action repeatedly happens at a certain time and/or at a certain place.

✎ Work Out 2

Choose the correct option to complete each sentence.

1. Wǒ měi _____ yuè dōu qù Zhōngguó. 我每个月都去中国。

   (*I go to China every month.*)

   a. ge个

   b. tiáo条

   c. none

2. Tā měi _____ nián bā yuè dōu lái Měiguó. 他每年八月都来美国。

   (*He comes to the US in August every year.*)

   a. ge个

   b. tiáo条

   c. none

3. Měi _____ rén dōu yǒu fángzi. 每个人都有房子。

   (*Everyone has a house.*)

   a. ge个

b. tiáo 条

c. bù 不

4. Měi _____ fángzi dōu hěn piàoliang. 每个房子都很漂亮。

   (Every house is very pretty.)

   a. ge 个

   b. tiáo 条

   c. none

5. Měi _____ lǎoshī dōu shì Zhōngguórén. 每个老师都是中国人。

   (Every teacher is Chinese.)

   a. ge 个

   b. tiáo 条

   c. none

6. Měi _____ lù dōu hěn cháng. 每条路都很长。 *(Every road is very long.)*

   a. ge 个

   b. tiáo 条

   c. none

7. Wǒ měi _____ xīngqī dōu tiàowǔ. 我每个星期都跳舞。 *(I dance every week.)*

   a. ge 个

   b. tiáo 条

   c. none

8. Wǒ měi _____ tiān zuòfàn. 我每天做饭。 *(I cook everyday.)*

   a. ge 个

Xǐhuan/bù xǐhuan 喜欢/不喜欢
(to like/not like)

Superlatives with **zuì** 最

Zài 在 and **zhe** 着

Question word
shénme (*what*)

b. tiáo 条

c. none

ANSWER KEY

1. a; 2. c; 3. a; 4. a; 5. a; 6. b; 7. a; 8. c

 Drive It Home

Form sentences with the given subject and time expression, using the verbs in parentheses. For example, with Wáng tàitai 王太太, měitiān 每天 (shàngbān 上班, xué Zhōngwén 学中文, kàn diànyǐng 看电影), you would write: Wáng tàitai měitiān shàngbān王太太每天上班, Wáng tàitai měitiān xué Zhōngwén王太太每天学中文, Wáng tàitai měitiān kàn diànyǐng王太太每天看电影.

1. yéye 爷爷, lǐbài sān xiàwǔ 礼拜三下午 (xué tiàowǔ 学跳舞, zuòfàn 做饭, yóuyǒng 游泳) _____

   _____

2. wǒmen 我们, měi ge zhōumò 每个周末 (qù cānguǎn 去餐馆, kāichē 开车, chànggē 唱歌) _____

   _____

3. Wáng tàitai 王太太, měi nián xiàtiān 每年夏天 (qù Fǎguó 去法国, kànshū 看书, xué Yīngwén 学英文) _____

   _____

ANSWER KEY

1. Yéye lǐbài sān xiàwǔ xué tiàowǔ. 爷爷礼拜三下午学跳舞。 Yéye lǐbài sān xiàwǔ zuòfàn. 爷爷礼拜三下午做饭。 Yéye lǐbài sān xiàwǔ yóuyǒng. 爷爷礼拜三下午游泳。 2. Wǒmen měi ge zhōumò qù cānguǎn. 我们每个周末去餐馆。 Wǒmen měi ge zhōumò kāichē. 我们每个周末开车。 Wǒmen měi ge zhōumò chànggē. 我们每个周末唱歌。 3. Wáng tàitai měi nián xiàtiān qù Fǎguó. 王太太每年夏天去法国。 Wáng tàitai měi nián xiàtiān kàn shū. 王太太每年夏天看书。 Wáng tàitai měi nián xiàtiān xué Yīngwén. 王太太每年夏天学英文。

How Did You Do?

By now, you should know:

☐ Some common verbs and how to use them.
(Still unsure? Go back to 83.)

☐ Expression of time that will help you talk about your routine.
(Still unsure? Go back to 90.)

 Word Recall

Match the English word in the left column with its appropriate translation in the left column.

1. *to know (a person), to meet*	a. hē shuǐ 喝水
2. *every year*	b. miǎo 秒
3. *to sing*	c. chīfàn 吃饭
4. *second*	d. rènshi 认识
5. *hour*	e. yínháng 银行
6. *everything*	f. zǒu 走
7. *to understand*	g. xiǎoshí/zhōngtóu 小时/钟头
8. *to dance*	h. měi tiān 每天
9. *to see*	i. tiàowǔ 跳舞
10. *every day*	j. jiǎnchá 检查
11. *bank*	k. míngbai 明白
12. *to examine, to check*	l. chànggē 唱歌
13. *to eat*	m. yīqiè 一切
14. *to leave/to walk*	n. jiàn 见
15. *to drink water*	o. měi nián 每年

ANSWER KEY
1. d; 2. o; 3. l; 4. b; 5. g; 6. m; 7. k; 8. i; 9. n; 10. h; 11. e; 12. j; 13. c; 14. f; 15. a

Xǐhuan/bù xǐhuan 喜欢/不喜欢
(to like/not like)

Superlatives with **zuì** 最

Zài 在 and **zhe** 着

Question word
shénme (*what*)

Lesson 7: Sentences

In this lesson, you'll learn:

☐ How to express likes and dislikes.

☐ How to express an ongoing action or state.

Sentence Builder 1

▶ 7A Sentence Builder 1 (CD 4, Track 27)

Wǒ xǐhuan chūntiān.	我喜欢春天。	*I like spring.*
Wǒ bù xǐhuan xiàtiān.	我不喜欢夏天。	*I don't like summer.*
Wǒ xǐhuan měi tiān tiàowǔ.	我喜欢每天跳舞。	*I like dancing/to dance every day.*
Wǒ měi ge zhōumò yóuyǒng.	我每个周末游泳。	*I swim every weekend.*
Wáng Tàitai hé Wáng Xiānsheng xǐhuan chànggē.	王太太和王先生喜欢唱歌。	*Mrs. Wang and Mr. Wang like singing.*
Wǒ de lǎoshī xǐhuan zuòfàn.	我的老师喜欢做饭。	*My teacher likes cooking.*
Tāmen xǐhuan Zhōngguó.	他们喜欢中国。	*They like China.*
Nǐ xǐhuan tā ma?	你喜欢他吗?	*Do you like him?*
Wǒmen xǐhuan lǐbài yī tiàowǔ.	我们喜欢礼拜一跳舞。	*We like to dance on Monday.*

Ⅱ

Take It Further

Remember that verb forms in Chinese do not change as much as in English. So tiàowǔ 跳舞 can be translated as *dance, dances, to dance, danced,* or *dancing,* depending on the subject and the grammatical context. For instance, in the sentence Wǒ xǐhuan měi tiān tiàowǔ 我喜欢每天跳舞, the subject wǒ 我 (*I*) is followed by the verb xǐhuan 喜欢 (*to like*), so the sentence could be translated as *I like dancing every day* or *I like to dance every day*.

✎ Sentence Practice 1

Translate the English sentences into pīnyīn.

1. *We like to sing.* _____

   _____

2. *I don't like to swim.* _____

   _____

3. *He likes to cook every night.* _____

   _____

4. *They like to watch movies every weekend.* _____

   _____

5. *My older sister likes to read books every night.* ____

   _____

ANSWER KEY
1. Wǒmen xǐhuan chànggē. 我们喜欢唱歌。 2. Wǒ bù xǐhuan yóuyǒng. 我不喜欢游泳。 3. Tā xǐhuan měi tiān wǎnshang zuòfàn. 他喜欢每天晚上做饭。 4. Tāmen xǐhuan měi ge zhōumò kàn diànyǐng. 他们喜欢每个周末看电影。 5. Wǒ jiějie xǐhuan měi tiān wǎnshang kànshū. 我姐姐喜欢每天晚上看书。

Xǐhuan/bù xǐhuan 喜欢/不喜欢
(to like/not like)

Superlatives with **zuì** 最

Zài 在 and **zhe** 着

Question word
shénme (*what*)

Grammar Builder 1
XǏHUAN/BÙ XǏHUAN 喜欢/不喜欢 (*TO LIKE/NOT LIKE*)

▶ 7B Grammar Builder 1 (CD 4, Track 28)

The verb xǐhuan 喜欢 means *to like* in Chinese. It can be followed by a noun or a verb, just as in English.

Wǒ xǐhuan píngguǒ.
我喜欢苹果。
I like apples.

Wǒ xǐhuan zuòfàn.
我喜欢做饭。
I like to cook.

In order to express a dislike, simply add the negative particle bù 不 (*not*) before xǐhuan 喜欢 to form bù xǐhuan 不喜欢 (*do/does/did not like*).

Tā bù xǐhuan huā.
他不喜欢花。
He doesn't like flowers.

Wǒ bù xǐhuan měi tiān shàngbān.
我不喜欢每天上班。
I don't like to go to work everyday.

Tā yǐqián bù xǐhuan huā.
她以前不喜欢花。
She didn't like flowers in the past.

⏸

✎ Work Out 1

Translate the following sentences into English.

1. Wáng Tàitai měi tiān zuòfàn. 王太太每天做饭。 _____

   _____

2. Nǐmen xǐhuan chànggē ma? 你们喜欢唱歌吗? _____

   _____

3. Tā de dìdi xǐhuan měi ge zhōumò tiàowǔ. 他的弟弟喜欢每个周末跳舞。

   _____

4. Wǒ měi nián qù Zhōngguó. 我每年去中国。 _____

   _____

5. Tāmen bù xǐhuan yīshēng ma? 他们不喜欢医生吗? _____

   _____

6. Gǒu bù xǐhuan māo. 狗不喜欢猫。 _____

   _____

7. Wǒ de māma xǐhuan wǒ de bàba. 我的妈妈喜欢我的爸爸。 _____

   _____

ANSWER KEY

1. *Mrs. Wang cooks everyday. 2. Do you (pl.) like to sing (singing)? 3. His younger brother likes to dance (dancing) every weekend. 4. I go to China every year. 5. Don't they like doctors? 6. Dogs don't like cats. 7. My mother likes my father.*

Xǐhuan/bù xǐhuan 喜欢/不喜欢
(to like/not like)

Superlatives with zuì 最

Zài 在 and zhe 着

Question word
shénme (what)

Sentence Builder 2

▶ 7C Sentence Builder 2 (CD 4, Track 29)

Wǒ zài kàn diànshì.	我在看电视。	*I'm watching television.*
Tāmen zài chīfàn.	他们在吃饭。	*They are eating (a meal).*
Wáng Xiānsheng hé Wáng tàitai zài tiàowǔ.	王先生和王太太在跳舞。	*Mr. Wang and Mrs. Wang are dancing.*
Nǐ zài tīng ma?	你在听吗?	*Are you listening?*
Tā zuòzhe.	她坐着。	*She is sitting.*
Zhāng lǎoshī názhe yī běn shū.	张老师拿着一本书。	*Teacher Zhang is holding a book.*
Tā de jiějie kànzhe wǒ.	她的姐姐看着我。	*Her older sister is looking at me.*
Tā názhe yī běn shū chànggē.	她拿着一本书唱歌。	*She is holding a book to sing.*
Tā zhànzhe ma?	他站着吗?	*Is he standing?*

⏸

✎ Sentence Practice 2

Fill in the blanks in the sentences below based upon the sentences above. The characters are provided for additional help and practice.

1. Zhāng lǎoshī _____ yī běn shū.

张老师拿着一本书。

2. Tāmen _____ chīfàn.

他们在吃饭。

Unit 2 Lesson 7: Sentences

99

3. Wáng xiānsheng _____ Wáng tàitai zài _____.

王先生和王太太在跳舞。

4. Wǒ _____ kàn diànshì.

我在看电视。

5. Tā zuò _____.

她坐着。

ANSWER KEY

1. názhe 拿着; 2. zài 在; 3. hé 和, tiàowǔ 跳舞; 4. zài 在; 5. zhe 着

Grammar Builder 2
ZÀI 在 AND ZHE 着

▶ 7D Grammar Builder 2 (CD 4, Track 30)

In Chinese, the word zài 在 or zhe 着 can be combined with a verb to indicate an ongoing action (zài 在) or state of being (zhe 着), much in the same way as *-ing* does in English. As the examples above show, zhe 着 is placed after the verb, and zài 在 comes before the verb.

Wǒ zài hē kāfēi.
我在喝咖啡。
I am drinking coffee.

Tā zài zuò gōngkè.
他在做功课。
He is doing his homework.

Tā tǎngzhe bù dòng.
他躺着不动。
He is lying motionless.

Xǐhuan/bù xǐhuan 喜欢/不喜欢
(to like/not like)

Superlatives with zuì 最

Zài 在 and **zhe** 着

Question word
shénme (*what*)

Dàmén chǎngzhe.

大门敞着。

The front door is open. (lit., The door is opening.)

The difference between zài 在 and zhe 着 is subtle. Remember that zài 在 refers to an ongoing and continuous action, while zhe 着 usually refers to an ongoing state of being. Here are a few examples to illustrate this difference.

Tā de jiějie zài chuān hóng xiézi.

她的姐姐在穿红鞋子。

Her older sister is putting on red shoes. (action)

Tā de jiějie chuānzhe hóng xiézi.

她的姐姐穿着红鞋子。

Her older sister is wearing red shoes. (state)

Tā zài guān mén.

他在关门。

He is closing the door. (action)

Dàmén guānzhe.

大门关着。

The front door is closed. (state)

Note that zài 在 is not only used to indicate an ongoing or continuous action in the present tense. It can also indicate a past action, in which case it would be translated as *was/were … -ing* in English:

Tā zuótiān zài kāichē.

他昨天在开车。

He was driving yesterday.

Notice in the example above that the verb kāichē 开车 doesn't change form to show past tense, as it would in English. Instead, it is only the presence of the adverb zuótiān 昨天 (*yesterday*) that indicates tense. We'll come back to expressing tense in Chinese later, but for now keep in mind that adverbs of time often play the role of tense endings like *-ed* in English.

(II)

✎ Work Out 2

Fill in the blanks in the following sentences using zhe 着 or zài 在. The translations are given to help you.

1. Wǒ _____ kànshū.

   我在看书。

   (*I am reading.*)

2. Lǐ xiānsheng _____ chī shuǐguǒ.

   李先生在吃水果。

   (*Mr. Li is eating fruit.*)

3. Nǐ hé mèimei _____ tiàowǔ.

   你和妹妹在跳舞。

   (*You and your younger sister are dancing.*)

4. Tā zhàn _____.

   他站着。

   (*He is standing.*)

Xǐhuan/bù xǐhuan 喜欢/不喜欢
(to like/not like)

Superlatives with **zuì** 最

Zài 在 and **zhe** 着

Question word
shénme (*what*)

5. Tāmen _____ tīng yīnyuè.

他们在听音乐。

(*They are listening to music.*)

6. Tā de gǒu _____ shuìjiào.

她的狗在睡觉。

(*Her dog is sleeping.*)

7. Wǒ kàn _____ Wǒ de línjū de huā.

我看着我的邻居的花。

(*I am looking at my neighbor's flowers.*)

8. Wáng Tàitai _____ zuòfàn.

王太太在做饭。

(*Mrs. Wang is cooking.*)

ANSWER KEY
1. zài 在; 2. zài 在; 3. zài 在; 4. zhe 着; 5. zài 在; 6. zài 在; 7. zhe 着; 8. zài 在

Culture Note

It's not common in Chinese to use the word ài 爱 (*to love*) colloquially to say that you care about someone. Instead, the verb xǐhuan 喜欢 (*to like*) is more often used to express such feelings.

Wǒ xǐhuan nǐ.
我喜欢你。
I like you./I love you.

Wǒ hěn xǐhuan nǐ.
我很喜欢你。
I like you very much./I love you very much.

✎ Drive It Home

Form sentences with zài 在 and zhe 着 using the simple sentences provided. For example, for zài 在 and wǒ tiàowǔ 我跳舞 (*I dance*), you would write wǒ zài tiàowǔ 我在跳舞 (*I am dancing*).

For zài 在:

1. Wǒmen kāichē. 我们开车。 _____

   _____

2. Tā chīfàn. 他吃饭。 _____

   _____

3. Wàigōng chànggē. 外公唱歌。 _____

   _____

4. Nǐ gōngzuò. 你工作。 _____

   _____

For zhe 着:

1. Shūshu tīng yīnyuē. 叔叔听音乐。 _____

   _____

2. Wǒ ná shū. 我拿书。 _____

   _____

3. Wáng Xiānsheng shuìjiào. 王先生睡觉。 _____

   _____

Xǐhuan/bù xǐhuan 喜欢/不喜欢
(to like/not like)

Superlatives with **zuì** 最

zài 在 and **zhe** 着

Question word
shénme (*what*)

4. Nǐmen hēshuǐ. 你们喝水。 _____

ANSWER KEY

For zài 在:

1. Wǒmen zài kāichē. 我们在开车。 2. Tā zài chīfàn. 他在吃饭。 3. Wàigōng zài chànggē. 外公在唱歌。 4. Nǐ zài gōngzuò. 你在工作。

For zhe 着:

1. Shūshu tīngzhe yīnyue. 叔叔听着音乐。 2. Wǒ názhe shū. 我拿着书。 3. Wáng Xiānsheng shuìzhe jiào. 王先生睡着觉。 4. Nǐmen hēzhe shuǐ. 你们喝着水。

How Did You Do?

By now, you should know:

☐ How to express likes and dislikes.
(Still unsure? Go back to 97.)

☐ How to express an ongoing action or state.
(Still unsure? Go back to 100.)

✎ Word Recall

Match the English word in the left column with its appropriate translation in the right column.

1. *to shut, to close*   a. tǎng 躺

2. *yesterday*   b. ná 拿

3. *to dislike*   c. gōngkè 功课

4. *to lie down*   d. zhàn 站

5. *at; particle indicating an ongoing action*   e. xǐhuan 喜欢

6. *to love*   f. guān 关

7. *to stand*   g. zài 在

8. *homework*   h. ài 爱

9. *fruit*   i. zhe 着

10. *to like*   j. zuótiān 昨天

11. *to hold*   k. bù xǐhuan 不喜欢

12. *particle indicating an ongoing state*   l. shuǐguǒ 水果
   of being

ANSWER KEY
1. f; 2. j; 3. k; 4. a; 5. g; 6. h; 7. d; 8. c; 9. l; 10. e; 11. b; 12. i

Lesson 8: Conversations

In this lesson, you'll learn:

☐ How to express *the most* in Chinese.

☐ How to use the question word shénme 什么 (*what*).

Conversation 1

▶ 8A Conversation 1 (CD 4, Track 31-Chinese, Track 32-Chinese and English)

Wang Hai and Jess are practicing Chinese.

Hǎi:	Jiéxī, nǐ zài zuò shénme?
海:	洁希, 你在做什么?
Jiéxī:	Wǒ zài liànxí Zhōngwén.
洁希:	我在练习中文。
Hǎi:	Hǎo, ràng wǒ kǎokǎo nǐ.
海:	好, 让我考考你。
Jiéxī:	Hǎo ba.
洁希:	好吧。
Hǎi:	Yī nián yǒu jǐ ge yuè?
海:	一年有几个月?

Zài 在 and **zhe 着**

Jiéxī:	Shí'èr ge yuè.
洁希:	十二个月。
Hǎi:	Yī ge lǐbài yǒu jǐ tiān?
海:	一个礼拜有几天?
Jiéxī:	Qī tiān.
洁希:	七天。
Hǎi:	Jīntiān shì jǐ hào, lǐbài jǐ?
海:	今天是几号，礼拜几?
Jiéxī:	Jīntiān shì shí'èr yuè sì hào, lǐbài yī.
洁希:	今天是十二月四号，礼拜一。
Hǎi:	Nǎge yuè zuì lěng?
海:	哪个月最冷?
Jiéxī:	Èr yuè.
洁希:	二月。

Hai:	*Jess, what are you doing?*
Jess:	*I'm practicing (my) Chinese.*
Hai:	*Okay. Let me test you.*
Jess:	*Alright.*
Hai:	*How many months are there in a year?*
Jess:	*Twelve months.*
Hai:	*How many days are there in a week?*
Jess:	*Seven days.*
Hai:	*What's today's date and what day of the week is it?*
Jess:	*Today is Monday, December 4th.*
Hai:	*Which month is the coldest?*
Jess:	*February.*

Ⓜ

Unit 2 Lesson 8: Conversations

107

Take It Further

Ràng wǒ 让我 means *let me*. It is always followed by another verb, in this case the verb kǎo 考 (*to give a test*).

Notice that the veb kǎo 考 is doubled: ràng wǒ kǎokǎo nǐ. 让我考考你。 This is called verb reduplication, and it's used in Chinese to signify that something is being done a little bit, or to a lesser degree than might be expected. Here, it means *let me give you a little quiz* rather than a long, formal examination. Here are some other examples of verb reduplication:

Wǒmen tántan.
我们谈谈。
We're having a little chat.

Wǒ qīnglǐ qīnglǐ fángzi.
我清理清理房子。
I'm tidying up the house a bit.

The expression hǎo ba 好吧 literally means *fine*. You can translate it as *okay*, *alright*, or *go ahead*, depending on the context.

The question word jǐ 几 (*how many*) requires the use of a measure word when combined with a noun, as in the case of jǐ ge yuè 几个月 (*how many months*). Another question word meaning *how many* in Chinese is duōshǎo 多少, which is used in everday conversation to ask how much something costs (duōshǎo qián? 多少钱？). You will learn more about these question words in Unit 4.

Nǎ 哪 is a demonstrative question pronoun. When combined with a noun and its measure word, it means *which* as can be seen in the phrase nǎge yuè 哪个月 (*which month*).

Xǐhuan/bù xǐhuan 喜欢/不喜欢
(to like/not like)

Superlatives with **zuì** 最

Zài 在 and zhe 着

Question word
shénme (*what*)

✎ Conversation Practice 1

Fill in the blanks with the missing words in pīnyīn. The characters are provided for additional help and practice. Refer to the conversation with Hai and Jess.

1. Jiéxī zài _____ Zhōngwén.

   洁希在练习中文。

2. Hǎi zài _____ Jiéxī.

   海在考洁希。

3. Jīntiān shì _____ yī.

   今天是礼拜一。

4. Jīntiān shì _____ sì hào.

   今天是十二月四号。

5. Èr yuè _____ lěng.

   二月最冷。

ANSWER KEY
1. liànxí 练习; 2. kǎo 考; 3. lǐbài 礼拜; 4. shí'èr yuè 十二月; 5. zuì 最

Grammar Builder 1
SUPERLATIVES WITH ZUÌ 最

Zuì 最 means *the most* and is placed before an adjective to indicate the superlative, or the *-est* form in English. Here are some examples:

▶ 8B Grammar Builder 1 (CD 4, Track 33)

Tā zuì piàoliang.
她最漂亮。
She is the prettiest.

Měiguó chē zuì guì.

美国车最贵。

American cars are the most expensive.

Ⓟ

Notice the word order in the last example. The adjective Měiguó 美国 (*American*), which describes chē 车 (*cars*), comes right before the noun, just as in English. The particle de 的 that generally follows disyllabic adjectives is usually omitted when the adjective is the name of a country, a language, or a place of origin. The phrase zuì guì 最贵 (*most expensive*) comes at the end of the sentence, also just as in English. The major difference of course is that there is no verb *is* in Chinese in adjective sentences such as this.

✎ Work Out 1

A. Answer the following questions in English.

1. Jīntiān shì jǐ hào? 今天是几号? _____

   _____

2. Yī nián yǒu jǐ ge yuè? 一年有几个月? _____

   _____

3. Yī ge lǐbài yǒu jǐ tiān? 一个礼拜有几天? _____

   _____

4. Shí'èr yuè yǒu jǐ tiān? 十二月有几天? _____

   _____

Xǐhuan/bù xǐhuan 喜欢/不喜欢
(to like/not like)

Superlatives with zuì 最

Zài 在 and **zhe** 着

Question word
shénme (*what*)

B. Insert the word zuì into the following sentences to make a superlative statement.

1. Wǒ gāo. 我高。 _____

2. Tā de chē kuài. 他的车快。 _____

3. Nàxiē fángzi dà. 那些房子大。 _____

4. Nà bǎ yǐzi xiǎo. 那把椅子小。 _____

ANSWER KEY
A: 1. *It depends on today's date.* 2. *twelve*; 3. *seven*; 4. *thirty-one*
B: 1. Wǒ zuì gāo. 我最高。 2. Tā de chē zuì kuài. 他的车最快。 3. Nàxiē fángzi zuì dà. 那些房子最大。
4. Nà bǎ yǐzi zuì xiǎo. 那把椅了最小。

⌕ Conversation 2

▶ 8C Conversation 2 (CD 4, Track 34-Chinese, CD 5, Track 1-Chinese and English)

Hai and Jess are talking about Jess' birthday.

Hǎi: Jiéxī, nǐ de shēngrì shì nǎ tiān?
海: 洁希, 你的生日是哪天？

Jiéxī: Shí'èr yuè shíwǔ hào.
洁希: 十二月十五号。

Hǎi: Jīntiān shì jǐ hào?
海: 今天是几号？

Jiéxī: Shí'èr yuè shíwǔ hào.
洁希: 十二月十五号。

Hǎi: Shēngrì kuàilè.
海: 生日快乐。

Jiéxī:	Xièxie!
洁希:	谢谢！
Hǎi:	Nǐ xǐhuan shénme shēngrì dàngāo?
海:	你喜欢什么生日蛋糕？
Jiéxī:	Wǒ xǐhuan qiǎokèlì. Nǐ ne?
洁希:	我喜欢巧克力。 你呢？
Hǎi:	Wǒ bù xǐhuan qiǎokèlì. Wǒ xǐhuan xiāngcǎo.
海:	我不喜欢巧克力。 我喜欢香草。

Hai:	*Jess, what day is your birthday?*
Jess:	*December 15th.*
Hai:	*Oh, what's today's date?*
Jess:	*December 15th.*
Hai:	*Happy birthday!*
Jess:	*Thank you!*
Hai:	*What (kind of) birthday cake do you like?*
Jess:	*I like chocolate. How about you?*
Hai:	*I don't like chocolate. I like vanilla.*

(II)

Take It Further

Happy birthday is expressed in Chinese as shēngrì kuàilè 生日快乐. The word order here is the exact opposite of English since shēngrì kuàilè 生日快乐 literally translates as *birthday happy*.

Notice the word order of Chinese questions with question words:

Nǐ de shēngrì shì nǎ tiān?
你的生日是哪天？
lit., Your birthday is what day?

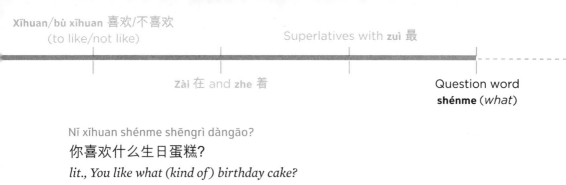

Xǐhuan/bù xǐhuan 喜欢/不喜欢
(to like/not like)

Superlatives with **zuì** 最

Zài 在 and **zhe** 着

Question word
shénme (*what*)

Nǐ xǐhuan shénme shēngrì dàngāo?

你喜欢什么生日蛋糕?

lit., You like what (kind of) birthday cake?

In English, question words typically come at the beginning of the questions, but not in Chinese. We'll take a closer look at this in the Grammar Builder section.

✎ Conversation Practice 2

Fill in the blanks with the missing words in pīnyīn. Refer to the second conversation with Hai and Jess. The characters are provided for additional help and practice.

1. Jiéxī de _____ shì shí'èr yuè shíwǔ _____.

   洁希的生日是十二月十五号。

2. Jīntiān shì _____ de shēngrì.

   今天是洁希的生日。

3. Jiéxī _____ qiǎokèlì _____.

   洁希喜欢巧克力蛋糕。

4. Hǎi _____ xǐhuan _____ dàngāo.

   海不喜欢巧克力蛋糕。

5. Hǎi xǐhuan _____.

   海喜欢香草蛋糕。

   ANSWER KEY
   1. shēngrì 生日, hào 号; 2. Jiéxī 洁希; 3. xǐhuan 喜欢, dàngāo 蛋糕; 4. bù 不, qiǎokèlì 巧克力;
   5. xiāngcǎo 香草, dàngāo 蛋糕

Grammar Builder 2
QUESTION WORD SHÉNME 什么 (WHAT)

Let's take a look at the very important and useful question word shénme 什么 (what), As you saw in the dialogue, question words in Chinese are not placed at the beginning of questions. So literally, questions in Chinese sound like English "echo" questions: *You ate what? They did what?*

▶ 8D Grammar Builder 2 (CD 5, Track 2)

Nà shì shénme?

那是什么?

What is that?

Nǐ chī shénme?

你吃什么?

What do you eat?

Nǐmen zài zuò shénme?

你们在做什么?

What are you doing?

Tā xǐhuan kàn shénme shū?

她喜欢看什么书?

What does she like to read?

Note that shénme 什么 can also be translated as *what kind of*:

Nǐ xǐhuan shénme shuǐguǒ?

你喜欢什么水果?

What kind of fruit do you like?

Superlatives with **zuì** 最

Zài 在 and **zhe** 着

Question word
shénme (*what*)

Tā xǐhuan shénme diànyǐng?
他喜欢什么电影?
What kind of movies does he like?

✎ Work Out 2
Translate the following sentences into English.

1. Nǐ xǐhuan chī shénme? 你喜欢吃什么? _____

_____

2. Tā de dìdi zài zuò shénme? 他／她的弟弟在做什么? _____

_____

3. Zhè shì shénme? 这是什么? _____

_____

4. Tā bù xǐhuan shénme? 他不喜欢什么? _____

_____

5. Nǐ hē shénme? 你喝什么? _____

_____

6. Tā kàn shénme shū? 他看什么书? _____

_____

ANSWER KEY
1. What do you like to eat? 2. What is his/her younger brother doing? 3. What is this? 4. What does he dislike? 5. What do you drink? 6. What book does he read?

✎ Drive It Home

Form question sentences with shénme 什么 and a noun based upon the sentences provided. For example, if the sentence is Tā kànshū. 他看书, you would write Tā kàn shénme shū? 他看什么书?

1. Gēge hē jiǔ. 哥哥喝酒。 _____

   _____

2. Tā chīfàn. 他吃饭。 _____

   _____

3. Nǐmen xǐhuan kàn diànyǐng. 你们喜欢看电影。 _____

   _____

4. Lǎoshī qù cānguǎn. 老师去餐馆。 _____

5. Nǐ kāichē. 你开车。 _____

   _____

6. Wǒmen zài lǚguǎn. 我们在旅馆。 _____

   _____

ANSWER KEY
1. Gēge hē shénme jiǔ? 哥哥喝什么酒? 2. Tā chī shénme fàn? 他吃什么饭? 3. Nǐmen xǐhuan kàn shénme diànyǐng? 你们喜欢看什么电影? 4. Lǎoshī qù shénme cānguǎn? 老师去什么餐馆? 5. Nǐ kāi shénme chē? 你开什么车? 6. Wǒmen zài shénme lǚguǎn? 我们在什么旅馆?

Xǐhuan/bù xǐhuan 喜欢/不喜欢
(to like/not like)

Superlatives with **zuì** 最

Zài 在 and **zhe** 着

Question word
shénme (*what*)

How Did You Do?

By now, you should know:

☐ How to express *the most* in Chinese. (Still unsure? Go back to 109.)

☐ How to use the question word shénme (*what*). (Still unsure? Go back to 114.)

✎ Word Recall

Match the English word in the left column with its appropriate translation in the right column.

1. the most	*a.* liànxí 练习
2. cake	*b.* ràng 让
3. how many months	*c.* kǎo 考
4. to clean, to tidy	*d.* hǎo ba 好吧
5. to allow, to let	*e.* zuì 最
6. how much (money)?	*f.* lěng 冷
7. to practice	*g.* tántan 谈谈
8. thank you	*h.* qīnglǐ 清理
9. to have a chat, to discuss	*i.* jǐ ge yuè 几个月
10. cold	*j.* duōshǎo 多少
11. Happy Birthday	*k.* duōshǎo qián? 多少钱?
12. ok, alright, go ahead	*l.* shēngrì 生日
13. chocolate	*m.* shēngrì kuàilè 生日快乐
14. birthday	*n.* xièxie 谢谢
15. to test	*o.* dàngāo 蛋糕
16. vanilla	*p.* qiǎokèlì 巧克力
17. how much	*q.* xiāngcǎo 香草

ANSWER KEY

1. e; 2. o; 3. i; 4. h; 5. b; 6. k; 7. a; 8. n; 9. g; 10. f; 11. m; 12. d; 13. p; 14. l; 15. c; 16. q; 17. j

Unit 2 Essentials

Vocabulary Essentials

Test your knowledge of the key material in this unit by filling in the blanks in the following charts. Once you've completed these pages, you'll have tested your retention, and you'll have your own reference for the most essential vocabulary. This is also a great time to practice a few Chinese characters. Fill in the middle column with the characters that you remember. Or, if you only remember the pīnyīn , go back through the unit to find the character.

DAYS OF THE WEEK

PĪNYĪN	CHARACTER	
		Monday
		Tuesday
		Wednesday
		Thursday
		Friday
		Saturday
		Sunday

MONTHS OF THE YEAR

PĪNYĪN	CHARACTER	
		January
		February
		March
		April
		May

PĪNYĪN	CHARACTER	
		June
		July
		August
		September
		October
		November
		December

COMMON VERBS

PĪNYĪN	CHARACTER	
		eat (a meal)
		swim
		drive (a car)
		dance (a dance)
		sing (a song)
		cook (a meal)
		go to school
		go to work
		read a book
		sleep/go to bed
		come
		go
		drink water

If you're having a hard time remembering this vocabulary, don't forget to check out the flashcards, games and quizzes for this unit online. Go to **www.livinglanguage. com/languagelab** for a great way to help you practice what you've learned.

Grammar Essentials

Here is a reference for the key grammar that was covered in Unit 2. Make sure you understand the summary and can use all of the grammar it covers.

TWO-SYLLABLE VERBS

Verb-object verbs are composed of a verb directly followed by an object.

Wáng tàitai xǐhuan tiàowǔ hé chànggē.	王太太喜欢跳舞和唱歌。	*Mrs. Wang likes dancing and singing.*
Wǒ zuòfàn.	我做饭。	*I cook.*
Tā kāichē qù Niǔyuē.	他开车去纽约。	*He drives to New York.*

Verb-Object verbs can be split by an adverb or particle. Regular two-syllable verbs cannot be split by an adverb or particle.

Wǒ tiàole liǎng nián de wǔ.	我跳了两年的舞。	*I have danced for two years.*
Wǒ tiàowǔ tiàole liǎng nián.	我跳舞跳了两年。	*I have danced for two years.*
Wǒ jiǎnchá le.	我检查了。	*I checked.*

ZÀI 在 AND ZHE 着

Zài 在 refers to an ongoing and continuous action, while zhe 着 usually refers to an ongoing state of being.

Wǒ zài hē kāfēi.	我在喝咖啡。	*I am drinking coffee.*
Tā zài zuò gōngkè.	他在做功课。	*He is doing his homework.*
Tā tǎng zhe bù dòng.	他躺着不动。	*He is lying motionlessly.*
Dàmén chǎngzhe.	大门敞着。	*The front door is open. (lit., The door is opening.)*

EXPRESSING LIKES AND DISLIKES

| Wǒ xǐhuan chūntiān. | 我喜欢春天。 | *I like spring.* |
| Wǒ bù xǐhuan xiàtiān. | 我不喜欢夏天。 | *I don't like summer.* |

Character Essentials

To practice the Chinese characters you learned in Unit 2, Conversations 1 and
2 are repeated here without pīnyīn or English translations. Translate as many
characters as you can. Check your answers by listening to the conversations from
your audio. Don't worry if you can't remember all of the characters. Just try to
remember as many as you can.

Conversation 1

8A Conversation 1 (CD 4, Track 31-Chinese, Track 32-Chinese and English)

海: 洁希, 你在做什么?

_____

_____

洁希: 我在练习中文。

_____

_____

海: 好, 让我考考你。

_____

_____

洁希: 好吧。

海: 一年有几个月?

洁希: 十二个月。

海: 一个礼拜有几天?

洁希: 七天。

海: 今天是几号, 礼拜几?

洁希:　　　今天是十二月四号, 礼拜一。

_____

_____

海:　　　哪个月最冷?

_____

_____

洁希:　　　二月。

_____

_____

Ⓘ

ⓐ Conversation 2

▶ 8C Conversation 2 (CD 4, Track 34-Chinese, CD 2, Track 1-Chinese and English)

海:　　　洁希, 你的生日是哪天?

_____

_____

洁希:　　　十二月十五号。

_____

_____

海:　　　今天是几号?

_____

_____

洁希:　　　十二月十五号。

海:　　　生日快乐。

洁希:　　　谢谢!

海:　　　你喜欢什么生日蛋糕?

洁希:　　　我喜欢巧克力。 你呢?

海:　　　我不喜欢巧克力。 我喜欢香草。

Unit 2 Quiz

A. Translate the following sentences and phrases into Chinese.

1. *Today is Sunday.* _____

_____

2. *Thursday evening* _____

_____

3. *July 28* _____

_____

4. *March 16 is a weekday.* _____

_____

B. Fill in the blank with the correct verb or measure word. Write the pīnyīn and the character.

1. Wǒmen 我们 _____ *(eat)*

2. Tā 他 _____ *(dance)*

3. Wǒ měi _____ yuè dōu qù Zhōngguó.

   我每 _____ 月都去中国。*(I go to China every month.)*

4. Měi _____ lù dōu hěn cháng.

   每 _____ 路都很长。*(Every road is very long.)*

C. Translate the following sentences into English.

1. Wáng Tàitai xǐhuan yīshēng ma? 王太太喜欢医生吗? _____

_____

2. Wǒ de māma xǐhuan gǒu. 我的妈妈喜欢狗。 _____

_____

3. Tā de dìdi xǐhuan měi tiān zuòfàn. 他的弟弟喜欢每天做饭。 _____

_____

4. Wǒ zài kànshū. 我在看书。 _____

_____

5. Tā zhànzhe. 他站着。 _____

_____

6. Tāmen tīngzhe yīnyue. 他们听着音乐。 _____

_____

D. Fill in the blank with zuì 最 or shénme 什么.

1. Nǐ xǐhuan chī _____?

   你喜欢吃 _____?

2. Tā de mèimei _____ gāo.

   他的妹妹 _____ 高。

3. Nǐ hē _____?

   你喝 _____?

4. Tā kàn _____ shū?

   她看 _____ 书?

5. Nà liàng chē _____ kuài ma?

那辆车_____快吗?

6. Nǎ ge fángzi _____ xiǎo?

哪个房子_____小?

How did you do?

Give yourself a point for every correct answer, then use the following key to tell whether you're ready to move on:

0-7 points: It's probably a good idea to go back through the lesson again. You may be moving too quickly, or there may be too much "down time" between your contact with Chinese. Remember that it's better to spend 30 minutes with Chinese three or four times a week than it is to spend two or three hours just once a week. Find a pace that's comfortable for you, and spread your contact hours out as much as you can.

8-12 points: You would benefit from a review before moving on. Go back and spend a little more time on the specific points that gave you trouble. Re-read the Grammar Builder sections that were difficult, and do the Work Outs one more time. Don't forget about the online supplemental practice material, either. Go to **www.livinglanguage.com/languagelab** for games and quizzes that will reinforce the material from this unit.

13-17 points: Good job! There are just a few points that you might consider reviewing before moving on. If you haven't worked with the games and quizzes on **www.livinglanguage.com/languagelab**, please give them a try.

18-20 points: Great! You're ready to move on to the next unit.

 **points**

 Don't forget to practice and reinforce what you've learned by visiting **www.livinglanguage.com/languagelab** for flashcards, games, and quizzes.

Unit 3: Going Shopping

Gòuwù
购物

In Unit 3, you'll learn how to talk about colors, clothing, and money. You'll also learn some essential expressions for shopping and more about numbers and negation.

Let's get started!

Lesson 9: Words

In this lesson, you'll learn:

☐ Essential vocabulary related to clothing.

☐ Measure words for clothes.

☐ How to talk about colors.

Word Builder 1

▶ 9A Word Builder 1 (CD 5, Track 3)

yīfu	衣服	*clothes, clothing*
mǎi	买	*to buy*
chuān	穿	*to wear*
T-xùshān/hànshān	T-恤衫/汗衫	*T-shirt*
chènshān	衬衫	*shirt*

kùzi	裤子	*pants*
liányīqún	连衣裙	*dress*
qúnzi	裙子	*skirt*
qúnkù	裙裤	*culottes, skort*
wàitào	外套	*coat*
jiákè	夹克	*jacket*
yǔyī	雨衣	*raincoat*
qípáo	旗袍	*traditional Chinese dress*
wàzi	袜子	*socks*
xiézi	鞋子	*shoes*
xuēzi	靴子	*boots*
yùndòngxié	运动鞋	*sneakers*
màozi	帽子	*hat*
pídài	皮带	*belt*
nèikù	内裤	*underpants*
shǒubiǎo	手表	*watch*
jièzhi	戒指	*ring*

⏸

✎ Word Practice 1

Match the English word in the left column with its appropriate translation in the
right column.

1. *to wear*   a. kùzi 裤子

2. *pants*   b. chènshān 衬衫

3. *skirt*   c. chuān 穿

4. *shirt*   d. xiézi 鞋子

5. *shoes*   e. qúnzi 裙子

ANSWER KEY
1. c; 2. a; 3. e; 4. b; 5. d

Grammar Builder 1
MEASURE WORDS FOR CLOTHING AND ACCESSORIES

As you know, a measure word needs to be placed before a noun if it is preceded
by a number or demonstrative. In the previous units, you learned some important
measure words and how measure words work with some time expressions and other
phrases. Now, let's see how measure words are used when you talk about clothing.

Generally, two measure words are used when describing articles of clothing in
Chinese: jiàn 件 and tiáo 条. Jiàn 件 is used for garments worn over the upper part
or full length of the body, and tiáo 条 is used for garments worn over the lower
half of the body:

▶ 9B Grammar Builder 1 (CD 5, Track 4)

yī jiàn chènshān 一件衬衫	*one/a shirt*
zhè jiàn wàitào 这件外套	*this overcoat*
sì tiáo qúnzi 四条裙子	*four skirts*
yī tiáo kùzi 一条裤子	*a/one pair of pants*

When talking about shoes and footwear, however, the measure word shuāng 双
(*pair*) is normally used. If you want to specify a particular number of shoes, socks,
or boots other than a pair, use the measure word zhī 只:

yī shuāng xiézi 一双鞋子	*a pair of shoes*
yī zhī xiézi 一只鞋子	*one shoe*

Here are some more examples of measure words used with clothing:

Wǒ yǒu yī jiàn T-xùshān.

我有一件T-恤衫。

I have a T-shirt.

Wǒ chuānzhe yī jiàn yǔyī.

我穿这一件雨衣。

I'm wearing a raincoat.

Wǒ yǒu yī tiáo kùzi.

我有一条裤子。

I have a pair of pants.

Wǒ yǒu qī shuāng wàzi.

我有七双袜子。

I have seven pairs of socks.

Wǒ yǒu yī zhī xuēzi.

我有一只靴子。

I have one boot.

Note that yī tiáo 一条 is translated as *a pair of* with certain articles of clothing, such as pants. Keep in mind that it's not the same *a pair of* that is used with footwear, which is yī shuāng 一双.

There are different measure words used for accessories and other types of clothing. Here are the most common ones:

yī ge shǒubiǎo 一个手表	*a watch*
yī duì ěrhuán 一对耳环	*a pair of earrings*
yī tiáo xiàngliàn 一条项链	*a necklace*
yī zhī zhúozi 一只镯子	*a bracelet*

| yī ge jièzhi 一个戒指 | *a ring* |
| yī dǐng màozi 一顶帽子 | *a hat* |

✎ Work Out 1

Complete the following phrases with the appropriate measure word in pīnyīn and Chinese characters, and then translate the phrase into English.

1. Yī _____ qúnzi (ge/jiàn/tiáo) 一 _____ 裙子 (个/件/条)

   _____

2. Yī _____ chènshān (ge/jiàn/tiáo) 一 _____ 衬衫 (个/件/条)

   _____

3. Yī _____ jiákè (ge/jiàn/tiáo) 一 _____ 夹克 (个/件/条)

   _____

4. Yī _____ xiézi (shuāng/jiàn/tiáo) 一 _____ 鞋子 (双/件/条)

   _____

5. Yī _____ kùzi (shuāng/jiàn/tiáo) 一 _____ 裤子 (双/件/条)

   _____

6. Yī _____ ěrhuán (duì/jiàn/tiáo) 一 _____ 耳环 (对/件/条)

   _____

7. Yī _____ shǒubiǎo (ge/jiàn/tiáo) 一 _____ 手表 (个/件/条)

   _____

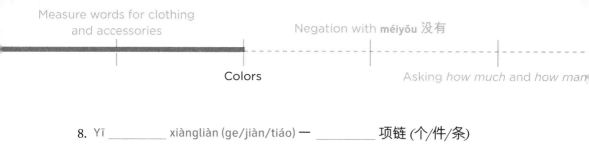
8. Yī _____ xiàngliàn (ge/jiàn/tiáo) 一 _____ 项链 (个/件/条)

ANSWER KEY

1. tiáo 条 (*a skirt*); 2. jiàn 件 (*a shirt*); 3. jiàn 件 (*a jacket*); 4. shuāng 双 (*a pair of shoes*); 5. tiáo 条 (*a pair of pants*); 6. duì 对 (*a pair of earrings*); 7. ge 个 (*a watch*); 8. tiáo 条 (*a necklace*)

Word Builder 2

▶ 9C Word Builder 2 (CD 5, Track 5)

hóngsè	红色	*red*
chéngsè	橙色	*orange*
huángsè	黄色	*yellow*
lǜsè	绿色	*green*
lánsè	蓝色	*blue*
zǐsè	紫色	*purple*
fěnhóngsè	粉红色	*pink*
zōngsè	棕色	*brown*
hēisè	黑色	*black*
báisè	白色	*white*
huīsè	灰色	*grey*
yínsè	银色	*silver*
jīnsè	金色	*gold*
shēn	深	*dark*
shēn lánsè	深蓝色	*dark blue*
qiǎn	浅	*light*
qiǎn lǜsè	浅绿色	*light green*

⏸

✎ Word Practice 2

Match the English word in the left column with its appropriate translation in the
right column.

1. *blue*

2. *gray*

3. *red*

4. *brown*

5. *yellow*

a. **huīsè** 灰色

b. **hóngsè** 红色

c. **lánsè** 蓝色

d. **huángsè** 黄色

e. **zōngsè** 棕色

ANSWER KEY
1. c; 2. a; 3. b; 4. e; 5. d

Grammar Builder 2
COLORS

▶ 9D Grammar Builder 2 (CD 5, Track 6)

Colors are expressed in Chinese as a combination of one or two syllables that
identify a specific hue, along with the additional syllable **sè** 色, which generically
means *color*. The use of **sè** 色 is usually necessary.

Zhè běn shū shì hóngsè de.
这本书是红色的。
This book is red.

Nà xiē kùzi shì lánsè de.
那些裤子是蓝色的。
Those pants are blue.

The syllable **de** 的 is also necessary when a color is used as a descriptive adjective
right before a noun:

Wǒ yǒu yī běn hóngsè de shū.

我有一本红色的书。

I have a red book.

Tā chuānzhe yī tiáo lánsè de kùzi.

她穿着一条蓝色的裤子。

She's wearing blue pants.

Note that hóngsè 红色 and lánsè 蓝色 are both composed of two syllables. In general, if an adjective with two syllables directly precedes a noun, then de 的 usually has to be placed in between the adjective and the noun. If, however, the adjective only has one syllable, then de is frequently omitted. For example: dà bízi 大鼻子 (*big nose*).

Also note that both sè 色 and de 的 are normally omitted when adjectives describing color are used in combination with certain monosyllabic nouns where the color is an intrinsic property of the noun.

yī duǒ hóng huā 一朵红花	*a red flower*
lǜ cǎo 绿草	*green grass*
lán tiān 蓝天	*blue sky*
bái yún 白云	*white cloud*

⏸

🖊 Work Out 2

Match the Chinese colors on the left with their English translations on the right.

1. báisè   a. *pink*

2. lǜsè   b. *blue*

3. lánsè   c. *white*

4. fěnhóngsè   d. *grey*

5. hóngsè   e. *red*

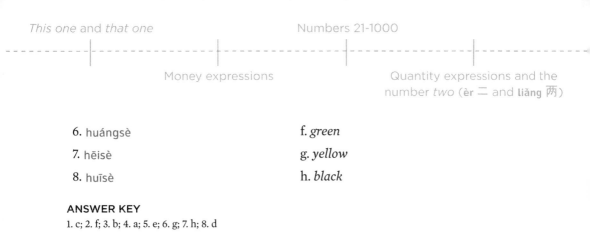
6. huángsè   f. *green*

7. hēisè   g. *yellow*

8. huīsè   h. *black*

ANSWER KEY
1. c; 2. f; 3. b; 4. a; 5. e; 6. g; 7. h; 8. d

🌐 Culture Note

Colors can have very different meanings in different traditions. For example, to the Chinese, red symbolizes luck, happiness and prosperity, and is therefore commonly used for celebrations such as birthdays, New Year festivities and weddings. By contrast, white and black are the traditional colors of funerals in China, so they're not considered appropriate for celebrating a marriage, as they are in the Western tradition. However, with the growing popularity of Western culture in China, many young couples have challenged the tradition by opting for a white bridal gown and black tuxedo at their wedding.

✎ Drive It Home

Form phrases using the number phrase or demonstrative and the list of clothing and accessories provided. For example, with zhè 这 and jiákè 夹克 and xuēzi 靴子, you would write zhè jiàn jiákè 这件夹克 and zhè shuāng xuēzi 这双靴子.

1. zhè tiáo 这条 (kùzi 裤子, xiàngliàn 项链, qúnzi 裙子, pídài 皮带) _____

   _____

2. sān shuāng 三双 (xiézi 鞋子, wàzi 袜子, xuēzi 靴子) _____

   _____

3. yī jiàn 一件 (chènshān 衬衫, wàitào 外套, yǔyī 雨衣, qípáo 旗袍) _____

   _____

4. sì zhī 四只 (érhuán 耳环, zhuózi 镯子) _____

_____

ANSWER KEY

1. zhè tiáo kùzi 这条裤子, zhè tiáo xiàngliàn 这条项链, zhè tiáo qúnzi 这条裙子, zhè tiáo pídài 这条皮带 2. sān shuāng xiézi 三双鞋子, sān shuāng wàzi 三双袜子, sān shuāng xuēzi 三双靴子 3. yī jiàn chènshān 一件衬衫, yī jiàn wàitào 一件外套, yī jiàn yǔyī 一件雨衣, yī jiàn qípáo 一件旗袍 4. sì zhī érhuán 四只耳环, sì zhī zhuózi 四只镯子

How Did You Do?

By now, you should know:

☐ Essential vocabulary related to clothing.
(Still unsure? Go back to 129.)

☐ Measure words for clothes.
(Still unsure? Go back to 131.)

☐ How to talk about colors.
(Still unsure? Go back to 135.)

 # Word Recall

Match the English word in the left column with its appropriate translation in the right column.

1. *measure word for pair*

2. *orange*

3. *pink*

4. *clothes, clothing*

5. *sneakers*

6. *white*

7. *coat*

8. *dress*

9. *underpants*

a. chéngsè 橙色

b. yǔyī 雨衣

c. qiǎn 浅

d. chuān 穿

e. shuāng 双

f. liányīqún 连衣裙

g. jiàn 件

h. fěnhóngsè 粉红色

i. nèikù 内裤

10. *to wear*	j. yīfu 衣服
11. *socks*	k. báisè 白色
12. *dark*	l. wàitào 外套
13. *raincoat*	m. zǐsè 紫色
14. *gold*	n. kùzi 裤子
15. *purple*	o. wàzi 袜子
16. *pants*	p. shēn 深
17. *light (in color)*	q. yùndòngxié 运动鞋
18. *measure word for garments worn over upper part or entire body*	r. jīnsè 金色

ANSWER KEY

1. e; 2. a; 3. h; 4. j; 5. q; 6. k; 7. l; 8. f; 9. i; 10. d; 11. o; 12. p; 13. b; 14. r; 15. m; 16. n; 17. c; 18. g

Lesson 10: Phrases

In this lesson, you'll learn:

☐ How to make negative sentences with the verb yǒu 有 *(have)*.

☐ Measure words for food items.

☐ How to ask *how much* and *how many*.

Phrase Builder 1

 10A Phrase Builder 1 (CD 5, Track 7)

Duōshǎo qián?	多少钱?	*How much (money)?*
Duōshǎo?	多少?	*How much?/How many?*
… yǒu méiyǒu … ?	… 有没有 … ?	*Do (you) have … ?*

méiyǒu	没有	*don't/doesn't have*
láojià	劳驾	*excuse me (asking for a favor)*
bùcuò	不错	*pretty good, not bad*
Bù hǎoyìsi.	不好意思。	*I'm sorry. (lit., to find it embarrassing to do something)*
… hǎo bù hǎo?	… 好不好?	*… is it alright?*
Méiyǒu wèntí.	没有问题。	*No problem.*
dǎzhé	打折	*to give a discount*

(II)

✎ Phrase Practice 1

Fill in the blank of the following phrases. The Chinese characters are provided for additional help.

1. yǒu méi_____ 有没有

2. méiyǒu _____ 没有问题

3. _____shǎo qián 多少钱

4. _____jià 劳驾

5. dǎ_____ 打折

ANSWER KEY

1. yǒu; 2. wèntí; 3. duō; 4. láo; 5. zhé

Grammar Builder 1
NEGATION WITH MÉIYǑU 没有

 10B Grammar Builder 1 (CD 5, Track 8)

You've already learned that you can make a verb negative by placing the particle
bù 不 in front of it:

Wǒ bù qù yīyuàn.
我不去医院。
I don't go to the hospital.

However, you can't negate yǒu 有 (*to have*) with bù 不. Instead you have to use
the form méiyǒu 没有 (*doesn't/don't/didn't have*).

Wǒ méiyǒu chē.
我没有车。
I don't have a car.

Wáng Tàitai méiyǒu Yīngwén shū.
王太太没有英文书。
Mrs. Wang doesn't have an English book.

Tā de gēge méiyǒu lǎoshī.
他的哥哥没有老师。
His older brother doesn't have a teacher.

Tā jīntiān zǎoshang méiyǒu kè.
她今天早上没有课。
She didn't have class this morning.

✎ Work Out 1

Make the following sentences negative. Then try to give the English translations of your answers.

1. Tā de xuésheng yǒu bǐ. 她的学生有笔。 _____

   _____

2. Wǒ yǒu yī zhī gǒu. 我有一只狗。 _____

   _____

3. Jīntiān shì lǐbài èr. 今天是礼拜二。 _____

   _____

4. Chén xiānsheng yǒu tàitai. 陈先生有太太。 _____

   _____

5. Tā chànggē. 他唱歌。 _____

   _____

6. Měiguórén xué Zhōngwén. 美国人学中文。 _____

   _____

7. Tā kāichē qù Niǔyuē (*New York*). 他开车去扭约。 _____

   _____

8. Tā rènshi wǒ de lǎoshī. 她认识我的老师。 _____

   _____

ANSWER KEY

1. Tā de xuésheng méiyǒu bǐ. 她的学生没有笔。 (*Her students don't have pens.*) 2. Wǒ méiyǒu yī zhī gǒu. 我没有一只狗。 (*I don't have a/one dog.*) 3. Jīntiān bù shì lǐbài èr. 今天不是礼拜二。 (*Today is not Tuesday.*) 4. Chén xiānsheng méiyǒu tàitai. 陈先生没有太太。 (*Mr. Chen doesn't have a wife.*) 5. Tā bù chànggē. 他不唱歌。 (*He doesn't sing.*) 6. Měiguórén bù xué Zhōngwén. 美国人不学中文。 (*Americans*

don't study Chinese.) 7. Tā bù kāichē qù Niǔyuē. 他不开车去扭约。 (*He doesn't drive to New York.*) 8. Tā bù rènshi wǒ de lǎoshī. 她不认识我的老师。 (*She doesn't know my teacher.*)

Phrase Builder 2

▶ 10C Phrase Builder 2 (CD 5, Track 9)

Here are some useful words that will come in handy when you go grocery shopping.

yī hé màipiàn	一盒麦片	*one/a box of cereal*
yī hé niúnǎi	一盒牛奶	*one/a carton of milk*
yī guàn tāng	一罐汤	*one/a can of soup*
yī bāo táng	一包糖	*one/a bag of sugar*
yī ge píngguǒ	一个苹果	*one/an apple*
yī ge júzi	一个橘子	*one/an orange*
yī tiáo xiāngjiāo	一条香蕉	*one/a banana*
yī chuàn pútao	一串葡萄	*one/a bunch of grapes*
yī bàng báicài	一磅白菜	*one/a pound of napa cabbage*
yī bàng fānqié	一磅番茄	*one/a pound of tomatoes*
yī bàng tǔdòu	一磅土豆	*one/a pound of potatoes*
yī bàng yángcōng	一磅洋葱	*one/a pound of onions*
yī bàng suàntóu	一磅蒜头	*one/a pound of garlic*
yī bàng hóngluóbo	一磅红萝卜	*one/a pound of carrots*

⏸

Take It Further

The measure word gè 个 is used for most fruits. For instance, yī ge lí 一个梨 (*a pear*), yī ge lǐzi 一个李子 (*a plum*), yī ge shìzi 一个柿子 (*a persimmon*), and yī ge xīguā 一个西瓜 (*a watermelon*). This is because most fruits are large and round in shape, which is what the measure word gè 个 denotes (note that although gè 个 is in the fourth tone, it is often spoken and written without any tone: ge 个). Not surprisingly, grapes and bananas therefore use different measure words which apply more accurately to objects that are small and round (chuàn 串) or long and narrow (tiáo 条).

The measure words used for vegetables are based on units of weight rather than on size or shape, such as bàng 磅 (*pound*) or gōngjīn 公斤 (*kilogram*). However, you can also use the measure word kē 颗 for vegetables (or for plants in general) when speaking of them piecemeal or as a general category: yī kē báicài 一颗白菜 (*a head of napa cabbage*) or yī kē shù 一棵树 (*a tree*). Note that, although they sound the same, when written in character form, the kē 颗 for small items like nappa cabbage and the kē 棵 for plants and trees are different characters.

✎ Phrase Practice 2

Translate the following English phrases into pīnyīn. Chinese characters are provided in the answer key for additional practice.

1. *A kilo of potatoes* _____

2. *A pound of apples* _____

3. *A bag of oranges* _____

4. *Two pounds of tomatoes* _____

5. *Two bunches of grapes* _____

ANSWER KEY
1. yī gōngjīn tǔdòu 一公斤土豆; 2. yī bàng píngguǒ 一磅苹果; 3. yī bāo júzi 一包橘子; 4. liǎng bàng fānqié 两磅番茄; 5. liǎng chuàn pútao 两串葡萄

Grammar Builder 2
ASKING *HOW MUCH* AND *HOW MANY*

▶ 10D Grammar Builder 2 (CD 5, Track 10)

In Chinese, the word jǐ 几 (*how many*) is used with countable nouns to ask about the number of people or objects. Jǐ 几 is always followed by a measure word, and these two words come before the countable noun.

Jǐ 几 is only used when there are fewer than ten of something. For example:

Nǐ yǒu jǐ tiáo qúnzi?
你有几条裙子？
How many skirts do you have?

Wǒ yǒu sān tiáo qúnzi.
我有三条裙子。
I have three skirts.

Here are some other questions with jǐ 几:

Tā yǒu jǐ tiáo hóngsè de qúnzi?
她有几条红色的裙子？
How many red skirts does she have?

Jīntiān nǐ mǎi le jǐ běn shū?
今天你买了几本书？
How many books did you buy today?

Nǐ chīle jǐ ge píngguǒ?
你吃了几个苹果？
How many apples did you eat?

Nǐ mǎile jǐ bàng báicài?

你买了几磅白菜?

How many pounds of nappa cabbage did you buy?

Nǐ yǒu jǐ ge péngyou xǐhuan chī Zhōngguó cài?

你有几个朋友喜欢吃中国菜?

How many of your friends like Chinese food?

For countable nouns of any or unlimited number, the word duōshǎo 多少 (*how many*) is used. It is placed right before the countable noun without a measure word. So, in other words, for countable nouns with quantities below ten, you use either jǐ 几 (plus a measure word) or duōshǎo 多少 (on its own), and for quantities above ten, you may only use duōshǎo 多少.

Nǐ shāole jǐ ge fānqié?

你烧了几个番茄?

OR

Nǐ shāole duōshǎo fānqié?

你烧了多少番茄?

How many tomatoes did you cook?

Wǒ shāole liù ge.

我烧了六个。

I cooked six (of them).

Nàge nóngfū zhòngle duōshǎo fānqié?

那个农夫种了多少番茄?

How many tomatoes did that farmer grow?

Nàge nóngfū zhòngle yīwàn ke fānqié.

那个农夫种了一万棵番茄。

The farmer grew ten thousand tomatoes.

To ask about uncountable things, like miànbāo 面包 (*bread*), kōngqì 空气 (*air*), shuǐ 水 (*water*), yóu 油 (*oil*), and so on, use duōshao 多少. In this case, it is translated as *how much* and it goes right before the noun, without any measure word:

Nǐ kěyǐ chī duōshǎo miànbāo?
你可以吃多少面包?
How much bread can you eat?

Wǒ kěyǐ chī wǔ piàn.
我可以吃五片。
I can eat five pieces.

Nǐ yào duōshǎo shuǐ?
你要多少水?
How much water do you need?

Wǒ yào yī píng.
我要一瓶。
I need one bottle (of water).

Here are some more examples of duōshǎo 多少 used with both countable and uncountable nouns:

Nǐ hē duōshǎo kāfēi?
你喝多少咖啡?
How much coffee do you drink?

Zuótiān xiàle duōshǎo yǔ?
昨天下了多少雨?
How much rain fell yesterday?

Nǐ mǎile duōshǎo yóu?

你买了多少油?

How much oil did you buy?

Tā shàng cì mǎile duōshǎo shuāng hóngsè de xuēzi?

他上次买了多少双红色的靴子?

How many red boots did he buy last time?

Note, however, that duōshǎo 多少 is probably most frequently used in Chinese when asking for the price of something. In this case, duōshǎo 多少 is used along with qián (*money*) to form the phrase duōshǎo qián 多少钱 (*how much money*):

Nǐ yǒu duōshǎo qián?

你有多少钱?

How much (money) do you have?

Zhè xiē píngguǒ duōshǎo qián?

这些苹果多少钱?

How much are these apples?

Nà tiáo hóngsè de qúnzi duōshǎo qián?

那条红色的裙子多少钱?

How much is that red skirt?

⑪

✎ Work Out 2

Match the Chinese sentences in the column on the left with the English translations on the right.

1. Tā yǒu jǐ shuāng báisè de xuēzi?
   他/她有几双白色的靴子?

2. Nǐ yào duōshǎo shuǐ?
   你要多少水?

3. Nǐmen de xuéxiào yǒu duōshǎo xuésheng?
   你们的学校有多少学生?

4. Nǐ de fángzi duōshǎo qián?
   你的房子多少钱?

5. Niǔyuē yǒu duōshǎo rén?
   纽约有多少人?

6. Nǐ yǒu duōshǎo qián? 你有多少钱?

7. Tā kěyǐ chī jǐ ge píngguǒ?
   他/她可以吃几个苹果?

8. Zuótiān nǐ mǎile jǐ běn shū?
   昨天你买了几本书?

a. *How much is your house?*

b. *How many pairs of white boots does he/she have?*

c. *How many apples can he/she eat?*

d. *How many students are there in your school?*

e. *How many books did you buy yesterday?*

f. *How much water do you need?*

g. *How much (money) do you have?*

h. *How many people are there in New York?*

ANSWER KEY
1. b; 2. f; 3. d; 4. a; 5. h; 6. g; 7. c; 8. e

✎ Drive It Home

For each item provided, form two question sentences, one using duōshao 多少 and the other using jǐ 几 and the appropriate measure word in parentheses. For example, with nǐ hē shuǐ (píng), you would write: Nǐ hē duōshao shui? 你喝多少水? Nǐ hē jǐ píng shuǐ? 你喝几瓶水?

1. Nǐ mǎi kāfēi (bēi) 你买咖啡 (杯) _____

   _____

2. Tā yǒu hóngluóbo (bàng) 他有红萝卜(磅) _____

   _____

3. Nǐ kěyǐ chī pútao (chuàn) 你可以吃葡萄 (串) _____

   _____

4. Wǒmen diǎn jiǔ (píng) 我们点酒 (瓶) _____

   _____

5. Tāmen yào niúnǎi (hé) 他们要牛奶 (盒) _____

   _____

ANSWER KEY

1. Nǐ mǎi duōshao kāfēi? 你买多少咖啡？ Nǐ mǎi jǐ bēi kāfēi? 你买几杯咖啡？ 2. Tā yǒu duōshao hóngluóbo? 他有多少红萝卜？ Tā yǒu jǐ bàng hóngluóbo? 他有几磅红萝卜？ 3. Nǐ kěyǐ chī duōshao pútao? 你可以吃多少葡萄？ Nǐ kěyǐ chī jǐ chuàn pútao? 你可以吃几串葡萄？ 4. Wǒmen diǎn duōshao jiǔ? 我们点多少酒？ Wǒmen diǎn jǐ píng jiǔ? 我们点几瓶酒？ 5. Tāmen yào duōshao niúnǎi? 他们要多少牛奶？ Tāmen yào jǐ hé niúnǎi? 他们要几盒牛奶？

How Did You Do?

By now, you should know:

☐ How to make negative sentences with the verb yǒu 有 (*have*).
(Still unsure? Go back to 141.)

☐ Measure words for food items.
(Still unsure? Go back to 143.)

☐ How to ask *how much* and *how many*.
(Still unsure? Go back to 145.)

✎ Word Recall

Match the English word in the left column with its appropriate translation in the right column.

1. *sugar*	a. Duōshǎo qián? 多少钱?
2. *pound (weight unit)*	b. guàn 罐
3. *No problem.*	c. fānqié 番茄
4. *can (container)*	d. júzi 橘子
5. *milk*	e. bùcuò 不错
6. *bag*	f. láojià 劳驾
7. *box, carton*	g. bàng 磅
8. *tomato*	h. niúnǎi 牛奶
9. *Do (you) have … ?*	i. duōshao 多少
10. *orange*	j. méiyǒu 没有
11. *measure word for plants and vegetables*	k. bāo 包
12. *How much/how many?*	l. hé 盒
13. *don't/doesn't have*	m. yángcōng 洋葱
14. *excuse me (asking for a favor)*	n. Méiyǒu wèntí. 没有问题。
15. *How much (money)?*	o. kē 棵
16. *onions*	p. chuàn 串
17. *pretty good, not bad*	q. táng 糖
18. *bunch, cluster*	r. … yǒu méiyǒu … ? …有没有…?

ANSWER KEY

1. q; 2. g; 3. n; 4. b; 5. h; 6. k; 7. l; 8. c; 9. r; 10. d; 11. o; 12. i; 13. j; 14. f; 15. a; 16. m; 17. e; 18. p

Lesson 11: Sentences

In this lesson, you'll learn:

☐ How to express *this one* and *that one*.

☐ Essential expressions for using money and shopping.

Sentence Builder 1

▶ 11A Sentence Builder 1 (CD 5, Track 11)

Nǐmen yǒu shénme yánsè de qúnzi?	你们有什么颜色的裙子？	*What color skirts do you have?*
Wǒ yǒu yī tiáo hóngsè de qúnzi.	我有一条红色的裙子。	*I have a red skirt.*
Nǐmen yǒu zǐsè de màozi ma?	你们有紫色的帽子吗？	*Do you have purple hats?*
Wǒ xǐhuan hóng huā.	我喜欢红花。	*I like red flowers.*
Tā xǐhuan zhè tiáo yínsè de xiàngliàn.	她喜欢这条银色的项链。	*She likes the silver (colored) necklace.*
Wǒ de māma chàng "Yínsè de yuèguāng."	我的妈妈唱 "银色的月光。"	*My mother sings "Silver moonlight."*
Wáng xiǎojiě hé Chén xiǎojiě xǐhuan jīnsè de zhuózi.	王小姐和陈小姐喜欢金色的镯子。	*Miss Wang and Miss Chen like gold (colored) bracelets.*
Nà jiàn huángsè de chènshān shì tā de.	那件黄色的衬衫是他的。	*That yellow shirt is his.*
Zhè tiáo hēisè de kùzi shì wǒ de.	这条黑色的裤子是我的。	*This pair of black pants is mine.*

Intermediate Chinese

Méiguì yǒu duōshǎo zhǒng yánsè?	玫瑰有多少种颜色?	*How many colors of roses are there?*
Cǎihóng yǒu jǐ zhǒng yánsè?	彩虹有几种颜色?	*How many colors are there in the rainbow?*
Cǎihóng yǒu qī zhǒng yánsè.	彩虹有七种颜色。	*A rainbow has seven colors.*
Wǒ kěyǐ kànkàn qítā yánsè de qúnzi ma?	我可以看看其它颜色的裙子吗?	*Can I take a look at a skirt in a different color?*
Wǒ bù xǐhuan zhège yánsè.	我不喜欢这个颜色。	*I don't like this color.*
Wǒ gěi nín dǎzhé.	我给您打折。	*I'm giving you a discount.*

Take It Further

You learned earlier that colors in Chinese usually contain the syllable sè 色, as in hēisè 黑色 (*black*) or hóngsè 红色 (*red*). Note that the word yánsè 颜色 is used to mean *color* when no specific hue is indicated, as in Cǎihóng yǒu jǐ zhǒng yánsè? 彩虹有几种颜色? (*How many colors are there in the rainbow?*) Also note that measure word zhǒng 种 (*kind*) is used when yánsè 颜色 refers to multiple colors.

✎ Sentence Practice 1

Translate the following English sentences into Chinese.

1. *How many yellow skirts do you (pl.) have?* _____

_____

2. *She likes that gold (colored) necklace.*

3. *Will you give me a discount?*

4. *I like that purple shirt.*

5. *Can we look at pants in a different color?*

ANSWER KEY

1. Nǐmen yǒu jǐ tiáo huáng qúnzi? 你们有几条黄裙子？ 2. Tā xǐhuan nà tiáo jīnsè de xiàngliàn. 她喜欢那条金色的项链。 3. Nǐ gěi wǒ dǎzhé ma? 你给我打折吗？ 4. Wǒ xǐhuan nà jiàn zǐsè de chènshān. 我喜欢那件紫色的衬衫。 5. Wǒmen kěyǐ kànkan qítā yánsè de kùzi ma? 我们可以看看其它颜色的裤子吗？

Grammar Builder 1
THIS ONE AND THAT ONE

▶ 11B Grammar Builder 1 (CD 5, Track 12)

As you know, the demonstratives in Chinese are zhè 这 (*this*) and nà 那 (*that*). They are always followed by a measure word. In other words, *this book* and *that book* are expressed as zhè běn shū 这本书 and nà běn shū 那本书 in Chinese.

Remember also that the plural forms are zhèxiē 这些 (*these*) and nàxiē 那些 (*those*) and since xiē 些 serves as the measure word for both, no additional measure word is needed: Wǒ xǐhuan nàxiē shū. 我喜欢那些书。 (*I like those books*).

So far, we have only talked about demonstratives that directly precede a noun: *this person, that pen*. In English, these are known as demonstrative adjectives. Demonstratives that stand on their own—*this is mine, I want these, I like this one*— are known as demonstrative pronouns. In English, the word *one* (*this one, that one, those ones*) is sometimes added after the demonstrative to help indicate that it is a demonstrative pronoun.

As in English, Chinese demonstratives can be used as both adjectives and pronouns. In other words, you can use the same words for both. Here are some examples:

Zhège shì yī kuài.
这个是一块。
This one is one yuan.

Zhège duōshǎo qián?
这个多少钱?
How much is this?

Gěi wǒ nàxiē.
给我那些。
Give me those.

Wǒ mǎi wùlǐ kèběn. Zhè běn duōshǎo qián?
我买物理课本。 这本多少钱?
I'm buying a physics textbook. How much is this one?

Note that there is no context in the first two examples, so ge 个 is used as a general measure word. However, in the last sentence, it is clear the speaker is referring to a textbook, so the measure word běn 本 is used.

Also note that although the word *one* is added onto the demonstrative in one of the above sentences in English, only the demonstrative and the measure word are needed in Chinese.

⏸

✎ Work Out 1

Match the Chinese sentences in the right column with the English translations on the left.

1. *Give me these.*

a. Gěi wǒ nàge. 给我那个。

2. *My mother likes this pair of earrings.*

b. Zhèxiē báisè de xuēzi shì wǒ de. 这些白色的靴子是我的。

3. *That woman is my teacher.*

c. Zhège. 这个。

4. *I'm buying this one.*

d. Wǒ de māma xǐhuan zhè duì ěrhuán. 我的妈妈喜欢这对耳环。

5. *How much are those skirts?*

e. Nàxiē qúnzi duōshǎo qián? 那些裙子多少钱?

6. *Give me that one.*

f. Nàge nǚrén shì wǒ de lǎoshī. 那个女人是我的老师。

7. *These white boots are mine.*

g. Wǒ mǎi zhège. 我买这个。

8. *This one.*

h. Gěi wǒ zhèxiē. 给我这些。

ANSWER KEY
1. h; 2. d; 3. f; 4. g; 5. e; 6. a; 7. b; 8. c

Sentence Builder 2

▶ 11C Sentence Builder 2 (CD 5, Track 13)

Zhège duōshǎo qián?	这个多少钱?	*How much is this?*
Xīguā yī ge duōshǎo qián?	西瓜一个多少钱?	*How much does a watermelon cost?*
Júzi yī bàng duōshǎo qián?	橘子一磅多少钱?	*How much is a pound of oranges?*
Zhège yī kuài (qián).	这个一块(钱).	*This one is/costs one yuan.*

Xīguā yī ge qī kuài wǔ máo.	西瓜一个七块五毛。	*Watermelons are 7.50 RMB each (lit., for one).*
Júzi yī bàng jiǔ máo jiǔ (fēn).	橘子一磅九毛九(分)。	*Oranges are/cost 0.99RMB a pound.*
Kùzi yī tiáo bāshísì kuài líng yī (fēn).	裤子一条八十四块零一(分).	*One pair of pants is/costs 84.01 RMB.*
Tài guì le!	太贵了!	*That's too expensive!*
Hěn piányi!	很便宜!	*That's cheap! (lit., Very cheap!)*
Tài duō le.	太多了。	*That's too much. (lit., Too much.)*
Jiàqian dī yīdiǎn ba.	价钱低一点吧。	*Can you lower your price a little bit? (lit., Price lower a little bit.)*
Wǒ yǒu yī máo.	我有一毛。	*I have 0.10 RMB.*
Wǒ méiyǒu sān máo wǔ (fēn).	我没有三毛五 (分)。	*I don't have 0.35 RMB.*
Zhèlǐ shi shí kuài.	这里十块。	*Here is 10 RMB. (lit., Give you 10 RMB.)*
Zhǎo nín sān kuài yī máo sān.	找您三块一毛三。	*Here's your 3.13 RMB in change. (lit., Find your 3.13 RMB in change.)*
Wǒ kěyǐ shuākǎ ma?	我可以刷卡吗?	*Can I pay by credit card?*
Bù kěyǐ. Wǒmen zhǐ shōu xiànjīn.	不可以。 我们只收现金。	*You can't. We only accept cash.*
Yínháng zài nǎli?	银行在哪里?	*Where is a bank?*
Tíkuǎnjī zài nǎli?	提款机在哪里?	*Where is an ATM machine?*

(II)

✎ Sentence Practice 2

Fill in the blanks of the sentences in pīnyīn, and then translate them into English. The Chinese characters are provided for additional help.

1. Zhè _____ kùzi duōshǎo _____?

   这条裤子多少钱?

2. Jià _____ tài _____ le.

   价钱太贵了。

3. Wǒkěyǐ _____ kǎ ma?

   我可以刷卡吗?

4. Tāmen zhǐ _____ xiàn _____.

   他们只收现金。

5. Zhè _____ yǒu _____ ma?

   这里有银行吗?

ANSWER KEY

1. tiáo, qián (*How much does this pair of pants cost?*); 2. qian, guì (*The price is too expensive*); 3. shuā (*Can I use my credit card?*) 4. shōu, jīn (*They only take cash.*); 5. lǐ, yínháng (*Is there a bank here?*)

Grammar Builder 2
MONEY EXPRESSIONS

▶ 11D Grammar Builder (CD 5, Track 14)

Rénmínbì 人民币 (RMB), which literally means *people's currency*, is the official currency in China. The basic unit is the yuán 元, which is usually known as kuài 块 in colloquial Chinese. One yuán 元 is divided into ten jiǎo 角, which is also referred to colloquially as máo 毛. One jiǎo 角 is further divided into ten fēn

分. Comparing these monetary units to American currency, the yuán 元 is the equivalent of the dollar, the jiǎo 角 the dime, and the fēn 分 the penny.

When mentioning Chinese currency in everyday conversation, yuán 元 and kuài 块 are equally used, as are jiǎo 角 and máo 毛, although in different areas people have different preferences.

Note that it is optional to place fēn 分 and qián 钱 (*money*) at the end in conversation. For example, 8.57 RMB could be spoken as bā kuài wǔ máo qī fēn qián 八块五毛七分钱 or just bā kuài wǔ máo qī 八块五毛七.

Here are some other useful constructions involving money:

fù xiànjīn 付现金	*to pay in cash*
yòng zhīpiào fùqián 用支票付钱	*to pay by check*
shuākǎ 刷卡	*to pay by credit card*
Wǒmen bù zhǎo líng. 我们不找零。	*We need exact change/the exact amount. (lit., We can't make change.)*
měi ge wǔ kuài 每个五块	*5 RMB (5 yuan) each*
wǔ kuài shí ge 五块十个	*ten for 5 RMB (5 yuan)*
èrshí kuài 二十块	*20 RMB (20 yuan)*

⑪

✎ Work Out 2

Translate the following prices into English based on the example below.
Ex. shíjiǔ kuài 十九块
19 RMB

1. jiǔ kuài 九块 _____

2. sì máo 四毛 _____

3. qī yuán wǔ jiǎo 七元五角 _____

4. bā kuài wǔ máo 八块五毛 _____

5. sān kuài líng sān fēn 三块零三分 _____

6. liù kuài bā máo 六块八毛 _____

7. yī kuài bā máo wǔ 一块八毛五 _____

8. shí'èr kuài 十二块 _____

ANSWER KEY
1. 9 RMB; 2. 0.40 RMB; 3. 7.50 RMB; 4. 8.50 RMB; 5. 3.03 RMB; 6. 6.80 RMB; 7. 1.85 RMB; 8. 12.00 RMB

⊕ Culture Note

Until recently, people in China paid for all their daily purchases in cash. That's why you may hear that Chinese people like to carry a lot of cash with them when they go shopping. Nowadays, paying by bank card is acceptable in the stores in cities. However, credit cards are still not very popular and paying by check is a new concept that has only recently been introduced to China.

Major banks in China are owned and run by the government. The most popular national bank is called Zhōngguó Jiànshè Yínháng 中国建设银行 (*China Construction Bank*), which has branches in every province throughout the country.

✎ Drive It Home

For each price provided, write out three money expressions in pīnyīn, starting with just the expression using kuài 块, then add máo 毛, and finally fēn 分. For example, with 1.23 RMB, you would write: yī kuài 一块, yī kuài èr máo 一块二毛, and yī kuài èr máo sān fēn 一块二毛三分.

Money expressions

1. *5.73 RMB* _____

2. *9.42 RMB* _____

3. *3.99 RMB* _____

4. *65.89 RMB* _____

5. *22.58 RMB* _____

ANSWER KEY

1. wǔ kuài 五块, wǔ kuài qī máo 五块七毛, wǔ kuài qī máo sān fēn 五块七毛三分; 2. jiǔ kuài 九块, jiǔ kuài sì máo 九块四毛, jiǔ kuài sì máo èr fēn 九块四毛二分; 3. sān kuài 三块, sān kuài jiǔ máo 三块九毛, sān kuài jiǔ máo jiǔ fēn 三块九毛九分; 4. liùshíwǔ kuài 六十五块, liùshíwǔ kuài bā máo 六十五块八毛, liùshíwǔ kuài bā máo jiǔ fēn 六十五块八毛九分; 5. èrshí'èr kuài 二十二块, èrshí'èr kuài wǔ máo 二十二块五毛, èrshí'èr kuài wǔ máo bā fēn 二十二块五毛八分

How Did You Do?

By now, you should know:

☐ How to express *this one* and *that one*.
(Still unsure? Go back to 154.)

☐ Essential expressions for using money and shopping.
(Still unsure? Go back to 158.)

✎ Word Recall

Match the English word in the left column with its appropriate translation in the right column.

1. *to pay by credit card*

2. *to give a discount*

3. *colloquial word for* jiǎo

4. *rainbow*

5. *official Chinese currency*

6. *colloquial word for* yuán

7. *rose*

8. *one one-hundredth of a* yuán, *equivalent to the cent*

9. *to be able to, allowed*

10. *cash*

11. *one tenth of a yuán, equivalent to the dime*

12. *change (monetary)*

13. *to pay*

14. *basic currency unit, equivalent to the dollar unit*

15. *check (payment)*

a. cǎihóng 彩虹

b. fēn 分

c. Rénmínbì 人民币

d. yuán 元

e. shuākǎ 刷卡

f. méiguì 玫瑰

g. língqián 零钱

h. jiǎo 角

i. fù 付

j. kuài 块

k. kěyǐ 可以

l. dǎzhé 打折

m. zhīpiào 支票

n. máo 毛

o. xiànjīn 现金

ANSWER KEY
1. e; 2. l; 3. n; 4. a; 5. c; 6. j; 7. f; 8. b; 9. k; 10. o; 11. h; 12. g; 13. i; 14. d; 15. m

Lesson 12: Conversations

In this lesson, you'll learn:

☐ Higher numbers.

☐ Quantity expressions.

🎧 Conversation 1

▶ 12A Conversation 1 (CD 5, Track 15-Chinese, Track 16-Chinese and English)

Jess wants to buy a purple dress, but her size is out of stock. The shopkeeper asks her to come back the next week.

Lǎobǎn:	Xiǎojie, nín yào shénme dōngxi?
老板:	小姐, 您要什么东西?
Jiéxī:	Nǐmen yǒu qúnzi ma?
洁希:	你们有裙子吗?
Lǎobǎn:	Yǒu. Qǐng guòlái. Zhè shì zuì xīn de kuǎnshì, yánsè bùcuò, jiàqian yě bù guì.
老板:	有。 请过来。这是最新的款式, 颜色不错, 价钱也不贵。
Jiéxī:	Hěn piàoliang. Zhè tiáo qúnzi duōshǎo qián?
洁希:	很漂亮。这条裙子多少钱?
Lǎobǎn:	Liǎng bǎi wǔshí kuài. Wǒ gěi nǐ dǎ zhé, yī bǎi bāshíbā.
老板:	两百五十块。我给你打折, 一百八十八。
Jiéxī:	Wǒ xǐhuan zǐsè. Nǐmen yǒu zǐsè de qúnzi ma?
洁希:	我喜欢紫色。你们有紫色的裙子吗?
Lǎobǎn:	Ràng wǒ kànkan. Zǐsè zhǐyǒu zhōnghào, nín chuān jǐhào?
老板:	让我看看。紫色只有中号, 您穿几号?
Jiéxī:	Wǒ chuān dàhào.
洁希:	我穿大号。

Lǎobǎn:	Bù hǎoyìsi. Wǒmen xiànzài méiyǒu dàhào, nǐ xiàge xīngqī zài guòlái hǎo bù hǎo?
老板:	不好意思。我们现在没有大号，你下个星期再过来好不好？
Jiéxī:	Hǎo ba. Qǐng nǐ bǎ qúnzi liú gěi wǒ, wǒ xiàge xīngqī zài guòlái.
洁希:	好吧。请你把裙子留给我，我下个星期再过来。
Lǎobǎn:	Méiyǒu wèntí. Zàijiàn.
老板:	没有问题。再见。
Jiéxī:	Zàijiàn.
洁希:	再见。

Shopkeeper:	*Miss, can I help you? (lit., What do you need?)*
Jess:	*Do you have any skirts?*
Shopkeeper:	*Yes. Please come over here. This is the latest style. The color is good and the price isn't high (lit., not expensive).*
Jess:	*Very pretty. How much is this skirt?*
Shopkeeper:	*250 RMB. I'll give you a discount. (You can have it for) 188 RMB.*
Jess:	*I like purple. Do you have the skirt in purple?*
Shopkeeper:	*Let me check. I only have purple in medium. What size do you wear?*
Jess:	*I wear large.*
Shopkeeper:	*I'm sorry. We don't have large now. Could you come back next week?*
Jess:	*Okay. Please keep the skirt for me. I'll come again next week.*
Shopkeeper:	*No problem. Goodbye.*
Jess:	*Goodbye.*

Take It Further

Note that, in Chinese, the word for size large is dàhào 大号, medium is zhōnghào 中号, and small is xiǎohào 小号。

Here are some more adjectives that you can use to describe clothing: piàoliang 漂亮 (*pretty*), xīn 新 (*new*), jiù 旧 (*old*), shímáo 时髦 (*fashionable, in style*), guòshí 过时 (*out of style*), jǐn 紧 (*tight*), tài xiǎo 太小 (*too small*), tài dà 太大 (*too large*).

✎ Conversation Practice 1

1. Jiéxī yào mǎi _____.

   洁希要买裙子。

2. Lǎobǎn de qúnzi shì zuì _____ de _____.

   老板的裙子是最新的款式。

3. Lǎobǎn gěi Jiéxī _____.

   老板给洁希打折。

4. Jiéxī yào _____ de qúnzi.

   洁希要紫色的裙子。

5. Zǐsè de qúnzi zhǐ yǒu _____.

   紫色的裙子只有中号。

6. Jiéxī chuān _____.

   洁希穿大号。

   ANSWER KEY
   1. qúnzi 裙子; 2. xīn 新, kuǎnshì 款式; 3. dǎzhé 打折; 4. zǐsè 紫色; 5. zhōnghào 中号; 6. dàhào 大号

Grammar Builder 1
NUMBERS 21-1000

Let's do something a bit easier and review numbers from twenty-one to a thousand in Chinese. For twenty, thirty, forty, and so on, simply add -shí 十 after a number from two to nine. For example, èr 二 (*two*) + shí 十 (*ten*) = èrshí 二十 (*twenty*). To add a number in the ones place after the tens place, as in 21 or 99, just say that number after -shí 十:

▶ 12B Grammar Builder 1 (CD 5, Track 17)

21 èrshíyī 二十一	*60* liùshí 六十
25 èrshíwǔ 二十五	*70* qīshí 七十
30 sānshí 三十	*80* bāshí 八十
40 sìshí 四十	*90* jiǔshí 九十
50 wǔshí 五十	*99* jiǔshíjiǔ 九十九

In Chinese, 100 and 1,000 are called yìbǎi 一百 and yìqiān 一千 respectively. Therefore, to say 200, 300, etc., just add bǎi 百 after a number from one through nine. For 2,000, 3,000, etc., add qiān 千 after the appropriate number.

For the numbers from 101 to 109, 201 to 209, 301 to 309, and so on, use the word líng 零 (*zero*) before the number in the ones place. For other numbers, simply add the number without saying hé 和 (*and*).

100 yībǎi 一百	*150* yībǎi wǔshí 一百五十
101 yībǎi líng yī 一百零一	*159* yībǎi wǔshíjiǔ 一百五十九
109 yībǎi líng jiǔ 一百零九	*200* èrbǎi 二百
110 yībǎi yīshí 一百一十	*300* sānbǎi 三百
111 yībǎi yīshíyī 一百一十一	*900* jiǔbǎi 九百
115 yībǎi yīshíwǔ 一百一十五	*999* jiǔbǎi jiǔshíjiǔ 九百九十九
120 yībǎi èrshí 一百二十	*1,000* yīqiān 一千
123 yībǎi èrshísān 一百二十三	

Money expressions   Quantity expressions and the number *two* (èr 二 and **liǎng** 两)

⊙

✎ Work Out 1

Translate the following numbers into English.

1. yībǎi bāshísān 一百八十三 _____

2. sìbǎi líng èr 四百零二 _____

3. wǔbǎi wǔshíwǔ 五百五十五 _____

4. liùbǎi 六百 _____

5. yīqiān 一千 _____

6. bābǎi liùshí 八百六十 _____

7. yībǎi yīshísān 一百一十三 _____

8. sānbǎi èrshí 三百二十 _____

ANSWER KEY
1. 183; 2. 402; 3. 555; 4. 600; 5. 1000; 6. 860; 7. 113; 8. 320

⒞ Conversation 2

▶ 12C Conversation 2 (CD 5, Track 18-Chinese, Track 19-Chinese and English)

Now listen as Jess buys groceries.

Tuīxiāoyuán:	Nín mǎi shénme dōngxi?
推销员:	您买什么东西?
Jiéxī:	Tǔdòu yī bàng duōshǎo qián?
洁希:	土豆一磅多少钱?
Tuīxiāoyuán:	Wǔ máo qián yī bàng.
推销员:	五毛钱一磅。
Jiéxī:	Gěi wǒ liǎng bàng. Nǐmen yǒu báicài ma?

Unit 3 Lesson 12: Conversations   167

洁希: 给我两磅。你们有白菜吗？

Tuīxiāoyuán: Yǒu. Jīntiān de báicài hěn xīnxiān. Nín yào duōshǎo?

推销员: 有。今天的白菜很新鲜。您要多少？

Jiéxī: Gěi wǒ sān bàng.

洁希: 给我三磅。

Tuīxiāoyuán: Yī kuài wǔ máo yī bàng. Sān bàng yào sì kuài wǔ máo. Hái yào shénme ma?

推销员: 一块五毛一磅。三磅要四块五毛。还要什么吗？

Jiéxī: Gěi wǒ sān ge fānqié.

洁希: 给我三个番茄。

Tuīxiāoyuán: Sān ge fānqié wǔ máo. Yīgòng liù kuài.

推销员: 三个番茄五毛。一共六块。

Jiéxī: Zhèlǐ shí kuài.

洁希: 这里十块。

Tuīxiāoyuán: Hǎo, zhǎo nín sì kuài. Xièxie.

推销员: 好，找您四块。谢谢。

Salesman: *What can I do for you? (lit., What things do you want to buy?)*

Jess: *How much is one/a pound of potatoes?*

Salesman: *0.5 RMB a pound.*

Jess: *Give me two pounds. Do you have nappa cabbage?*

Salesman: *Yes. The nappa cabbage is very fresh today. How much do you want?*

Jess: *Give me three pounds.*

Salesman: *It's 1.50 RMB a pound. That would be 4.50 RMB for three pounds. What else do you want?*

Jess: *Give me three tomatoes.*

Salesman: *It's 0.50 RMB for three tomatoes. The total is 6 RMB.*

Jess: *Here's 10.00 RMB.*

Salesman: *Okay, here's 4.00 RMB in change. Thank you.*

✎ Conversation Practice 2

Fill in the blanks with the missing words in pīnyīn. Refer to the conversation between
Jess and the salesman. The Chinese characters are provided for additional help

1. Tǔdòu _____ máo qián yī _____.

   土豆五毛钱一磅。

2. Jiéxī mǎi _____ bàng tǔdòu.

   洁希买两磅土豆。

3. Jīntiān de báicài hěn _____.

   今天的白菜很新鲜。

4. Sān bàng báicài yào sì _____ wǔ _____ qián.

   三磅白菜要四块五毛钱。

5. Jiéxī mǎi de cài _____ liù kuài.

   洁希买的菜一共六块钱。

ANSWER KEY
1. wǔ 五, bàng 磅; 2. liǎng 两; 3. xīnxiān 新鲜; 4. kuài 块, máo 毛; 5. yīgòng 一共

Grammar Builder 2
QUANTITY EXPRESSIONS AND THE NUMBER *TWO*
(ÈR 二 AND LIǍNG 两)

▶ 12D Grammar Builder 2 (CD 5, Track 20)

As you know, there are two ways of saying *two* in Chinese: èr 二 and liǎng
两。These two expressions serve different functions.

Èr 二 is used for counting when the number *two* stands alone. For example, when you say: yī 一, èr 二, sān 三 … (*one, two, three* …). Èr 二 is also used when it is combined with most cardinal numbers:

èrshí 二十	*twenty*
èrshí'èr 二十二	*twenty-two*
èrbǎi 二百	*two hundred*
yībǎi wǔshí'èr 一百五十二	*one hundred and fifty-two*

Liǎng 两 is used with a measure word when it quantifies a noun. In other words, liǎng is used when you say that there are two of something.

liǎng ge píngguǒ 两个苹果	*two apples*
liǎng běn shū 两本书	*two books*

However, keep in mind that you would say shí'èr ge píngguǒ 十二个苹果 (*twelve apples*), not shíliǎng ge píngguǒ 十两个苹果.

Also note that the number 2 is usually liǎng 两 when used with the money units yuán/kuài 元/块 and jiǎo/máo 角/毛.

Here are some more quantity-related expressions in Chinese.

yī dǎ jīdàn 一打鸡蛋	*one dozen eggs*
dàgài shí ge rén 大概十个人	*about ten people*
wǔshí liàng chē zuǒyòu 五十辆车左右	*around fifty cars*
bù gòu yībǎi bàng 不够一百磅	*fewer than 100 pounds*

�

✎ Work Out 2

Fill in the missing Chinese word in the following sentences, using the translations
as cues.

1. Wǒ yǒu _____ ge píngguǒ.

   我有 _____个苹果。

   (*I have two apples.*)

2. Tā _____ shí suì.

   他 _____十岁。

   (*He is twenty years old.*)

3. Yī jiā _____ děngyú sān.

   一加 _____等于三。

   (*One plus two equals to three.*)

4. Wáng tàitai méiyǒu _____ ge gēge.

   王太太没有 _____个哥哥。

   (*Mrs. Wang doesn't have two older brothers.*)

5. Wǒ hé Zhāng lǎoshī qù guò _____ ge dìfang.

   我和张老师去过 _____个地方。

   (*Teacher Zhang and I went to two places.*)

6. Wǒ de biǎojiě yǒu _____ tiáo gǒu.

   我的表姐有 _____条狗。

   (*My cousin has two dogs.*)

7. Zhè shì yībǎi líng _____ hào.

这是一百零 _____ 号。

(*This is number 102.*)

8. Māma měitiān chī _____ ge júzi.

妈妈每天吃 _____ 个橘子。

(*My mother eats two oranges every day.*)

ANSWER KEY

1. liǎng 两; 2. èr 二; 3. èr 二; 4. liǎng 两; 5. liǎng 两; 6. liǎng 两; 7. èr 二; 8. liǎng 两

✎ Drive It Home

Write out all the numbers between and including 30 and 39 in Chinese.

_____

_____

_____

_____

ANSWER KEY

sānshí 三十, sānshíyī 三十一, sānshí'èr 三十二, sānshísān 三十三, sānshísì 三十四, sānshíwǔ 三十五, sānshíliù 三十六, sānshíqī 三十七, sānshíbā 三十八, sānshíjiǔ 三十九

How Did You Do?

By now, you should know:

☐ Higher numbers.
(Still unsure? Go back to 166.)

☐ Quantity expressions.
(Still unsure? Go back to 169.)

✎ Word Recall

Match the English word in the left column with its appropriate translation in the right column.

1. *egg(s)*	a. shímáo 时髦
2. *large (size)*	b. yī dǎ 一打
3. *out of style*	c. kuǎnshì 款式
4. *again*	d. bú gòu 不够
5. *fashionable, in style*	e. dàgài 大概
6. *too small*	f. jīdàn 鸡蛋
7. *style*	g. zhōnghào 中号
8. *tight*	h. guòshí 过时
9. *fewer than (lit. not enough)*	i. dàhào 大号
10. *small (size)*	j. tài xiǎo 太小
11. *too large*	k. zài 再
12. *to come over*	l. jǐn 紧
13. *medium (size)*	m. xiǎohào 小号
14. *approximately, about*	n. tài dà 太大
15. *one dozen*	o. guòlái 过来

ANSWER KEY
1. f; 2. i; 3. h; 4. k; 5. a; 6. j; 7. c; 8. l; 9. d; 10. m; 11. n; 12. o; 13. g; 14. e; 15. b

Don't forget to practice and reinforce what you've learned by visiting **www.livinglanguage.com/ languagelab** for flashcards, games, and quizzes.

Unit 3 Essentials

Vocabulary Essentials

Test your knowledge of the key material in this unit by filling in the blanks in the following charts. Once you've completed these pages, you'll have tested your retention, and you'll have your own reference for the most essential vocabulary. This is also a great time to practice a few Chinese characters. Fill in the middle column with the characters that you remember. Or, if you only remember the pīnyīn, go back through the unit to find the character.

CLOTHING

PĪNYĪN	CHARACTER	
		T-shirt
		shirt
		pants
		dress
		skirt
		culottes, skort
		coat
		jacket
		raincoat
		traditional Chinese dress
		socks
		shoes
		boots
		sneakers
		hat
		belt

PĪNYĪN	CHARACTER	
		underpants
		watch
		ring

COLORS

PĪNYĪN	CHARACTER	
		red
		orange
		yellow
		green
		blue
		purple
		pink
		brown
		black
		white
		grey
		silver
		gold
		dark
		light

If you're having a hard time remembering this vocabulary, don't forget to check out the flashcards, games and quizzes for this unit online. Go to **www.livinglanguage. com/languagelab** for a great way to help you practice what you've learned.

Grammar Essentials

Here is a reference for the key grammar that was covered in Unit 3. Make sure you understand the summary and can use all of the grammar it covers.

MEASURE WORDS FOR FOOD

yī hé màipiàn	一盒麦片	one/a box of cereal
yī hé niúnǎi	一盒牛奶	one/a carton of milk
yī guàn tāng	一罐汤	one/a can of soup
yī bāo táng	一包糖	one/a bag of sugar
yī ge píngguǒ	一个苹果	one/an apple
yī ge júzi	一个橘子	one/an orange
yī tiáo xiāngjiāo	一条香蕉	one/a banana
yī chuàn pútao	一串葡萄	one/a bunch of grapes
.yī bàng fānqié	一磅番茄	one/a pound of tomatoes
yī bàng tǔdòu	一磅土豆	one/a pound of potatoes

MEASURE WORDS FOR CLOTHING

Jiàn 件 is used for garments worn over the upper part or full length of the body, and tiáo 条 is used for garments worn over the lower half of the body. Shuāng 双 (pair) is used for footwear.

yī jiàn chènshān 一件衬衫	one/a shirt
zhè jiàn wàitào 这件外套	this overcoat
sì tiáo qúnzi 四条裙子	four skirts
yī tiáo kùzi 一条裤子	a/one pair of pants
yī shuāng xiézi 一双鞋子	a pair of shoes

NEGATING *TO HAVE*

To negate yǒu 有 (*to have*) use the form méiyǒu 没有 (*doesn't/don't/didn't have*) instead of with bù 不.

Wǒ méiyǒu chē.	我没有车。	*I don't have a car.*
Wáng tàitai méiyǒu Yīngwén shū.	王太太没有英文书。	*Mrs. Wang doesn't have an English book.*
Tā jīntiān zǎoshang méiyǒu kè.	她今天早上没有课。	*She didn't have class this morning.*

ASKING *HOW MUCH/MANY*

Use jǐ 几 (*how many*) plus a measure word or duōshǎo 多少 (*how many*) to ask about countable nouns under ten and duōshǎo 多少 (*how many*) to ask about non-countable nouns and countable nouns of any quantity.

Nǐ shāole jǐ ge xīhóngshì?	你烧了几个西红柿?	*How many tomatoes did you cook?*
Nǐ shāole duōshǎo xīhóngshì?	你烧了多少西红柿?	*How many tomatoes did you cook?*
Wǒ shāole liù ge.	我烧了六个。	*I cooked six (of them).*
Nàge nóngfū zhòngle duōshǎo xīhóngshì?	那个农夫种了多少西红柿?	*How many tomatoes did that farmer grow?*
Nàge nóngfū zhòngle yīwàn ke xīhóngshì.	那个农夫种了一万棵西红柿。	*The farmer grew ten thousand tomatoes.*

NUMBERS

21 èrshíyī 二十一		*60* liùshí 六十	
25 èrshíwǔ 二十五		*70* qīshí 七十	
30 sānshí 三十		*80* bāshí 八十	
40 sìshí 四十		*90* jiǔshí 九十	

50 wǔshí 五十	*99* jiǔshíjiǔ 九十九
100 yībǎi 一百	*150* yībǎi wǔshí 一百五十
101 yībǎi líng yī 一百零一	*159* yībǎi wǔshíjiǔ 一百五十九
109 yībǎi líng jiǔ 一百零九	*200* èrbǎi 二百
110 yībǎi yīshí 一百一十	*300* sānbǎi 三百
111 yībǎi yīshíyī 一百一十一	*900* jiǔbǎi 九百
115 yībǎi yīshíwǔ 一百一十五	*999* jiǔbǎi jiǔshíjiǔ 九百九十九
120 yībǎi èrshí 一百二十	*1,000* yīqiān 一千
123 yībǎi èrshísān 一百二十三	

Character Essentials

To practice the Chinese characters you learned in Unit 3, Conversations 1 and 2 are repeated here without pīnyīn or English translations. Translate as many characters as you can. Check your answers by listening to the conversations from your audio. Don't worry if you can't remember all of the characters. Just try to remember as many as you can.

Conversation 1

▶ 12A Conversation 1 (CD 5, Track 15-Chinese, Track 16-Chinese and English)

老板:　　　小姐, 您要什么东西?

_____

_____

洁希:　　　你们有裙子吗?

_____

_____

老板:　　　　有。 请过来。 这是最新的款式,颜色不错,价钱也不贵。

洁希:　　　　很漂亮。 这条裙子多少钱?

老板:　　　　两百五十块。 我给你打折,一百八十八。

洁希:　　　　我喜欢紫色。 你们有紫色的裙子吗?

老板:　　　　让我看看。 紫色只有中号,您穿几号?

洁希:　　　　我穿大号。

老板: 不好意思。 我们现在没有大号, 你下个星期再过来好不好?

_____

_____

洁希: 好吧。 请你把裙子留给我, 我下个星期再过来。

_____

_____

老板: 没有问题。 再见。

_____

_____

洁希: 再见。

_____

_____

Conversation 2
12C Conversation 2 (CD 5, Track 18-Chinese, Track 19-Chinese and English)

推销员: 您买什么东西?

_____

_____

洁希: 土豆一磅多少钱?

_____

_____

推销员: 五毛钱一磅。

_____

_____

洁希: 给我两磅。 你们有白菜吗?

_____

_____

推销员: 有。 今天的白菜很新鲜。 您要多少?

_____

_____

洁希: 给我三磅。

_____

_____

推销员: 一块五毛一磅。 三磅要四块五毛。 还要什么吗?

_____

_____

洁希: 给我三个番茄。

_____

_____

推销员:　　　三个番茄五毛。一共六块。

_____

_____

洁希:　　　这里十块。

_____

_____

推销员:　　　好，找您四块。谢谢。

_____

_____

Unit 3 Quiz

A. Complete the following phrases with the appropriate measure word, and then translate them into English.

1. Yī _____ xuēzi. (ge/shuāng/tiáo)

   _____ 靴子。(个/双/条)

   _____

2. Yī _____ pídài. (ge/jiàn/tiáo)

   _____皮带。(个/件/条)

   _____

3. Yī _____ qípáo. (ge/jiàn/tiáo)

   _____ 旗袍。(个/件/条)

   _____

4. Yī _____ yùndòngxié. (shuāng/jiàn/tiáo)

   _____ 运动鞋。(双/件/条)

   _____

B. Make the following sentences negative. Then give the English translations of the negative sentences.

1. Tā rènshi wǒ de xuésheng. 他认识我的学生。_____

   _____

2. Wáng Xiānsheng yǒu yī zhī māo. 王先生有一只猫。_____

   _____

3. Tā tiàowǔ. 她跳舞。 _____

_____

4. Nǐmen yǒu sān zhāng zhǐ. 你们有三张纸。 _____

_____

5. Jīntiān shì xīngqī liù. 今天是星期六。 _____

_____

C. Translate the following price expressions into English.

1. wǔ kuài bā máo 五块八毛 _____

2. sān kuài sān máo èr fēn 三块三毛二分 _____

3. jiǔshíjiǔ kuài 九十九块 _____

4. liù máo 六毛 _____

5. qī kuài sì máo yī fēn 七块四毛一分 _____

D. Fill in the missing Chinese word for *two* in the following sentences, using the translations as cues.

1. Wǒ yǒu _____ tiáo gǒu.

我有 _____ 条狗。

(*I have two dogs.*)

2. Tā _____ shí'èr suì.

他 _____ 十二岁。

(*He is twenty-two years old.*)

3. Wáng Tàitai měitiān chī _____ ge píngguǒ.

王太太每天吃 _____ 个苹果。

4. Zhè shì yī bǎi líng _____ hào.

这是一百零_____号。

(This is number 102.)

5. Wǒmen mǎile _____ chuàn pútao.

我们买了_____串葡萄。

(We bought two bunches of grapes.)

6. Jīntiān shì sān yuè _____ hào.

今天是三月_____号。

(Today is March 2nd.)

How Did You Do?

Give yourself a point for every correct answer, then use the following key to tell whether you're ready to move on:

0-7 points: It's probably a good idea to go back through the lesson again. You may be moving too quickly, or there may be too much "down time" between your contact with Chinese. Remember that it's better to spend 30 minutes with Chinese three or four times a week than it is to spend two or three hours just once a week. Find a pace that's comfortable for you, and spread your contact hours out as much as you can.

8-12 points: You would benefit from a review before moving on. Go back and spend a little more time on the specific points that gave you trouble. Re-read the Grammar Builder sections that were difficult, and do the Work Outs one more time. Don't forget about the online supplemental practice material, either. Go to **www.livinglanguage.com/languagelab** for games and quizzes that will reinforce the material from this unit.

13-17 points: Good job! There are just a few points that you might consider reviewing before moving on. If you haven't worked with the games and quizzes on **www.livinglanguage.com/languagelab**, please give them a try.

18-20 points: Great! You're ready to move on to the next unit.

points

Negating completed
actions: **méiyǒu** 没有   Asking questions about completed
actions with **yǒu méiyǒu** 有没有

Unit 4: Doctors and Health

Yīshēng hé jiànkāng

医生和健康

In this unit, you'll learn how to talk about your health and lots of useful
vocabulary related to the body. You'll also learn more about negation, how to
express commands, and how to ask *how* and *how long*. Plus, you will learn how to
express completed actions in Chinese. Let's get started!

Lesson 13: Words

In this lesson, you'll learn:

☐ Essential vocabulary related to the body.

☐ How to use bù 不 and bùshì 不是 before adjectives and adverbs.

☐ Commands.

Word Builder 1

▶ 13A Word Builder 1 (CD 5, Track 21)

yǎnjing	眼睛	*eye*
ěrduo	耳朵	*ear*
zuǐba	嘴巴	*mouth*
zuǐchún	嘴唇	*lips*
liǎn	脸	*face*

bízi	鼻子	*nose*
bózi	脖子	*neck*
étóu	额头	*forehead*
sǎngzi	嗓子	*throat*
liǎnjiá	脸颊	*cheek*
yáchǐ	牙齿	*tooth*
shétou	舌头	*tongue*

✎ Word Practice 1

Fill in the blank in each word. The characters are provided for additional help and practice.

1. sǎng_____

   嗓子

2. _____ chǐ

   牙齿

3. _____chún

   嘴唇

4. _____jing

   眼睛

5. zuǐ _____

   嘴巴

ANSWER KEY
1. zi 子; 2. yá 牙; 3. zuǐ 嘴; 4. yǎn 眼睛; 5. ba 巴

Grammar Builder 1:
NEGATION WITH BÙ 不 AND BÚSHÌ 不是 BEFORE ADJECTIVES AND ADVERBS

▶ 13B Grammar Builder 1 (CD 5, Track 22)

You already know that you can negate most verbs by placing the negative particle bù 不 before the verb. You can also use bù 不 before an adjective, with a similar negative meaning.

Zhège nǚháizi měi.
这个女孩子美。
This girl is pretty.

Nàge nǚháizi bù měi.
那个女孩子不美。
That girl is not pretty.

Note, however, that when an adjective is modified by an adverb expressing quantity or degree, such as hěn 很 (*very*), bù 不 can no longer be used to form the negative. Instead, the word bùshì 不是 is placed before the modifying adverb in order to negate the sentence.

Wǒ de jiějie hěn měi.
我的姐姐很美。
My older sister is very pretty.

Wǒ de jiějie bùshì hěn měi.
我的姐姐不是很美。
My older sister is not very pretty.

Měiguó hěn dà.

美国很大。

America is very big.

Měiguó bùshì hěn dà.

美国不是很大。

America is not very big.

Rìběn chē tài guì.

日本车太贵。

Japanese cars are too expensive.

Rìběn chē bùshì tài guì.

日本车不是太贵。

Japanese cars are not too expensive.

⏸

✎ Work Out 1

Negate the following sentences by adding ₍bùshì₎ 不是 or ₍bù₎ 不.

1. ₍Dìguódàshà hěn gāo.₎ 帝国大厦很高。 *(The Empire State Building is very tall.)*

2. ₍Nà jiàn wàitào tài guì.₎ 那件外套太贵。 *(That coat is too expensive.)*

3. ₍Tā cōngmíng.₎ 她聪明。 *(She is intelligent.)*

Negating completed
actions: **méiyǒu** 没有 | Asking questions about completed
actions with **yǒu méiyǒu** 有没有

4. Zhège fángzi tài guì. 这个房子太贵。(*This house is too expensive.*) _____

_____

5. Nà liàng chē hěn kuài. 那辆车很快。(*That car is fast.*) _____

6. Zhèxiē píngguǒ hěn xiāng. 这些苹果很香。(*These apples are very aromatic.*)

_____

7. Tā de gǒu xiǎo. 她的狗小。(*Her dog is small.*) _____

ANSWER KEY

1. Dìguódàshà bùshì hěn gāo. 帝国大厦不是很高。2. Nà jiàn wàitào bùshì tài guì. 那件外套不是太贵。3. Tā bù cōngmíng. 她不聪明。4. Zhège fángzi bùshì tài guì. 这个房子不是太贵。5. Nà liàng chē bùshì hěn kuài. 那辆车不是很快。6. Zhèxiē píngguǒ bùshì hěn xiāng. 这些苹果不是很香。7. Tā de gǒu bù xiǎo. 她的狗不小。

Word Builder 2

▶ 13C Word Builder 2 (CD 5, Track 23)

shǒu	手	*hand*
shǒuzhǐ	手指	*finger*
tuǐ	腿	*leg*
xiǎotuǐ	小腿	*calf*
jiǎo	脚	*foot*
zhǐjia	指甲	*fingernail*
zhǒu	肘	*elbow*
shǒuwàn	手腕	*wrist*
dàtuǐ	大腿	*thigh*
zúgēn	足跟	*heel*
dùzi	肚子	*belly*

bèibù	背部	*back*
jiānbǎng	肩膀	*shoulder*
xiōngbù	胸部	*chest*

✎ Word Practice 2

Match the English word in the left column with its appropriate translation in the right column.

1. *shoulder*

2. *leg*

3. *hand*

4. *fingernail*

5. *belly*

a. dùzi 肚子

b. zhǐjia 指甲

c. jiānbǎng 肩膀

d. tuǐ 腿

e. shǒu 手

ANSWER KEY
1. c; 2. d; 3. e; 4. b; 5. a

Grammar Builder 2
COMMANDS

▶ 13D Grammar Builder 2 (CD 5, Track 24)

The imperative, or command form, in Chinese is very easy. Just use the basic verb form without any subject. Qǐng 请 (*please*) can be used to make the command more polite.

Qǐng zài shuō yī cì.
请再说一次。
Please repeat that. (lit., Please say it once again.)

Qǐng zhāngkāi zuǐba.

请张开嘴巴。

Please open your mouth.

To form a negative command, bù 不 is not used. Instead, the negative particle bié 别 (*don't*) is placed in front of the verb. Bié 别 and the verb are usually placed at the head of the sentence.

Bié kàn tài duō diànshì.

别看太多电视。

Don't watch too much TV.

Bié chī lěng de dōngxi.

别吃冷的东西。

Don't eat cold food.

Bié qù.

别去。

Don't go.

You can also use the word búyào 不要 in Chinese to make negative commands. Like bié 别, búyào 不要 is placed in front of the verb at the beginning of the sentence. Bié 别 and búyào 不要 are interchangeble:

Búyào pèng nà tiáo gǒu.

不要碰那条狗。

Don't touch that dog.

Bié pèng nà tiáo gǒu.

别碰那条狗。

Don't touch that dog.

Unit 4 Lesson 13: Words

Ⓘ

✎ Work Out 2

Choose the appropriate negative particle (bié 别 or bù 不) in the following sentences.

1. Nàli tài wēixiǎn. Nǐ _____ qù.

   (It's too dangerous there. Don't go.)

2. Wǒmen _____ chī ròu.

   (We don't eat meat.)

3. Zhège fángzi tài guì. Wǒ _____ mǎi.

   (This house is too expensive. I'm not buying it.)

4. Tiānqì tài lěng. Tā _____ qù shàngxué.

   (The weather is too cold. He is not going to school.)

5. Nǐ _____ shūfu. _____ hē jiǔ.

   (You don't feel well. Don't drink wine.)

6. Tā de huā _____ guì.

   (His flowers are not expensive.)

7. Lǎoshī láile. _____ shuìjiào.

   (The teacher is coming. Don't sleep.)

   ANSWER KEY
   1. bié 别; 2. bù 不; 3. bù 不; 4. bù 不; 5. bù 不, Bié 别; 6. bù 不; 7. Bié 别

✎ Drive It Home

Write out sentences with bié 别 and bù 不 using the phrases provided. Then give the English translation.

1. bié别 (chuān nà tiáo qúnzi 穿那条裙子, qù nàge shìchǎng 去那个市场, mǎi tài duō cài 买太多菜, chī zhège fānqié 吃这个番茄) _____

    _____

2. bù不 (tā hē píjiǔ 他喝啤酒, wǒmen xiàwǔ shuìjiào 我们下午睡觉, wǒ de jiějie kàn diànshì 我的姐姐看电视, nǐ xǐhuan chī ròu 你喜欢吃肉) _____

    _____

ANSWER KEY

1. Bié chuān nà tiáo qúnzi. 别穿那条裙子。(*Don't wear that skirt.*) Bié qù nàge shìchǎng. 别去那个市场。(*Don't go to that market.*) Bié mǎi tài duō cài. 别买太多菜。(*Don't buy too many vegetables.*) Bié chī zhège fānqié. 别吃这个番茄。(*Don't eat that tomato.*) 2. Tā bù hē píjiǔ. 他不喝啤酒。(*He doesn't drink beer.*) Wǒmen xiàwǔ bù shuìjiào. 我们下午不睡觉。(*We don't sleep in the afternoon.*) Wǒ de jiějie bù kàn diànshì. 我的姐姐不看电视。(*My older sister doesn't watch television.*) Nǐ bù xǐhuan chī ròu. 你不喜欢吃肉。(*You don't like to eat meat.*)

How Did You Do?

By now you should know:

☐ Essential vocabulary related to the body.
    (Still unsure? Go back to 187.)

☐ How to use bù 不 and bùshì 不是 before adjectives and adverbs.
    (Still unsure? Go back to 189.)

☐ Commands.
    (Still unsure? Go back to 192.)

✎ Word Recall

Match the English word in the left column with its appropriate translation in the right column.

1. *chest*	a. ěrduo 耳朵
2. *face*	b. tuǐ 腿
3. *belly*	c. bízi 鼻子
4. *thigh*	d. sǎngzi 嗓子
5. *neck*	e. xiōngbù 胸部
6. *leg*	f. zhǒu 肘
7. *eye*	g. bózi 脖子
8. *hand*	h. étóu 额头
9. *foot*	i. liǎn 脸
10. *nose*	j. dàtuǐ 大腿
11. *elbow*	k. yǎnjing 眼睛
12. *tongue*	l. shǒu 手
13. *forehead*	m. jiǎo 脚
14. *throat*	n. shétou 舌头
15. *ear*	o. dùzi 肚子

ANSWER KEY
1. e; 2. i; 3. o; 4. j; 5. g; 6. b; 7. k; 8. l; 9. m; 10. c; 11. f; 12. n; 13. h; 14. d; 15. a

Lesson 14: Phrases

In this lesson, you'll learn:

☐ Essential vocabulary related to illness.

☐ How to talk about completed actions.

☐ How to ask *how long*.

Phrase Builder 1

▶ 14A Phrase Builder 1 (CD 5, Track 25)

bù shūfu	不舒服	to not feel well
zháoliáng	着凉	to catch a cold
fāshāo	发烧	to have a fever
lā dùzi	拉肚子	to have diarrhea
wèi tòng/dùzi tòng	胃痛/肚子痛	to have a stomachache/ abdominal pain
tóuyūn	头晕	to feel dizzy
tóu tòng	头痛	to have a headache
yǒu yìdiǎnr késou	有一点儿咳嗽	to have a slight cough
tùle hěn duō cì	吐了很多次	to vomit many times
ěxin	恶心	to feel nauseous
sǎngzi tòng	嗓子痛	to have a sore throat
xiōngbù tòng	胸部痛	to have chest pain
chū zhěn	出诊	to make a medical house call (a doctor)
fādǒu	发抖	to shiver

liúxiě	流血	*to bleed*
fāyán	发炎	*inflammation*
qù yīyuàn	去医院	*to go to the hospital*
qù zhěnsuǒ	去诊所	*to go to a clinic*
zěnme yàng?	怎么样?	*how …?*

(II)

✎ Phrase Practice 1

Fill in the blank of the pīnyīn phrases: The characters are provided for additional help and practice.

1. qùyī _____

   去医院

2. bù _____ fu

   不舒服

3. fā _____

   发烧

4. fā _____

   发炎

5. _____ dùzi

   拉肚子

ANSWER KEY
1. yuàn 院; 2. shū 舒; 3. shāo 烧; 4. yán 炎; 5. lā 拉

Grammar Builder 1
EXPRESSING A COMPLETED ACTION WITH LE 了

▶ 14B Grammar Builder 1 (CD 5, Track 26)

A common way to express the simple past (*-ed*) or the present perfect tense (*have*
+ verb) in Chinese is to add the particle le 了 immediately after the verb. This
particle indicates that an action has been completed.

Tā chīle yào.
他吃了药。
He took (lit., ate) the medicine.

Wǒ qùle Zhōngguó.
我去了中国。
I went to China.

Tāmen chàngle sān shǒu Yīngwén gē.
他们唱了三首英文歌。
They have sung three English songs.

But be careful. Le 了 doesn't always refer to the past. It stresses completion of an
action, so it can also refer to an action that will be completed in the future.

Lǐbài sān wǒ yǐjīng fēidào le Zhōngguó.
礼拜三我已经飞到了中国。
I will already have flown to China by Wednesday.

Tā jīntiān wǎnshang bā diǎn yǐjīng shuì le.
她今天晚上八点已经睡了。
She'll already have slept by 8pm tonight.

Le 了 can also be used to indicate that a current situation or condition is different from the way things were in the immediate past. It's typically used in Chinese to indicate a change in time, weather or season.

Dōngtiān lái le.
冬天来了。
It's winter. (lit., Winter has come.)

Wǔ diǎn le.
五点了。
It's five o'clock.

Xiàyǔ le.
下雨了。
It's raining.

Wǒ méiyǒu qián le.
我没有钱了。
I don't have money now.

Of course, it is also possible to simply say wǒ méiyǒu qián 我没有钱. (*I don't have money*). The difference in meaning between that phrase and wǒ méiyǒu qián le 我没有钱了 is that the addition of le 了 stresses that the current situation is different. So, wǒ méiyǒu qián le 我没有钱了 implies that the person recently had money but doesn't now.

When le is added after an adjective, however, it implies has become + adjective. When le is added after shì 是 (*to be*), it means to be ... now. For example:

Tā pàng le.
他胖了。
He has become fat. (He was not fat before.)

Wǒ de dìdi gāo le.

我的弟弟高了。

My younger brother has become tall. (He was not tall before.)

Tā shì xuésheng le.

他是学生了。

He is a student now. (He was not before.)

✎ Work Out 1

A. Translate the following sentences into English, paying careful attention to the meaning expressed by ₗₑ 了.

1. Tā lái Měiguó wǔ nián le. 他/她来美国五年了。 _____

   _____

2. Wáng Tàitai qùle yīyuàn. 王太太去了医院。 _____

   _____

3. Zhāng lǎoshī mǎile liǎng běn shū. 张老师买了两本书。 _____

   _____

4. Xīngqī sān le. 星期三了。 _____

   _____

5. Dìdi chīle yào. 弟弟吃了药。 _____

   _____

6. Nàge rén mǎile sān tiáo qúnzi. 那个人买了三条裙子。 _____

   _____

7. Wǒ míngbái le. 我明白了。 _____

_____

8. Tā de péngyou qùle zhěnsuǒ. 他/她的朋友去了诊所。 _____

_____

B. Change the tense of these sentences by using le 了.

1. Liù diǎn bàn. 六点半。 _____

_____

2. Wǒmen chīfàn. 我们吃饭。 _____

_____

3. Tā shāngxué. 他上学。 _____

_____

4. Nǐ mǎi shénme cài? 你买什么菜? _____

_____

5. Xuésheng qù xìyuàn. 学生去戏院。 _____

_____

ANSWER KEY

A. 1. *He/She has been in the U.S. for five years.* 2. *Mrs. Wang went to the hospital.* 3. *Teacher Zhang bought two books.* 4. *It's Wednesday.* 5. *My younger brother took the medicine.* 6. *That person bought three skirts.* 7. *I understand now.* 8. *His/Her friend went to the clinic.*
B. 1. Liù diǎn bàn le. 六点半了。 (*It's six thirty.*) 2. Wǒmen chīfàn le. 我们吃饭了。 (*We ate.*)
3. Tā shāngxué le. 他上学了。 (*He went to school.*) 4. Nǐ mǎile shénme cài? 你买了什么菜? (*What vegetables did you buy?*) 5. Xuésheng qùle xìyuàn. 学生去了戏院。 (*The student went to the theater.*)

Asking *how?*

Asking *where?*

Negating completed
actions: **méiyǒu** 没有

Asking questions about completed
actions with **yǒu méiyǒu** 有没有

Phrase Builder 2

▶ 14C Phrase Builder 2 (CD 5, Track 27)

bìngle	病了	to be sick
dǎ zhēn	打针	to give/get an injection
liáng tǐwēn	量体温	to take (someone's) temperature
bǎmài	把脉	to check (someone's) pulse
chī yào	吃药	to take medicine
bāozā shāngkǒu	包扎伤口	to bind up a wound, to apply a bandage (to a wound)
dǎ shígāo	打石膏	to have a plaster cast
féngxiàn	缝线	to stitch up (a wound)
zuò xīndiàntú	做心电图	to take a cardiogram
duōjiǔ	多久	how long?
fàn qián fú	饭前服	(medication) to be taken before a meal
fàn hòu fú	饭后服	(medication) to be taken after a meal

⏸

✎ Phrase Practice 2

Translate the following English phrases into pīnyīn.

1. *to stitch up* _____

2. *to be sick* _____

3. *to take medicine* _____

4. *how long?* _____

5. *to take someone's temperature* _____

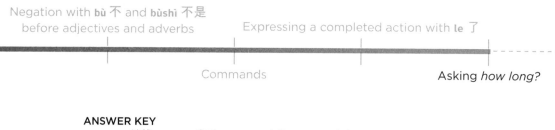

Grammar Builder 2
ASKING *HOW LONG?*

▶ 14D Grammar Builder 2 (CD 5, Track 28)

Use the phrase duōjiǔ 多久, which literally means *how long*, to ask about the duration of something. Notice that you can ask about both a completed action and an uncompleted action by using le 了.

Nǐ bìngle duōjiǔ?
你病了多久?
How long have you been sick?

Nǐ kéle duōjiǔ?
你咳了多久?
How long have you been coughing?

Wǒ yào děng duōjiǔ?
我要等多久?
How long do I need to wait?

Nǐ děngle duōjiǔ?
你等了多久?
How long have you been waiting?

Nǐ xuéle duōjiǔ Zhōngwén?
你学了多久中文?
How long have you been studying Chinese?

⏸

Asking *how?*   Asking *where?*

Negating completed
actions: **méiyǒu** 没有   Asking questions about completed
actions with **yǒu méiyǒu** 有没有

✎ Work Out 2

Pick sentences from the column on the right that best answer each question in the
column on the left.

1. Nǐ bàba yǒu chē ma?
   你爸爸有车吗?

   a. Wǒ qùle liǎng nián.
   我去了两年。

2. Nǐ qùle Zhōngguó duōjiǔ?
   你去了中国多久?

   b. Liǎng tiān.
   两天。

3. Nǐ chīle fàn méiyǒu?
   你吃了饭没有?

   c. Wǒ míngbái.
   我明白。

4. Tā bìngle duōjiǔ?
   他病了多久?

   d. Tā chāngle wǔ ge zhōngtóu.
   他唱了五个钟头。

5. Nǐ xuéle duōjiǔ Zhōngwén?
   你学了多久中文?

   e. Tā yǒu.
   他有。

6. Zhège duōshǎo qián?
   这个多少钱?

   f. Shí kuài.
   十块。

7. Nǐ míngbái ma?
   你明白吗?

   g. Wǒ xuéle sān ge yuè.
   我学了三个月。

8. Tā gēge chāngle duōjiǔ?
   他哥哥唱了多久?

   h. Wǒ chī le.
   我吃了。

ANSWER KEY
1. e; 2. a; 3. h; 4. b; 5. g; 6. f; 7. c; 8. d.

Take It Further

You've already seen how verb-object verbs are two-syllable words that consist of
a verb followed by an object that clarifies the purpose of an action. Chīfàn 吃饭 (*to
eat*) and chànggē 唱歌 (*to sing*) are two examples of verb-object verbs. The nouns
fàn 饭 (*meal, food*) and gē 歌 (*song*) are used as objects to clarify and emphasize
what is being eaten (chī 吃) and what is being sung (chàng 唱).

Remember that these object syllables can be attached to the verb, or separated from it, without affecting meaning at all. This is particularly evident when the particle le 了 is added to indicate a completed action.

Wǒ chīle fàn.
我吃了饭。
I ate the/a meal.

As you know, there's another category of two-syllable verbs in Chinese that do not show this flexibility, so they're grammatically distinct from verb-object verbs. Examples of inseparable two-syllable verbs include míngbái 明白 (*to understand*) and rènshi 认识 (*to know someone*).

Tā míngbái wǒ de Zhōngwén.
他明白我的中文。
He understands my Chinese.

Tā míngbái le wǒ de huà.
他明白了我的话。
He understood what I said.

Wǒ rènshi Wáng tàitai.
我认识王太太。
I know Mrs. Wang.

Tāmen rènshi le sān nián.
他们认识了三年。
They have known (each other) for three years.

Notice that the particle le 了 (or anything else) can never separate bái 白 from míng 明 or shi 识 from rèn 认.

✎ Drive It Home

Let's practice. Use each of the following verbs in a sentence with the given subject
and the particle le 了. First, practice with a few verb-object constructions that
can be separated. Then try the same thing with a few inseparable two-syllable/
verb-object verbs.

1. chīfàn(wǒmen, nǐmen, nà ge xuésheng) 吃饭 (我们, 你们, 那个学生) _____

_____

2. hē jiǔ (nǐ, wǒ, tā de tàitai) 喝酒 (你, 我, 他的太太) _____

_____

3. chànggē (zhège lǎoshī, nǐ de dìdi, tāmen) 唱歌 (这个老师, 你的弟弟, 他们)

_____

4. rènshi(wǒmen, nǐmen, tāmen) 认识 (我们, 你们, 他们) _____

_____

5. míngbái(nǐ, wǒ, Zhāng Lǎoshi) 明白 (你, 我, 张老师) _____

_____

6. zháoliáng(Wǒ de mèimei, nàge nǚháir, tā) 着凉 (我的妹妹, 那个女孩儿, 她)

ANSWER KEY
1. Wǒmen chīle fàn. 我们吃了饭。 Nǐmen chīle fàn. 你们吃了饭。 Nàge xuésheng chīle fàn. 那个学生
吃了饭。 2. Nǐ hēle jiǔ. 你喝了酒。 Wǒ hēle jiǔ. 我喝了酒。 Tā de tàitai hēle jiǔ. 他的太太喝了酒。
3. Zhège lǎoshī chàngle gē. 这个老师唱了歌。 Nǐ de dìdi chàngle gē. 你的弟弟唱了歌。 Tāmen
chàngle gē. 他们唱了歌。 4. Wǒmen rènshi le. 我们认识了。 Nǐmen rènshi le. 你们认识了。 Tāmen
rènshi le. 他们认识了。 5. Nǐ míngbái le. 你明白了。 Wǒ míngbái le. 我明白了。 Zhāng lǎoshi míngbái
le. 张老师明白了。 6. Wǒ de mèimei zháoliáng le. 我的妹妹着凉了。 Nàge nǚháir zháoliáng le. 那个
女孩儿着凉了。 Tā zháoliáng le. 她着凉了。

How Did You Do?

By now you should know:

☐ Essential vocabulary related to illness.
(Still unsure? Go back to xx.)

☐ How to talk about completed actions.
(Still unsure? Go back to xx.)

☐ How to ask *how long*.
(Still unsure? Go back to xx.)

✎ Word Recall

Match the English word in the left column with its appropriate translation in the
right column.

1. *to take (someone's) temperature*   a. fàn hòu fú 饭后服

2. *to have a headache*   b. xiōngbù tòng 胸部痛

3. *to go to a clinic*   c. zháoliáng 着凉

4. *to take medicine*   d. dǎ zhēn 打针

5. *to have a plaster cast*   e. liáng tǐwēn 量体温

6. *to catch cold*   f. chū zhěn 出诊

7. *to give/get an injection*   g. fàn qián fú 饭前服

8. *(medication) to be taken before a meal* h. fāshāo 发烧

9. *(medication) to be taken after a meal*   i. dǎ shígāo 打石膏

10. *to have a fever*   j. chī yào 吃药

11. *to shiver*   k. zuò xīndiàntú 做心电图

12. *to make a medical house call (a doctor)* l. tóu tòng 头痛

13. *to take a cardiogram*   m. fādǒu 发抖

14. *to have chest pain*   n. duōjiǔ 多久

15. *how long?*   o. qù zhěnsuǒ 去诊所

ANSWER KEY
1. e; 2. l; 3. o; 4. j; 5. i; 6. c; 7. d; 8. g; 9. a; 10. h; 11. m; 12. f; 13. k; 14. b; 15. n

Lesson 15: Sentences

In this lesson, you'll learn:

☐ How to talk about illness.

☐ Asking *how*.

☐ How to negate completed actions with méiyǒu 没有.

Sentence Builder 1

 15A Sentence Builder 1 (CD 6, Track 1)

Nǐ nǎli bù shūfu?	你哪里不舒服？	*What's troubling you? (lit., Where don't you feel well?)*
Wǒ fāshāo.	我发烧。	*I have a fever.*
Wǒ tóu tòng hé dùzi tòng.	我头痛和肚子痛。	*I have a headache and abdominal pain.*
Nǐ tòngle duōjiǔ?	你痛了多久？	*How long have you been in pain?*
Tòngle liǎngtiān.	痛了两天。	*I've been in pain for two days.*
Nǐ xiànzài juéde zěnme yàng?	你现在觉得怎么样？	*How do you feel now?*
Wǒ yǒudiǎnr bù shūfu.	我有点儿不舒服。	*I don't feel very well.*
Wǒ xiǎng tù.	我想吐。	*I'm nauseous./I'm sick to my stomach.*

Wǒ hěn lèi.	我很累。	*I'm very tired.*
Nǐ de màibó yǒudiǎnr kuài.	你的脉搏有点儿快。	*Your pulse is a little fast.*
Nǐ zuìjìn zěnme yàng?	你最近怎么样?	*How have you been doing recently?*
Wǒ hěn máng.	我很忙。	*I'm very busy.*

Ⓜ

✎ Sentence Practice 1

Fill in the blanks of the following conversation. Use the translations as cues.

A: Wǒ yǒudiǎnr bù_____.

我有点儿不舒服。

(*I don't feel very well.*)

B: Nǐ_____bù shūfu?

你哪里不舒服?

(*What's troubling you?*)

A: Wǒ _____ tòng.

我肚子痛。

(*My stomach/abdomen hurts.*)

B: Nǐ tòngle _____ ?

你痛了多久?

(*How long have you been in pain?*)

A: _____ le sān tiān.

痛了三天。

(*I've been in pain for three days.*)

B: Xiǎng _____ ma?

想吐吗？

(*Do you feel nauseous?*)

A: Bù _____ tù.

不想吐。

(*No, I don't feel nauseous.*)

ANSWER KEY
A: shūfu; B: nǎli; A: dùzi; B: duōjiǔ; A: tòng; B: tù; A: xiǎng

Grammar Builder 1
ASKING *HOW?*

▶ 15B Grammar Builder 1 (CD 6, Track 2)

The phrase zěnme yàng? 怎么样？ (sometimes shortened to zěnyàng 怎样)
is used to ask the question *how?* It can be put in front of a verb to ask how
something is done, or after a noun to ask how someone is doing.

Nǐmen zěn(me) yàng qù kàn yīshēng?
你们怎(么)样去看医生？
How do you go to (see) the doctor?

Wǒmen zuò gōngchē qù kàn yīshēng.
我们做公车去看医生。
We take a bus to go to (see) the doctor.

Nǐ de bàba xiànzài zěnme yàng?

你的爸爸现在怎么样？

How is your father doing now?

✎ Work Out 1

Pick sentences from the column on the right that best answer each question in the column on the left. Translate the answer that you choose.

1. Tā méiyǒu qián. Tā zěnyàng qù Niǔyuē?
   他/她没有钱。 他/她怎样去纽约？

   a. Tā měitiān zuò gōngchē.
   他/她每天做公车。

2. Nín zuìjìn zěnme yàng?
   您最近怎么样？

   b. Tài guì.
   太贵。

3. Nàge xuésheng měitiān zěnme yàng shàngxué?
   那个学生每天怎么样上学？

   c. Tā bù zuòfàn. Tā qù péngyou de jiā chīfàn.
   他/她不做饭。 他/她去朋友的家吃饭。

4. Zhège fángzi zěnme yàng?
   这个房子怎么样？

   d. Wǒ měi tiān kàn Zhōngwén shū.
   我每天看中文书。

5. Nǐ xiànzài juéde zěnme yàng?
   你现在觉得怎么样？

   e. Tā màile (*sold*) tā de chē qù Niǔyuē.
   他/ 她卖了他的车去纽约。

6. Tā zěnme yàng zuòfàn?
   他/她怎么样做饭？

   f. Wǒ xiǎng tù.
   我想吐。

7. Nǐ zěnyàng xué Zhōngwén?
   你怎样学中文？

   g. Wǒ hěn hǎo. Xièxie.
   我很好。 谢谢。

ANSWER KEY

1. e (*He/She sold his car to go to New York.*); 2. g (*I'm very well. Thank you.*); 3. a (*He/She takes the bus everyday.*); 4. b (*It's too expensive.*); 5. f (*I am feeling nauseous.*); 6. c (*He/She doesn't cook. He/She goes to his/her friend's home to eat.*); 7. d (*I read Chinese books everyday.*)

Sentence Builder 2

▶ 15C Sentence Builder 2 (CD 6, Track 3)

Tā chīle yào.	他吃了药。	*He took the medicine.*
Tā méiyǒu chī yào.	他没有吃药。	*He didn't take the medicine.*
Tā hái méiyǒu chī yào.	他还没有吃药。	*He hasn't taken the medicine yet.*
Wǒ de bàba mǎile yī liàng xīn chē.	我的爸爸买了一辆新车。	*My father bought a new car.*
Wǒ de bàba méiyǒu mǎi xīn chē.	我的爸爸没有买新车。	*My father didn't buy a new car.*
Wǒ de bàba hái méiyǒu mǎi xīn chē.	我的爸爸还没有买新车。	*My father hasn't bought a new car yet.*
Zhāng lǎoshī bìngle.	张老师病了。	*Teacher Zhang was sick.*
Zhāng lǎoshī méiyǒu bìng.	张老师没有病。	*Teacher Zhang was not sick.*

⏸

✎ Sentence Practice 2

Fill in the blanks with either méiyǒu 没有 or le 了, using the English translation as a clue.

1. Wǒ kànshū _____.

   我看书 _____。

   (*I read* [past] *a book.*)

2. Tāmen _____ qù mǎi kùzi.

   他们 _____ 去买裤子。

   (They didn't go to buy pants.)

3. Nǎinai _____ chuān wàitào.

   奶奶 _____ 穿外套。

   (Grandmother didn't wear a coat.)

4. Gēge shàngbān _____.

   哥哥上班 _____ 。

   (Older brother went to work.)

5. Chén Xiānsheng _____ hē jiǔ.

   陈先生 _____ 喝酒。

   (Mr. Chen didn't drink wine.)

   ANSWER KEY
   1. le 了; 2. méiyǒu 没有; 3. méiyǒu 没有; 4. le 了; 5. méiyǒu 没有

Grammar Builder 2
NEGATING COMPLETED ACTIONS: MÉIYǑU 没有

▶ 15D Grammar Builder 2 (CD 6, Track 4)

You learned that le 了 is used in Chinese to show that an action has been completed. To express negation of completed actions, the negative phrase méiyǒu 没有 is used. This typically expresses that someone failed to accomplish something, or never undertook it in the first place. Notice that le 了 is not used in the negative constructions.

Negating completed actions: méiyǒu 没有

Zhāng lǎoshī méiyǒu kàn diànshì.

张老师没有看电视。

Teacher Zhang didn't watch TV.

Tā méiyǒu qù.

他没有去。

He didn't go.

Don't forget the other use of méiyǒu 没有, which is the negative form of the verb yǒu 有 (*to have*). In those constructions, méiyǒu 没有 is followed by a noun. But in the constructions discussed here, méiyǒu 没有 is followed by a verb and is usually translated as *did not*.

You can add the word haí 还 (*still*) before méiyǒu 没有, forming the phrase hái méiyǒu 还没有 (*not yet*). Notice that this construction is usually translated into the English present perfect tense (*has/have done*).

Wǒ de māma hái méiyǒu chīfàn.

我的妈妈还没有吃饭。

My mother hasn't eaten yet.

Tā hái méiyǒu qù.

他还没有去。

He hasn't gone yet.

(II)

✎ Work Out 2

Use bù 不 or méiyǒu 没有 to negate the following sentences, and then translate your answers.

1. Wǒ qùle Zhōngguó. 我去了中国。 _____

   _____

2. Tā xǐhuan dǎ zhēn. 她喜欢打针。 _____

   _____

3. Nàge yīshēng chīle yào. 那个医生吃了药。 _____

   _____

4. Zhège Měiguórén mǎile sì běn Yīngwén shū. 这个美国人买了四本英文书。

   _____

5. Chén lǎoshī shàngxué. 陈老师上学。 _____

   _____

6. Wáng Tàitai lái le. 王太太来了。 _____

   _____

7. Wǒ de māma bìng le. 我的妈妈病了。 _____

   _____

8. Zhāng Tàitai qù kàn yīshēng. 张太太去看医生。 _____

   _____

ANSWER KEY

1. Wǒ méiyǒu qù Zhōngguó. 我没有去中国。 (*I didn't go to China.*) 2. Tā bù xǐhuan dǎ zhēn. 她不喜欢打针。 (*She doesn't like getting injections.*) 3. Nàge yīshēng méiyǒu chī yào. 那个医生没有吃药。 (*That doctor didn't take the medicine.*) 4. Zhège Měiguórén méiyǒu mǎi sì běn Yīngwén shū. 这个美国人没有买四本英文书。 (*This American didn't buy four English books.*) 5. Chén lǎoshī bù shàngxué. 陈老师不上

Negating completed
actions: **méiyǒu** 没有

学。(*Teacher Chen doesn't go to school.*) 6. Wáng Tàitai méiyǒu lái. 王太太没有来。(*Mrs. Wang didn't come.*) 7. Wǒ de māma méiyǒu bìng. 我的妈妈没有病。(*My mother was not sick.*) 8. Zhāng Tàitai bù qù kàn yīshēng. 张太太不去看医生。(*Mrs. Zhang isn't going to see a doctor.*)

✎ Drive It Home

Negate the following sentences with both bù 不 and méiyǒu 没有。For example, with Wǒ qù cānguǎn 我去餐馆, you would write Wǒ bù qù cānguǎn 我不去餐馆 and Wǒ méiyǒu qù cānguǎn 我没有去餐馆。Notice the two sentences differ in tense.

1. Tā kàn diànyǐng. 他看电影。(*He watches movies.*) _____

_____

2. Zhège yīshēng chū zhěn. 这个医生出诊。(*This doctor makes house calls.*) _____

_____

3. Wǒmen měitiān kāichē. 我们每天开车。(*We drive every day.*) _____

_____

4. Wǒ yào tīng yīnyuè. 我要听音乐。(*I want to listen to music.*) _____

_____

5. Tāmen chuān hóng xuēzi. 他们穿红靴子。(*They wear red boots.*) _____

_____

ANSWER KEY

1. Tā bù kàn diànyǐng. 他不看电影。(*He doesn't watch movies.*) Tā méiyǒu kàn diànyǐng. 他没有看电影。(*He didn't watch a movie.*) 2. Zhège yīshēng bù chū zhěn. 这个医生不出诊。(*This doctor does not make house calls.*) Zhège yīshēng méiyǒu chū zhěn. 这个医生没有出诊。(*This doctor didn't make a house call.*) 3. Wǒmen měitiān bù kāichē. 我们每天不开车。(*We don't drive every day.*) Wǒmen méiyǒu měitiān kāichē. 我们没有每天开车。(*We didn't drive every day.*) 4. Wǒ bù yào tīng yīnyuè. 我不要听音乐。(*I don't want to listen to music.*) Wǒ méiyǒu yào tīng yīnyuè. 我没有要听音乐。(*I didn't want to listen to music.*) 5. Tāmen bù chuān hóng xuēzi. 他们不穿红靴子。(*They don't wear red boots.*) Tāmen méiyǒu chuān hóng xuēzi. 他们没有穿红靴子。(*They didn't wear red boots.*)

Negation with **bù** 不 and **bùshì** 不是
before adjectives and adverbs
Expressing a completed action with **le** 了

Commands

Asking *how long?*

How Did You Do?

By now you should know:

☐ How to talk about illness.
(Still unsure? Go back to 209.)

☐ Asking *how*.
(Still unsure? Go back to 211.)

☐ How to negate completed actions with méiyǒu 没有.
(Still unsure? Go back to 214.)

✎ Word Recall

Match the English word in the left column with its appropriate translation in the right column.

1. *to eat*	a. yǒu 有
2. *to order (food)*	b. yào 要
3. *to understand*	c. qù 去
4. *to go to work*	d. chī 吃
5. *to listen*	e. kàn 看
6. *to have*	f. diǎn 点
7. *to go to school*	g. tīng 听
8. *to drive (a car)*	h. mǎi 买
9. *to cook*	i. chuān 穿
10. *to want*	j. rènshi 认识
11. *to be*	k. míngbái 明白
12. *to wear*	l. chànggē 唱歌
13. *to know (someone)*	m. tiàowǔ 跳舞
14. *to buy*	n. shàngbān 上班
15. *to see, to look, to read*	o. shǎngxué 上学

16. *to sing*

17. *to dance*

18. *to go*

p. shì 是

q. kāichē 开车

r. shāofàn 烧饭

ANSWER KEY

1. d; 2. f; 3. k; 4. n; 5. g; 6. a; 7. o; 8. q; 9. r; 10. b; 11. p; 12. i; 13. j; 14. h; 15. e 16. l; 17. m; 18. c

Lesson 16: Conversations

In this lesson, you'll learn:

☐ How to discuss an illness with a doctor.

☐ Asking *where*.

Conversation 1

▶ 16A Conversation 1 (CD 6, Track 5-Chinese, Track 6-Chinese and English)

Jess doesn't feel well, so she goes to the doctor's office.

Yīshēng: Nín nǎli bù shūfu?

医生: 您哪里不舒服?

Jiéxī: Wǒ jīntiān yǒu diǎnr tóu tòng, quánshēn dōu tòng.

洁希: 我今天有点儿头痛, 全身都痛。

Yīshēng: Nín de tǐwēn shì sānshíjiǔ dù, yǒu diǎnr fāshāo. Qǐng zhāngkāi zuǐba,
               ràng wǒ kàn yī kàn.

医生: 您的体温是三十九度, 有点儿发烧。请张开嘴巴, 让我看一
               看。

Jiéxī: Yīshēng, wǒ shì shénme bìng?

洁希: 医生, 我是什么病?

Yīshēng: Sǎngzi yǒu diǎnr fāyán. Nín jīntiān yǒu méiyǒu késou?

医生:	嗓子有点儿发炎。您今天有没有咳嗽？
Jiéxī:	Yǒu yīdiǎnr. Sǎngzi yě yǒu diǎnr tòng.
洁希:	有一点儿。嗓子也有点儿痛。
Yīshēng:	Shì gǎnmào.
医生:	是感冒。
Jiéxī:	Yào dǎ zhēn ma? Wǒ zuì pà dǎ zhēn.
洁希:	要打针吗？我最怕打针。
Yīshēng:	Bùyòng dǎ zhēn. Bié hē lěng de dōngxi, chī diǎnr yào, xiūxi yì liǎng tiān jiù kěyǐ le.
医生:	不用打针。别喝冷的东西, 吃点儿药, 休息一两天就可以了。

Doctor:	*What seems to be troubling/bothering you?*
Jess:	*I feel a little dizzy and have a headache. My whole body is aching.*
Doctor:	*Your temperature is 39 (degrees Celsius). You have a mild fever. Please open your mouth and let me take a look.*
Jess:	*Doctor, what's wrong with me?*
Doctor:	*Your throat is inflamed. Are you coughing?*
Jess:	*A little. My throat also hurts a bit.*
Doctor:	*You have a cold.*
Jess:	*Do I need a shot? I'm very (lit., most) afraid of getting injections.*
Doctor:	*It's not necessary to get an injection. Just don't drink anything cold, take this medication, give your body a good rest for one or two days, and you'll be fine.*

⏸

Take It Further

Wǒ shì shénme bìng? 我是什么病？, which can be translated as *What's wrong with me?*, literally means *What illness am I?* Another way of saying this is Wǒ yǒu shénme bìng? 我有什么病？ (lit., *What illness do I have?*).

Negating completed
actions: **méiyǒu** 没有

Yī liǎng tiān 一两天 can be translated as *one to two days* or *one or two days*. In order to express an approximate number of days, people, objects, etc., two consecutive numbers are joined together and then followed by the noun that they're quantifying: wǔ liù tiān 五六天 (*five to/or six days*), wǔ liù ge rén 五六个人 (*five to/ or six people*), sān sì ge yuè 三四个月 (*three to/or four months*). But don't forget to use a measure word after the last number. As you learned in Unit 3, the word tiān 天 itself can function as a measure word, so you don't need an additional measure word. But with yuè 月 and rén 人, you need the measure word ge 个.

✎ Conversation Practice 1

Fill in the blanks with the words from the conversation. The Chinese characters are given as a hint and for extra practice with characters.

1. Jiéxī de tóu hé _____ tòng.

   洁希的头和全身痛。

2. Jiéxī de _____ shì sānshíjiǔ dù.

   洁希的体温是三十九度。

3. Jiéxī de _____ yǒu diǎnr fāyán.

   洁希的嗓子有点儿发炎。

4. Yīshēng shuō Jiéxī yǒu _____.

   医生说洁希有感冒。

5. Jiéxīzuì _____ dǎ zhēn.

   洁希最怕打针。

6. Jiéxī de bìng bùyòng _____.

洁希的病不用打针。

ANSWER KEY
1. quánshēn 全身; 2. tǐwēn 体温; 3. sǎngzi 嗓子; 4. gǎnmào 感冒; 5. pà 怕; 6. dǎ zhēn 打针

Grammar Builder 1
ASKING *WHERE?*

▶ 16B Grammar Builder 1 (CD 6, Track 7)

You've already learned some useful question words such as shénme 什么 (*what*)
and duōshǎo 多少 (*how much*). Now let's look at nǎli 哪里, which is used to
ask the question *where?* in Chinese. Nǎli 哪里 is actually a combination of the
question word nǎ 哪 (*which*), which you learned in the last unit, and lǐ 里 (*place*).
So literally, nǎli 哪里 means *which place?* One thing to keep in mind is that if
you're asking for a location, the preposition zài 在 (*in, at, on*) needs to precede the
word nǎli 哪里. The answer would then include the same preposition.

Nǐ nǎli tòng?
你哪里痛?
Where does it hurt? (lit., Where do you feel pain?)

Nǐ zài nǎli?
你在哪里?
Where are you?

Zhāng Xiānsheng zài nǎli shàngbān?
张先生在哪里上班?
Where does Mr. Zhang work?

Wáng Tàitai zhù zài nǎli?

王太太住在哪里?

Where does Mrs. Wang live?

Wáng Tàitai zhù zài Fǎguó.

王太太住在法国。

Mrs. Wang lives in France.

Don't forget that zài 在 is also used as a particle to indicate continuous or ongoing actions, as you learned in Lesson 7. In that construction, it's combined with a verb. When it's combined with nǎli 哪里 or with a place, it expresses location.

Tāmen zài chànggē.

他们在唱歌。

They are singing.

Wǒ zhù zài Niǔyuē.

我住在纽约。

I live in New York.

Ⓘ

✎ Work Out 1

Pick sentences from the column on the right that best answer each question in the column on the left. Then translate the answer that you've chosen.

1. Tāmen qù nǎli kàn yīshēng?

   他们去哪里看医生?

2. Nǐ de lǎoshī zài nǎli jiāo (*teach*)
   Yīngwén?

   你的老师在哪里教英文?

a. Wǒ de bízi hěn tòng.

   我的鼻子很痛。

b. Wǒ de lǎoshī zài Zhōngguó jiāo
   Yīngwén.

   我的老师在中国教英文。

3. Nǐmen zài nǎli shuìjiào?
   你们在哪里睡觉?

4. Tā qùle nǎli?
   她去了哪里?

5. Nǐ nǎli bù shūfu?
   你哪里不舒服?

6. Wǒmen lǐbài tiān zài nǎli chīfàn?
   我们礼拜天在哪里吃饭?

7. Nǐ zài nǎli xué Zhōngwén?
   你在哪里学中文?

c. Wǒmen lǐbài tiān zài xuéxiào chīfàn.
   我们礼拜天在学校吃饭。

d. Niǔyuē Dàxué.
   纽约大学。 (*New York University.*)

e. Wǒmen zài wòfáng shuìjiào.
   我们在卧房睡觉。

f. Tāmen qù yīyuàn kàn yīshēng.
   他们去医院看医生。

g. Tā qùle Zhōngguó.
   她去了中国。

ANSWER KEY

1. f (*They go to the hospital to see a doctor.*) 2. b (*My teacher teaches English in China.*) 3. e (*We sleep in the bedroom.*) 4. g (*She went to China.*) 5. a (*My nose hurts.*) 6. c (*We eat at school on Sunday.*) 7. d (*New York University.*)

Conversation 2

▶ 16C Conversation 2 (CD 6, Track 8-Chinese, Track 9-Chinese and English)

Now listen to the following dialogue in which Hai asks Jess about her health.

Hǎi: Jiéxī, zuótiān nǐ yǒu méiyǒu shàng Hànyǔ kè?
海: 洁希, 昨天你有没有上汉语课?

Jiéxī: Wǒ méiyǒu shàngkè. Wǒ bìng le.
洁希: 我没有上课。我病了。

Hǎi: Nǐ shì shénme bìng? Nǐ kànle yīshēng méiyǒu?
海: 你是什么病? 你看了医生没有?

Jiéxī: Wǒ kànle yīshēng. Yīshēng shuō zhǐshì gǎnmào.
洁希: 我看了医生。医生说只是感冒。

Hǎi: Nǐ chīle yào méiyǒu?
海: 你吃了药没有?

Jiéxī: Wǒ wàng le. Xièxie nǐ tíxǐng wǒ.
洁希: 我忘了。谢谢你提醒我。

Hǎi:	Bùyòng kèqi. Hǎohao xiūxi, bié zài zháoliáng le.
海:	不用客气。好好休息, 别再着凉了。
Jiéxī:	Xièxie!
洁希:	谢谢!

Hai:	*Jess, did you attend Chinese class yesterday?*
Jess:	*No, I didn't. I was sick yesterday.*
Hai:	*What was wrong with you? Did you see a doctor?*
Jess:	*I did. The doctor said it was only a cold.*
Hai:	*Have you taken any medicine?*
Jess:	*I forgot to. Thank you for reminding me.*
Hai:	*You're welcome. Get a good rest and don't catch a cold again.*
Jess:	*Thanks!*

Take It Further

The verb wàng 忘 means *to forget*, and it's usually used in combination with the particle le 了. This is similar to the English expression *I forgot* or *I've forgotten*.

Tíxǐng 提醒 means *to remind*. In the set phrase Xièxie nǐ tíxǐng wǒ 谢谢你提醒我 (*Thank you for reminding me*), there is no equivalent in Chinese for the English preposition *for* and the *-ing* form of *to remind*.

Notice that zài 再 means *again* in Bié zài zháoliáng le 别再着凉了 (*Don't catch a cold again*). Even though this adverb zài 再 is pronounced (and spelled in pīnyīn) the same way as the particle/preposition zài 在, it's not the same word in written Chinese. When zài is used as a particle or a preposition, its written character is 在. But when zài is used as an adverb meaning *again*, the written character is 再. There are words like this in English as well; words that have the same pronunciation but different meanings and spellings. For instance, *bear/bare*, *here/hear*, and *for/four*.

✎ Conversation Practice 2

Fill in the blanks with the missing words in pīnyīn. Refer to the second conversation with Hai and Jess. The Chinese characters are provided for additional help and practice.

1. Hǎi hé Jiéxī zuótiān yǒu _____ kè.

   海和洁希昨天有汉语课。

2. Jiéxī méiyǒu _____.

   洁希没有上课。

3. Jiéxī de _____ shuō tā gǎnmào le.

   洁希的医生说她感冒了。

4. Hǎi _____ Jiéxī chī yào.

   海提醒洁希吃药。

5. Hǎi shuō bié zài _____ le.

   海说别再着凉了。

ANSWER KEY
1. Hànyǔ 汉语; 2. shàngkè 上课; 3. yīshēng 医生; 4. tíxǐng 提醒; 5. zháoliáng 着凉

Grammar Builder 2
ASKING QUESTIONS ABOUT COMPLETED ACTIONS WITH YǑU MÉIYǑU 有没有

▶ 16D Grammar Builder 2 (CD 6, Track 10)

You've already learned that you can change a statement into a yes/no question (simple question) by adding the particle ma 吗 at the end of the statement. This

Asking *how?*   Asking *where?*

Negating completed
actions: **méiyǒu** 没有   Asking questions about completed
actions with **yǒu méiyǒu** 有没有

construction is used in everyday Chinese regardless of verb tense, and it applies to
ongoing as well as completed actions. Here are a few examples that show how you
can ask whether something happened in the past using the particle ma 吗:

Tā qùle Niǔyuē.
他去了纽约。
He went to New York.

Tā qùle Niǔyuē ma?
他去了纽约吗?
Did he go to New York?

Wǒ de tóngxué kànle yīshēng.
我的同学看了医生。
My classmate saw a doctor.

Nǐ de tóngxué kànle yīshēng ma?
你的同学看了医生吗?
Did your classmate see a doctor?

Another way of asking whether an action has been completed is to add the phrase
yǒu méiyǒu 有没有 before the verb. This construction is used interchangeably
with the ma 吗 construction.

Nǐ yǒu méiyǒu chī yào?
你有没有吃药?
Did you take (your) medicine?

Tā yǒu méiyǒu qù yīyuàn?
他有没有去医院?
Did he go to the hospital?

Nǐ bàba yǒu méiyǒu lā dùzi?

你爸爸有没有拉肚子?

Did your father have diarrhea?

Nǐ bàba yǒu méiyǒu kàn yīshēng?

你爸爸有没有看医生?

Did your father see a doctor?

Note that when yǒu méiyǒu 有没有 is used to formulate a question about a past action, the particle le 了 is not needed, since yǒu méiyǒu 有没有 itself implies the past tense. However, if the yǒu is dropped and méiyǒu 没有 alone is used at the end of a question, the particle le 了 is necessary to indicate a past action. The structure is: verb + 了 + méiyǒu 没有, and the question can be translated into the present perfect tense (*have/has done*).

Nǐ chīle yào méiyǒu?

你吃了药没有?

Have you (already) taken your medicine?

Nǐ bàba kànle yīshēng méiyou?

你爸爸看了医生没有?

Has your father seen a doctor?

To summarize, there are three distinct ways of asking questions about past actions in Chinese. The first two (ma 吗 and yǒu méiyǒu 有没有) are used interchangeably to inquire about a completed action. The third (verb + le 了 + méiyǒu 没有) is used when you want to question whether something has already happened.

1) Tā qùle ma? 他去了吗?	*Did he go?*
2) Tā yǒu méiyǒu qù? 他有没有去?	*Did he go?*
3) Tā qùle méiyǒu? 他去了没有?	*Has he gone already?*

Note that when answering this last question in the negative, you must add the adverb hái 还 (*still*) before méiyǒu 没有 + verb in your answer:

Tā hái méiyǒu qù.
他还没有去。
He hasn't gone yet./He still hasn't gone.

✎ Work Out 2

Pick the question from the column on the right that best fits an answer in the column on the left. Translate the question that you've chosen.

1. Wǒ méiyǒu shuìjiào.
   我没有睡觉。

2. Tā de péngyou méiyǒu lā dùzi.
   他的朋友没有拉肚子。

3. Wǒ hái méiyǒu mǎi xiézi.
   我还没有买鞋子。

4. Zhāng Xiānsheng de línjū méiyǒu qù kàn yīshēng.
   张先生的邻居没有去看医生。

5. Chén Tàitai méiyǒu chī yào.
   陈太太没有吃药。

6. Lǐbài sān tā méiyǒu qù yīyuàn.
   礼拜三他没有去医院。

7. Tā jīntiān méiyǒu chīfàn.
   她今天没有吃饭。

8. Wǒmen méiyǒu hē jiǔ.
   我们没有喝酒。

a. Lǐbài sān tā yǒu méiyǒu qù yīyuàn?
   礼拜三他有没有去医院？

b. Zhāng Xiānsheng de línjū yǒu méiyǒu qù kàn yīshēng?
   张先生的邻居有没有去看医生？

c. Nǐmen yǒu méiyǒu hē jiǔ?
   你们有没有喝酒？

d. Nǐ yǒu méiyǒu shuìjiào?
   你有没有睡觉？

e. Tā de péngyou yǒu méiyǒu lā dùzi?
   他的朋友有没有拉肚子？

f. Nǐ mǎile xiézi méiyǒu?
   你买了鞋子没有？

g. Chén tàitai yǒu méiyǒu chī yào?
   陈太太有没有吃药？

h. Tā jīntiān yǒu méiyǒu chīfàn?
   她今天有没有吃饭？

ANSWER KEY

1. d (*Did you sleep?*) 2. e (*Did his friend have diarrhea?*) 3. f (*Did you buy shoes?*) 4. b (*Did Mr. Zhang's neighbor go to see a doctor?*) 5. g (*Did Mrs. Chen take the medicine?*) 6. a (*Did he go to the hospital on Wednesday?*) 7. h (*Did she eat today?*) 8. c (*Did you (pl.) drink wine?*)

🌐 Culture Note

In China, especially in rural areas where there has traditionally been a concern about having enough to eat, it is very common to hear people greet each other by asking Nǐ chīfàn le ma? 你吃饭了吗? (*Have you eaten yet?*). In reply to this question, people either answer Chīle 吃了 (*Yes, I've eaten*) or Hái méi chī 还没吃 (*No, I haven't eaten yet*). However, this dialogue doesn't literally refer to the act of eating. It is instead a way of opening conversation when you meet a friend or relative.

Nǐ hǎo ma? 你好吗? and Nǐ xiànzài zěnme yàng? 你现在怎么样? are two other popular ways of saying *Hello* in Chinese and are akin to the English expressions *How are you?* and *How are you doing?* respectively. While both of these greetings might seem to ask for information about someone's health, they are in fact inquiries into a person's overall mood or state of being. As in English, an equally general reply is expected. Consequently, in response to Nǐ hǎo ma? 你好吗? , you would usually say Hǎo 好(*fine/ok/great*). You could also say Bù tài hǎo 不太好 (*not very good*), but this is not often heard when people meet for the first time. Likewise, you might typically reply to the greeting Nǐ xiànzài zěnme yàng? 你现在怎么样? by saying Bùcuò 不错 (*pretty good*).

In fact, Chinese people generally don't mention personal health issues unless they are quite familiar with each other. This is especially true when it comes to sex-related health issues, which are still taboo in Chinese culture and are therefore rarely discussed in public. Most Chinese people are even highly uncomfortable talking to their doctors about these issues.

At the same time, the Chinese also pay a good deal of attention to traditional medicine and its treatments, which include zhēnjiǔ 针灸 (*acupuncture*), xuéwèi ànmó 穴位按摩 (*acupressure*), and bá huǒguàn 拔火罐 (*cupping*).

✎ Drive It Home

Change each sentence into a question about past actions using ma 吗, yǒu méiyǒu
有没有, and the verb + le 了 + méiyǒu 没有 construction.

1. Nǐ dǎ zhēn. 你打针。(*You get an injection.*) _____

_____

2. Tā zuòfàn. 他做饭。(*He cooks.*) _____

_____

3. Nǐ de dìdi qù shūdiàn. 你的弟弟去书店。(*Your younger brother goes to the*

bookstore.) _____

_____

4. Nàge hùshi mǎi màozi. 那个护士买帽子。(*That nurse buys a hat.*) _____

_____

ANSWER KEY

1. Nǐ dǎ zhēn le ma? 你打针了吗？　Nǐ yǒu méiyǒu dǎ zhēn? 你有没有打针？(*Did you get an
injection?*) Nǐ dǎ zhēn le méiyǒu? 你打针了没有？(*Did you get an injection already?*) 2. Tā zuòfàn le
ma? 他做饭了吗？Tā yǒu méiyǒu zuòfàn? 他有没有做饭？(*Did he cook?*) Tā zuòfàn le méiyǒu? 他做
饭了没有？(*Has he cooked already?*) 3. Nǐ de dìdi qù shūdiàn le ma? 你的弟弟去书店了吗？　Nǐ de
dìdi yǒu méiyǒu qù shudiàn 你的弟弟有没有去书店？(*Did your younger brother go to the bookstore?*)
Nǐ de dìdi qù shudiàn le méiyǒu? 你的弟弟去书店了没有？(*Has your younger brother gone to the
bookstore already?*) 4. Nàge hùshi mǎi màozi le ma? 那个护士买帽子了吗？　Nàge hùshi yǒu méiyǒu
mǎi màozi? 那个护士有没有买帽子？(*Did that nurse buy a hat?*) Nàge hùshi mǎi màozi le méiyǒu? 那
个护士买帽子了没有？(*Has that nurse bought a hat already?*)

How Did You Do?

By now you should know:

☐ How to discuss an illness with a doctor.
  (Still unsure? Go back to 219.)

☐ Asking *where*.
  (Still unsure? Go back to 222.)

✎ Word Recall

Match the English word in the left column with its appropriate translation in the right column.

1. *no need to*	a. zài 再
2. *illness*	b. quánshēn 全身
3. *a cold*	c. wàng 忘
4. *to be scared of, to fear*	d. bùyòng 不用
5. *whole body*	e. zhǐshì 只是
6. *to remind*	f. dù 度
7. *to open (the mouth)*	g. gǎnmào 感冒
8. *let me*	h. shàngkè 上课
9. *it's only*	i. tǐwēn 体温
10. *degree (for temperature)*	j. tíxǐng 提醒
11. *to rest*	k. pà 怕
12. *body temperature*	l. zhāngkāi 张开
13. *to forget*	m. ràng wǒ 让我
14. *to go to class*	n. xiūxi 休息
15. *again*	o. bìng 病

ANSWER KEY
1. d; 2. o; 3. g; 4. k; 5. b; 6. j; 7. l; 8. m; 9. e; 10. f; 11. n; 12. i; 13. c; 14. h; 15. a

Unit 4 Essentials

Vocabulary Essentials

Test your knowledge of the key material in this unit by filling in the blanks in the following charts. Once you've completed these pages, you'll have tested your retention, and you'll have your own reference for the most essential vocabulary. This is also a great time to practice a few Chinese characters. Fill in the middle column with the characters that you remember. Or, if you only remember the pīnyīn, go back through the unit to find the character.

PARTS OF THE BODY

PĪNYĪN	CHARACTER	
		eye
		ear
		mouth
		lips
		face
		nose
		neck
		throat
		tooth
		tongue
		hand
		finger
		leg
		foot
		thigh
		back

PĪNYĪN	CHARACTER	
		shoulder
		chest

If you're having a hard time remembering this vocabulary, don't forget to check out the supplemental flashcards for this unit online. Go to **www.livinglanguage.com/languagelab** for a great way to help you practice vocabulary.

Grammar Essentials

Here is a reference for the key grammar that was covered in Unit 4. Make sure you understand the summary and can use all of the grammar it covers.

TALKING ABOUT COMPLETED ACTIONS

Use le 了 to express that an action has been completed; use (hái) méiyǒu 还没有 to say that an action has not been completed (yet).

PĪNYĪN	CHARACTER	
Tā chīle yào.	他吃了药。	*He took the medicine.*
Tā méiyǒu chī yào.	他没有吃药。	*He didn't take the medicine.*
Tā hái méiyǒu chī yào.	他还没有吃药。	*He hasn't taken the medicine yet.*

COMMANDS

Use qǐng 请 to make a polite command, and bùyào 不要 or bié 别 to make a negative command.

PĪNYĪN	CHARACTER	
Qǐng zài shuō yī cì.	请再说一次。	*Please repeat that. (lit., Please say it once again.)*
Bié kàn tài duō diànshì.	别看太多电视。	*Don't watch too much TV.*
Bùyào pèng nà tiáo gǒu.	不要碰那条狗。	*Don't touch that dog.*

PĪNYĪN	CHARACTER	
Bié qù.	别去。	*Don't go.*

ASKING HOW AND HOW LONG

PĪNYĪN	CHARACTER	
Nǐ bìngle duōjiǔ?	你病了多久?	*How long have you been sick?*
Nǐ kéle duōjiǔ?	你咳了多久?	*How long have you been coughing?*
Nǐmen zěn(me) yàng qù kàn yīshēng?	你们怎(么)样去看医生?	*How do you go to (see) the doctor?*
Nǐ de bàba xiànzài zěnme yàng?	你的爸爸现在怎么样?	*How is your father doing now?*

ASKING NǍLI 哪里 (*WHERE*)

When asking about and answering with locations, the preposition zài 在 (*in, at, on*) precedes the word nǎli 哪里 (*where*).

PĪNYĪN	CHARACTER	
Nǐ nǎli tòng?	你哪里痛?	*Where does it hurt? (lit., Where do you feel pain?)*
Nǐ zài nǎli?	你在哪里?	*Where are you?*
Zhāng xiānsheng zài nǎli shàngbān?	张先生在哪里上班?	*Where does Mr. Zhang work?*
Wáng tàitai zhù zài nǎli?	王太太住在哪里?	*Where does Mrs. Wang live?*
Wáng tàitai zhù zài Fǎguó.	王太太住在法国。	*Mrs. Wang lives in France.*

THREE WAYS OF ASKING ABOUT THE PAST

1) Tā qùle ma? 他去了吗?	*Did he go?*
2) Tā yǒu méiyǒu qù? 他有没有去?	*Did he go?*
3) Tā qùle méiyǒu? 他去了没有?	*Has he gone already?*

Character Essentials

To practice the Chinese characters you learned in Unit 4, Conversations 1 and 2 are repeated here without pīnyīn or English translations. Translate as many characters as you can. Check your answers by listening to the conversations from your audio. Don't worry if you can't remember all of the characters. Just try to remember as many as you can.

Conversation 1

▶ 16A Conversation 1 (CD 6, Track 5-Chinese, Track 6-Chinese and English)

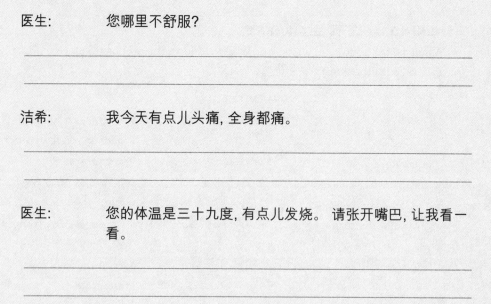

医生: 您哪里不舒服?

_____

_____

洁希: 我今天有点儿头痛, 全身都痛。

_____

_____

医生: 您的体温是三十九度, 有点儿发烧。 请张开嘴巴, 让我看一
         看。

_____

_____

洁希: 医生,我是什么病?

_____

_____

医生: 嗓子有点儿发炎。 您今天有没有咳嗽?

_____

_____

洁希: 有一点儿。 嗓子也有点儿痛。

_____

_____

医生: 是感冒。

_____

_____

洁希: 要打针吗? 我最怕打针。

_____

_____

医生: 不用打针。 别喝冷的东西,吃点儿药,休息一两天就可以
了。

_____

_____

◀ Conversation 2

▶ 16C Conversation 2 (CD 6, Track 8-Chinese, Track 9-Chinese and English)

海:　　　　洁希, 昨天你有没有上汉语课?

_____

_____

洁希:　　　我没有上课。 我病了。

_____

_____

海:　　　　你是什么病? 你看了医生没有?

_____

_____

洁希:　　　我看了医生。 医生说只是感冒。

_____

_____

海:　　　　你吃了药没有?

_____

_____

洁希:　　　我忘了。 谢谢你提醒我。

_____

_____

海: 不用客气。 好好休息, 别再着凉了。

_____

_____

洁希: 谢谢!

_____

_____

Don't forget to practice and reinforce what you've learned by visiting **www.livinglanguage.com/ languagelab** for flashcards, games, and quizzes.

Unit 4 Quiz

A. Fill in the blanks with the appropriate negative particle bié 别 or bù 不.

1. Tā de cài _____ guì.

   他的菜_____贵。

   (His vegetables are not expensive.)

2. Nǐ _____ shūfu. _____ qù xìyuàn.

   你 _____ 舒服。 _____ 去戏院。

   (You don't feel well. Don't go to the theater.)

3. Wǒmen _____ tīng yīnyuè.

   我们 _____ 听音乐。

   (We don't listen to music.)

4. _____ chī tài duō.

   _____ 吃太多。

   (Don't eat too much.)

5. _____ diǎn ròu. Tāmen _____ chī ròu.

   _____ 买肉。他们 _____ 吃肉。

   (Don't order meat. They don't eat meat.)

B. Change each sentence to past tense using le 了.

1. Wáng Tàitai qù yīyuàn. 王太太去医院。 _____

   _____

2. Nàge nǚháir mǎi sān shuāng wàzi. 那个女孩儿买三双袜子。 _____

   _____

3. Nǐ míngbái ma? 你明白吗? _____

   _____

4. Tā gēge chàng shénme gē? 他哥哥唱什么歌? _____

   _____

C. Use bù 不 or méiyǒu 没有 to negate the following sentences.

1. Tāmen qùle Zhōngguó. 他们去了中国。 _____

   _____

2. Wǒ xǐhuan chī yào. 我喜欢吃药。 _____

   _____

3. Tā jīntiān shàngbān. 她今天上班。 _____

   _____

4. Mèimei shàngxué le. 妹妹上学了。 _____

   _____

5. Zhège jǐngchá hēle shuǐ. 这个警察喝了水。 _____

   _____

D. Make each sentence into a question using the construction provided in parentheses.

1. Chén Tàitai kàn diànyǐng. 陈太太看电影。(ma 吗) _____

2. Nǐmen lǐbài sān qù yīyuàn. 你们礼拜三去医院。(yǒu méiyǒu 有没有) _____

3. Tā mǎi lán kùzi. 他买蓝裤子。(le ... méiyǒu 了... 没有) _____

4. Nǐ de péngyou fāshāo. 你的朋友发烧。(yǒu méiyǒu 有没有) _____

5. Zhāng Xiānsheng de línjū dǎzhēn. 张先生的邻居打针。(le ... méiyǒu 了... 没有 __

6. Tāmen zǎoshang xué Yīngwén. 他们早上学英文。(ma 吗) _____

ANSWER KEY

A. 1. bù 不; 2. bù 不, bié 别; 3. bù 不; 4. bié 别; 5. bié 别, bù 不

B. 1. Wáng Tàitai qùle yīyuàn. 王太太去了医院。 (*Mrs. Wang went to the hospital.*) 2. Nàge nǚháir mǎile sān shuāng wàzi. 那个女孩儿买了三双袜子。 (*That girl bought three pairs of socks.*) 3. Nǐ míngbái le ma? 你明白了吗？ (*Did you understand?*) 4. Tā gēge chàngle shénme gē? 他哥哥唱了什么歌？ (*What song did his older brother sing?*)

C. 1. Tāmen méiyǒu qù Zhōngguó. 他们没有去中国。 (*They did not go to China.*) 2. Wǒ bù xǐhuan chī yào. 我不喜欢吃药。 (*I don't like to take medicine.*) 3. Tā jīntiān bù shàngbān. 她今天不上班。 (*She does not go to work today.*) 4. Mèimei méiyǒu shàngxué. 妹妹没有上学。 (*Younger sister did not go to school.*) 5. Zhège jǐngchá méiyǒu hē shuǐ. 这个警察没有喝水。 (*This police officer did not drink water.*)

D. 1. Chén tàitai kàn diànyǐng ma? 陈太太看电影吗？ (*Does Mrs. Chen watch movies?*) 2. Nǐmen lǐbài sān yǒu méiyou qù yīyuàn? 你们礼拜三有没有去医院？ (*Did you go to the hospital on Wednesday?*) 3. Tā mǎile lán kùzi méiyǒu? 他买了蓝裤子没有？ (*Has he bought blue pants already?*) 4. Nǐ de péngyou yǒu méiyǒu fāshāo? 你的朋友有没有发烧？ (*Did your friend have a fever?*) 5. Zhāng Xiānsheng de línjū dǎ zhēn le méiyǒu? 张先生的邻居打针了没有？ (*Has Mr. Zhang's neighbor gotten a shot already?*) 6. Tāmen zǎoshang xué Yīngwén ma 他们早上学英文吗？ (*Do they study English in the morning?*)

How Did You Do?

Give yourself a point for every correct answer, then use the following key to tell whether you're ready to move on:

0-7 points: It's probably a good idea to go back through the lesson again. You may be moving too quickly, or there may be too much "down time" between your contact with Chinese. Remember that it's better to spend 30 minutes with Chinese three or four times a week than it is to spend two or three hours just once a week. Find a pace that's comfortable for you, and spread your contact hours out as much as you can.

8-12 points: You would benefit from a review before moving on. Go back and spend a little more time on the specific points that gave you trouble. Re-read the Grammar Builder sections that were difficult, and do the Work Outs one more time. Don't forget about the online supplemental practice material, either. Go to **www.livinglanguage.com/languagelab** for games and quizzes that will reinforce the material from this unit.

13-17 points: Good job! There are just a few points that you might consider reviewing before moving on. If you haven't worked with the games and quizzes on **www.livinglanguage.com/languagelab**, please give them a try.

18-20 points: Great! You're ready to move on to the next unit.

points

Unit 5: On the Phone and Making Appointments

Dǎ diànhuà hé yuēhuì

打电话和约会

In this unit, you'll learn how to tell time and how to make an appointment on the phone. You'll also learn key grammar, such as time expressions, the use of shéi 谁 (who), and the important verbs qù 去 (go) and lái 来 (come).

Lesson 17: Words

In this lesson, you'll learn:

☐ How to tell time.

☐ Use of time expressions and the auxiliary huì 会.

Word Builder 1

Here are some important words you will need to know to tell time in Chinese.

▶ 17A Word Builder 1 (CD 6, Track 11)

shízhōng	时钟	clock
shǒubiǎo	手表	watch
zhōngtóu	钟头	hour(s)
fēnzhōng	分钟	minute(s)
fēn	分	minute(s)

miǎo	秒	second(s)
diǎn	点	o'clock
kè	刻	quarter
bàn	半	half
xiànzài	现在	now
děng	等	to wait
dàyuē	大约	about
zuǒyòu	左右	around
chà (chà shí fēn yī diǎn)	差 (差十分一点)	to, before (ten minutes to/before one o'clock)

Word Practice 1

Match the English word in the left column with its appropriate translation in the right column.

1. *half*

2. *now*

3. *minute*

4. *about*

5. *hour*

a. xiànzài 现在

b. zhōngtóu 钟头

c. dàyuē 大约

d. fēnzhōng 分钟

e. bàn 半

ANSWER KEY

1. e; 2. a; 3. d; 4. c; 5. b

Grammar Builder 1
TELLING TIME

▶ 17B Grammar Builder 1 (CD 6, Track 12)

To ask what time it is, use the expression Xiànzài jǐdiǎn? 现在几点？ (*What time is it now?*) By itself, jǐdiǎn 几点 simply means *what time?* or *when?*

To answer with a full hour, use the word diǎn 点 right after the number. Don't forget that liǎng 两 is used in place of èr 二 to mean *two* when a noun is being counted or measured.

Xiànzài yī diǎn.
现在一点。
It's 1:00 now.

Xiànzài liǎng diǎn.
现在两点。
It's 2:00 now.

To answer with a half hour, use bàn 半 (*half*) or sānshí fēn 三十分 (*thirty minutes*).

| sì diǎn bàn 四点半 | 4:30 |
| wǔ diǎn sānshí fēn 五点三十分 | 5:30 |

To answer with a quarter hour, use yí kè 一刻 (*a quarter*) or shí wǔ fēn 十五分 (*fifteen minutes*).

| liǎng diǎn yī kè 两点一刻 | 2:15 |
| wǔ diǎn shíwǔ fēn 五点十五分 | 5:15 |

To say that it's a quarter to a certain hour, use sān kè 三刻 (*three quarters*) or sìshí wǔ fēn 四十五分 (*forty-five minutes*).

yī diǎn sān kè 一点三刻	1:45
wǔ diǎn sìshíwǔ fēn 五点四十五分	5:45

To say that it's a certain number of minutes past the hour, just give that number. You can also use the word fēn 分 (*minutes*).

wǔ diǎn èrshíwǔ fēn 五点二十五分	5:25
qī diǎn shíyī fēn 七点十一分	7:11

If the number of minutes after the hour is less than ten, then you generally add the word líng 零 (*zero*) before a single digit. For example:

liù diǎn líng wǔ fēn 六点零五分	6:05
bā diǎn líng sān fēn 八点零三分	8:03

If the number of minutes before the hour is ten or less, you can use the word chà 差 (*to*) before the number of minutes. Notice that the entire chà 差 phrase can come before or after the whole hour.

qī diǎn chà jiǔ fēn 七点差九分	6:51
chà jiǔ fēn qī diǎn 差九分七点	6:51

As you noticed in the word list, there are two different words in Chinese that mean *minute(s)*. The first, fēnzhōng 分钟, is used to talk about an amount of time (in minutes) that has passed. The second, fēn 分, is used to tell the time. Fēn 分 and fēnzhōng 分钟 are not interchangeable.

sān diǎn èrshí fēn 三点二十分	3:20
wǒ dúle èrshí fēnzhōng 我读了二十分钟	*I've read for twenty minutes.*

Note that a measure word does not need to be placed between fēnzhōng 分钟 and the quantifying number that precedes it.

As in English, *hours* and *o'clock* are also expressed in Chinese by two different words: zhōngtóu 钟头 and diǎn 点. Zhōngtóu 钟头 is used to talk about an amount of time (in hours) that has passed, and diǎn 点 is used for telling time:

| yī diǎn 一点 | *1:00* |
| Tā qùle yī ge zhōngtóu. 他去了一个钟头。 | *She went for an hour.* |

Note that in colloquial Chinese the measure word ge 个 must be placed between zhōngtóu 钟头 and the quantifying number that precedes it.

✎ Work Out 1

Match the Chinese word in the column on the right to the English word in the column on the left.

1. *clock*   a. kè 刻

2. *quarter*   b. shízhōng 时钟

3. *half*   c. děng 等

4. *o'clock*   d. zhōngtóu 钟头

5. *now*   e. bàn 半

6. *to wait*   f. diǎn 点

7. *hour*   g. chà 差

8. *to, before*   h. xiànzài 现在

Now match the time to the correct expression in Chinese.

9. *1:30*   a. liǎng diǎn líng yī fēn 两点零一分

10. *8:00*   b. chā shí fēn liù diǎn 差十分六点

11. *4:15*   c. liù diǎn shí fēn 六点十分

12. *2:01*   d. shíyī diǎn sìshísì fēn 十一点四十四分

13. *7:45*   e. bā diǎn 八点

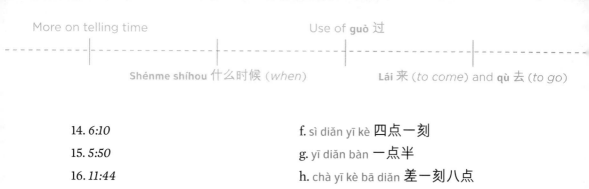
14. *6:10*

15. *5:50*

16. *11:44*

f. sì diǎn yī kè 四点一刻

g. yī diǎn bàn 一点半

h. chà yī kè bā diǎn 差一刻八点

ANSWER KEY

1. b; 2. a; 3. e; 4. f; 5. h; 6. c; 7. d; 8. g; 9. g; 10. e; 11. f; 12. a; 13. h; 14. c; 15. b; 16. d

Word Builder 2

Here are more useful time expressions. You should already be familiar with some of them.

▶ 17C Word Builder 2 (CD 6, Track 13)

jīntiān	今天	*today*
míngtiān	明天	*tomorrow*
zuótiān	昨天	*yesterday*
qiántiān	前天	*the day before yesterday*
hòutiān	后天	*the day after tomorrow*
zhōngwǔ	中午	*noon*
bànyè	半夜	*midnight*
yǐqián	以前	*ago*
zhīqián	之前	*before*
zhīhòu	之后	*after*
jīntiān zǎoshang	今天早上	*this morning*
jīntiān xiàwǔ	今天下午	*this afternoon*
jīntiān wǎnshang	今天晚上	*tonight, this evening*
zǒngshì	总是	*always*
cónglái méiyǒu	从来没有	*never*
tōngcháng	通常	*usually*
jīngcháng	经常	*often, frequently*

Ⅱ

✎ Word Practice 2

Fill in the blanks of the following phrases about time.

1. jīntiān _____ wǔ

   今天下午

   (*this afternoon*)

2. _____ cháng

   经常

   (*often, frequently*)

3. _____ tiān

   后天

   (*the day after tomorrow*)

4. _____ tiān

   昨天

   (*yesterday*)

5. zhī _____

   之前

   (*before*)

   ANSWER KEY
   1. xià 下; 2. jīng 经; 3. hòu 后; 4. zuó 昨; 5. qián 前

Grammar Builder 2
USE OF TIME EXPRESSIONS AND HUÌ 会

▶ 17D Grammar Builder 2 (CD 6, Track 14)

In English, time expressions are typically positioned after the verb, as in *I went to school yesterday*. In Chinese, though, time expressions such as jīntiān 今天 (*today*) and zuótiān 昨天 (*yesterday*) come before the verb:

Wǒ jīntiān shàngxué.
我今天上学。
I'm going to school today.

Wáng Tàitai zuótiān qùle Měiguó.
王太太昨天去了美国。
Mrs. Wang went to the U. S. yesterday.

Zhāng lǎoshī hé xuésheng míngtiān zhōngwǔ chīfàn.
张老师和学生明天中午吃饭。
Teacher Zhang and (his) students will eat together at noon tomorrow.

Wǒmen jīngcháng qù kàn diànyǐng.
我们经常去看电影。
We often go to a movie.

It's also possible to place the time expressions at the beginning of the sentence, before the subject:

Jīntiān wǒ shàngxué.
今天我上学。
Today I'm going to school.

Use of time expressions and **huì** 会

Zuótiān Wáng Tàitai qùle Měiguó.

昨天王太太去了美国。

Yesterday Mrs. Wang went to the U. S.

Míngtiān zhōngwǔ Zhāng lǎoshī hé xuésheng chīfàn.

明天中午张老师和学生吃饭。

Tomorrow at noon Teacher Zhang and (his) students will eat (lunch) together.

Where you place the time expression depends on what you want to emphasize. If you want to emphasize time, then you can put the time expression first, before the subject. If not, then the time word is generally placed after the subject, but before the verb.

The three examples above also show you something about time expressions and verb tense in Chinese. In English, verbs are inflected to show tense: *walks, walking, walked,* etc. As you know, however, Chinese verbs do not change form based on tense, or when the action is taking place. Instead, this job is done with particles, such as le 了, which you learned in Lesson 14, and time expressions. So for example, chīfàn 吃饭, which means *to eat,* can be translated as *will eat* when it's used with a time expression like míngtiān 明天 (*tomorrow*).

Chinese does also have a kind of auxiliary verb similar to *will* to express the future: huì 会. Ordinarily, huì 会 is used before the main verb to indicate the future tense when no other future time expression is used. But it's not necessary to add huì 会 to a sentence when a time word such as míngtiān 明天 (*tomorrow*) or hòutiān 后天 (*the day after tomorrow*) is used:

Zhāng lǎoshī hé xuésheng huì zài jiā lǐ chīfàn.

Teacher Zhang and (his) students will eat at home.

Zhāng lǎoshī hé xuésheng hòutiān zài jiā lǐ chīfàn.

Teacher Zhang and (his) students will eat at home the day after tomorrow.

Zhīqián 之前 *(before)* and zhīhòu 之后 *(after)* are time expressions whose placement might be confusing to English speakers. Both of these words come after the time that they qualify (1:00 after) rather than before it (after 1:00), as is the order in English:

Tā míngtiān yī diǎn zhīqián huì lái.
他明天一点之前会来。
He will come before one o'clock tomorrow.

Wǒ bànyè yī diǎn zhīhòu shuìjiào.
我半夜一点之后睡觉。
I go to bed after one o'clock in the morning (lit., one o'clock after midnight).

Yīqián 以前 *(ago)* is a time expression that is used to specify events that took place in the (relatively) distant past. As in the case of zhīqián 之前 and zhīhòu 之后, it is placed immediately after the period of time to which it refers:

Hěn jiǔ yǐqián tā mǎile zhège fángzi.
很久以前他买了这个房子。
He bought this house a long time ago.

Wǒmen sān ge zhōngtóu zhīqián chīle fàn.
我们三个钟头之前吃了饭。
We ate three hours ago.

(II)

✎ Work Out 2

Fill in the blanks by translating the words and phrases in parentheses. Then translate the complete sentences.

1. Wǒmen _____ (*yesterday*) qù kàn diànyǐng.

   我们 _____ 去看电影。

2. Nǐ _____ (*the day before yesterday*) yǒu méiyǒu shàngxué?

   你 _____ 有没有上学?

3. Wáng Xiānsheng _____ (*tomorrow*) qù Zhōngguó.

   王先生 _____ 去中国。

4. _____ (*This morning*) wǒ méiyǒu chī.

   _____ 我没有吃。

5. Nàge rén _____ (*tonight*) lái tiàowǔ.

   那个人 _____ 来跳舞

6. Tā hé lǎoshī _____ (*tomorrow afternoon*) yóuyǒng.

   他和老师 _____ 游泳。

7. Tā de línjū bā diǎn _____ (*after*) bù kàn diànshì.

   他的邻居八点 _____ 不看电视。

8. Wǒmen de xiǎogǒu liǎng diǎn _____ (*before*) xǐhuan chī xiāngjiāo.

   我们的小狗两点 _____ 喜欢吃香蕉。

ANSWER KEY

1. Wǒmen zuótiān qù kàn diànyǐng. 我们昨天去看电影。 (*We went to a movie yesterday.*) 2. Nǐ qiántiān yǒu méiyǒu shàngxué. 你前天有没有上学? (*Did you go to school the day before yesterday?*) 3. Wáng Xiānsheng míngtiān qù Zhōngguó. 王先生明天去中国。 (*Mr. Wang will go to China tomorrow.*) 4. Jīntiān zǎoshang wǒ méiyǒu chī. 今天早上我没有吃。 (*This morning I didn't eat.*)

5. Nàge rén jīntiān wǎnshang lái tiàowǔ. 那个人今天晚上来跳舞。(*That person will come and dance tonight.*) 6. Tā hé lǎoshī míngtiān xiàwǔ yóuyǒng. 他和老师明天下午游泳。(*He and his teacher will go swimming tomorrow afternoon.*) 7. Tā de línjū bā diǎn zhīhòu bù kàn diànshì. 他的邻居八点之后不看电视。(*His neighbor doesn't watch TV after eight o'clock.*) 8. Wǒmen de xiǎogǒu liǎng diǎn zhīqián xǐhuan chī xiāngjiāo. 我们的小狗两点之前喜欢吃香蕉。(*Our puppy likes eating bananas before two o'clock.*)

🌐 Culture Note

It's not appropriate to give a clock to a Chinese person on his or her birthday, especially if the person is elderly. This is because the expression to give a clock as a gift translates as sòng zhōng 送钟 in Chinese, which sounds exactly the same as another expression that means to bid farewell to someone at a funeral. These expressions are of course written differently in Chinese, but the pronunciation is identical. You can imagine how the recipient might feel if he or she received such a gift!

✎ Drive It Home

Translate the following phrases about the hour and day into pīnyīn.

1. *today at 12 o'clock* _____

2. *yesterday at 3:30 p.m.* _____

3. *the day after tomorrow at 9:45 a.m.* _____

4. *the day before yesterday at 1:15 p.m.* _____

5. *tomorrow at 5:50 a.m.* _____

ANSWER KEY

1. jīntiān shí'èr diǎn zhōng 今天十二点钟; 2. zuótiān xiàwǔ sān diǎn bàn 昨天下午三点半/zuótiān xiàwǔ sān diǎn sān shí fēn/昨天下午三点三十分; 3. hòutiān zǎoshang jiǔ diǎn sìshíwǔ fēn 后天早上九点四十五分/hòutiān zǎoshang jiǔ diǎn sān kè 后天早上九点三刻; 4. qiántiān xiàwǔ yī diǎn shíwǔ fēn 前天下午一点十五分/qiántiān xiàwǔ yī diǎn yī kè/前天下午一点一刻; 5. míngtiān zǎoshang wǔ diǎn wǔshí 明天早上五点五十

How Did You Do?

By now you should know:

☐ How to tell time.
(Still unsure? Go back to 246.)

☐ Use of time expressions and the auxiliary huì 会.
(Still unsure? Go back to 251.)

✎ Word Recall

Match the English word in the left column with its appropriate translation in the right column.

1. *hour*	a. tōngcháng 通常
2. *quarter*	b. zuótiān 昨天
3. *watch*	c. kè 刻
4. *before*	d. diǎn 点
5. *ago*	e. bànyè 半夜
6. *yesterday*	f. děng 等
7. *after*	g. shǒubiǎo 手表
8. *o'clock*	h. zhōngtóu 钟头
9. *today*	i. zhīhòu 之后
10. *always*	j. cónglái méiyǒu 从来没有
11. *usually*	k. jīntiān 今天
12. *midnight*	l. yǐqián 以前

13. *often*

14. *to wait*

15. *never*

m. zhīqián 之前

n. zǒngshì 总是

o. jīngcháng 经常

ANSWER KEY

1. h; 2. c; 3. g; 4. m; 5. l; 6. b; 7. i; 8. d; 9. k; 10. n; 11. a; 12. e; 13. o; 14. f; 15. j

Lesson 18: Phrases

In this lesson, you'll learn:

☐ More time expressions.

☐ Use of shéi 谁 *(who)*.

Phrase Builder 1

▶ 18A Phrase Builder 1 (CD 6, Track 15)

zhège xīngqī/lǐbài	这个礼拜	*this week*
shàng ge xīngqī/lǐbài	上个礼拜	*last week*
xià ge xīngqī/lǐbài	下个礼拜	*next week*
zhège yuè	这个月	*this month*
shàng ge yuè	上个月	*last month*
xià ge yuè	下个月	*next month*
jīnnián	今年	*this year*
qùnián	去年	*last year*
míngnián	明年	*next year*
qiánnián	前年	*the year before last*
hòunián	后年	*the year after next*

| èr líng yī líng nián | 二零一零年 | (year) 2010 |
| yī jiǔ jiǔ sān nián | 一九九三年 | (year) 1993 |

Ⅱ

✎ Phrase Practice 1

Fill in the blanks of the following phrases.

1. _____ ge yuè

   这个月

   (this month)

2. _____ ge lǐbài

   上个礼拜

   (last week)

3. _____ nián

   今年

   (this year)

4. _____ ge yuè

   下个月

   (next month)

5. _____ nián

   明年

   (next year)

   ANSWER KEY
   1. zhè 这; 2. shàng 上; 3. jīn 今; 4. xià 下; 5. míng 明

Grammar Builder 1
MORE ON TIME EXPRESSIONS

▶ 18B Grammar Builder 1 (CD 6, Track 16)

Note that nián 年 (*year*) and tiān 天 (*day*) do not require an additional measure word when combined with jīn 今, qù 去, or míng 明. As was mentioned in Unit 3, this is because nián 年 and tiān 天 are themselves measure words. However, it is necessary to add a measure word when placing zhè 这, shàng 上 or xià 下 before lǐbài 礼拜 (*week*) or yuè 月 (*month*) because neither of these are measure words and therefore they require the addition of ge 个.

Please also note that *this*, *last*, and *next* are each translated into different Chinese words, depending on whether you are qualifying nián 年 and tiān 天 or lǐbài 礼拜 and yuè 月.

	NIÁN 年 AND TIĀN 天	LǏBÀI 礼拜 AND YUÈ 月
this	jīn 今	zhè 这
next	míng 明	xià 下
last	qù 去	shàng 上

Wǒmen xià ge lǐbài zǒu.
我们下个礼拜走。
We're leaving next week.

Míngnián wǒ qù Zhōngguó.
明年我去中国。
Next year I'll go to China.

Tāmen shàng ge yuè kànle nàge diànyǐng.
他们上个月看了那个电影。
They saw that movie last month.

⏸

✏ Work Out 1

Choose the correct time expressions and then translate the complete sentences.

1. Wǒmen _____ (*year before last*) láile Zhōngguó. 我们 _____ 来了中国。

   a. qiánnián 前年

   b. qiántiān 前天

   c. hòunián 后年

2. Tā de māo _____ (*next month*) qù yīyuàn. 他的猫 _____ 去医院。

   a. shàng ge yuè 上个月

   b. xià ge yuè 下个月

   c. wǔ ge yuè 五个月

3. Zhāng Tàitai _____ (*this week*) bù zuòfàn. 张太太 _____ 不做饭。

   a. nàge lǐbài 那个礼拜

   b. nǎge lǐbài 哪个礼拜

   c. zhège lǐbài 这个礼拜

4. Wǒ de línjū de xiānsheng _____ (*last year*) mǎile yī liàng xīn chē. 我的邻居的先生 _____ 买了一辆新车。

   a. míngnián 明年

   b. qùnián 去年

   c. qiánnián 前年

5. Tā _____ *(last week)* bìngle, méiyǒu shàngxué. 他 _____ 病 了, 没有上学。

   a. xià ge lǐbài 下个礼拜

   b. shàng ge lǐbài 上个礼拜

   c. zhège lǐbài 这个礼拜

6. Nǐ de péngyou _____ *(next year)* qù Zhōngguó xué Zhōngwén. 你的朋 友 _____ 去中国学中文。

   a. míngnián 明年

   b. qùnián 去年

   c. qiánnián 前年

7. Nǐmen _____ *(last month)* qùle nǎli? 你们 _____ 去了哪里?

   a. jǐ ge yuè 几个月

   b. shàng ge yuè 上个月

   c. xià ge yuè 下个月

ANSWER KEY

1. a. Wǒmen qiánnián láile Zhōngguó. 我们前年来了中国。 *(We came to China the year before last.)* 2. b. Tā de māo xià ge yuè qù yīyuàn. 他的猫下个月去医院。 *(His cat will go to the hospital next month.)* 3. c. Zhāng Tàitai zhège lǐbài bù zuòfàn. 张太太这个礼拜不做饭。 *(Mrs. Zhang is not going to cook this week.)* 4. b. Wǒ de línjū de xiānsheng qùnián mǎile yī liàng xīn chē. 我的邻居的先生去年买了一辆新 车。 *(My neighbor's husband bought a new car last year.)* 5. b. Tā shàng ge lǐbài bìngle, méiyǒu shàngxué. 他上个礼拜病了, 没有上学。 *(He was sick last week and didn't go to school.)* 6. a. Nǐ de péngyou míngnián qù Zhōngguó xué Zhōngwén. 你的朋友明年去中国学中文。 *(Your friend will go to China to study Chinese next year.)* 7. b. Nǐmen shàng ge yuè qùle nǎli? 你们上个月去了哪里? *(Where did you (pl.) go last month?)*

Phrase Builder 2

▶ 18C Phrase Builder 2 (CD 6, Track 17)

yī huìr	一会儿	a while
liǎng diǎn	两点	two o'clock
sān diǎn bàn	三点半	half past three
wǔ diǎn yī kè	五点一刻	a quarter past five
wǔ diǎn shíwǔ fēn	五点十五分	five fifteen
liù diǎn sān kè	六点三刻	a quarter to seven (lit., three quarters past six)
liù diǎn sìshíwǔ fēn	六点四十五分	six forty-five
chà yī kè qī diǎn	差一刻七点	a quarter to seven
liǎng ge zhōngtóu	两个钟头	two hours
sān fēnzhōng	三分钟	three minutes
xià cì jiàn	下次见	see you next time
Děng huìr jiàn!	等会儿见!	See you later!
Huítóu jiàn!	回头见!	See you soon!
zhǔnshí	准时	on time
shéi	谁	who

⏸

✎ Phrase Practice 2

Match the English time expression in the left column with its appropriate translation in the right column.

1. *a quarter to seven (lit., three quarters past six)*

2. *three minutes*

3. *half past three*

a. sān fēnzhōng 三分钟

b. yī huìr 一会儿

c. liù diǎn sān kè 六点三刻

4. *see you next time*

5. *a while*

d. sān diǎn bàn 三点半

e. xià cì jiàn 下次见

ANSWER KEY
1. c; 2. a; 3. d; 4. e; 5. b

Grammar Builder 2
USE OF SHÉI 谁 (*WHO*)

(▶) 18D Grammar Builder 2 (CD 6, Track 18)

By now, you've learned the question words shénme 什么 (*what*), jǐ 几 (*how many*), duōshao 多少 (*how many/how much*), zěnme yàng 怎么样 (*how*), nǎ 哪 (*which*), duōjiǔ 多久 (*how long*), and nǎli 哪里 (*where*).

Now let's look at shéi 谁 (*who*):

Nǐ shì shéi?
你是谁?
Who are you?

Nàge rén shì shéi?
那个人是谁?
Who is that person?

Shéi shàng ge lǐbài qùle Měiguó?
谁上个礼拜去了美国?
Who went to the U.S. last week?

Shéi yǒu yī kuài?
谁有一块?
Who has one yuan?

Don't forget that question words in Chinese don't "move." In other words, the question word is in the same position in the question as it is in the answer. So, in Chinese, *Who are you?* literally means *You are who?*

✎ Work Out 2

Match each question from the column on the left to the best answer in the column on the right. Then translate the answers.

1. Qǐngwèn nǐ shì shéi?
   请问你是谁?

   a. Wǒ shíbā suì.
      我十八岁。

2. Nàge rén shì shéi?
   那个人是谁?

   b. Shí kuài qián.
      十块钱。

3. Nǐ jǐ suì?
   你几岁?

   c. Bùcuò. Nǐ ne?
      不错。你呢?

4. Nǐ yǒu mèimei ma?
   你有妹妹吗?

   d. Nàge rén shì wǒ de gēge.
      那个人是我的哥哥。

5. Nǐ zhù zài nǎli?
   你住在哪里?

   e. Wǒ zuì xǐhuan wǒ de māma.
      我最喜欢我的妈妈。

6. Zhège duōshǎo qián?
   这个多少钱?

   f. Wǒ shì Wáng Yǒu.
      我是王友。

7. Nǐ zuì xǐhuan shéi?
   你最喜欢谁?

   g. Wǒ yǒu sān ge mèimei.
      我有三个妹妹。

8. Nǐ zuìjìn zěnme yàng?
   你最近怎么样?

   h. Wǒ zhù zài Shànghǎi.
      我住在上海。

ANSWER KEY

1. f, (*I'm Wang You.*) 2. d, (*That person is my older brother.*) 3. a, (*I'm 18 years old.*) 4. g, (*I have three younger sisters.*) 5. h, (*I live in Shanghai.*) 6. b, (*[It's] 10 yuan.*) 7. e, (*I like my mother the most.*) 8. c, (*Very well. How about you?*)

✎ Drive It Home

For each question word or phrase given, form a question with the phrases given in the parentheses.

1. shéi 谁 (tā shì 她是, nǐ de gēge shì 你的哥哥是, nǐmen xǐhuan 你们喜欢) _____

   _____

2. zěnme yàng 怎么样 (tāmen 他们, zhège màozi 这个帽子, tā de yīshēng 他的医生)

   _____

3. duōshao (Nǐ yǒu ... shū? 你有...书？, tāmen chī ... yú? 他们吃 ... 鱼？ Jiějie chuān

   ... xiézi? 姐姐穿 ... 鞋子？) _____

ANSWER KEY

1. Tā shì shéi? 她是谁？ (*Who is she?*) Nǐ de gēge shì shéi? 你的哥哥是谁？ (*Who is your older brother?*) Nǐmen xǐhuan shéi? 你们喜欢谁？ (*Whom do you like?*) 2. Tāmen zěnme yàng? 他们怎么样？ (*How are they?*) Zhège màozi zěnme yàng? 这个帽子怎么样？ (*How is this hat?*) Tā de yīshēng zěnme yàng? 他的医生怎么样？ (*How is his doctor?*) 3. Nǐ yǒu duōshǎo shū? 你有多少书？ (*How many books do you have?*) Tāmen chī duōshǎo yú? 他们吃多少鱼？ (*How much fish do they eat?*) Jiějie chuān duōshǎo xiézi? 姐姐穿多少鞋子？ (*How many shoes does older sister wear?*)

How Did You Do?

By now you should know:

☐ More time expressions.
   (Still unsure? Go back to 259.)

☐ Use of shéi 谁 (who).
   (Still unsure? Go back to 263.)

✎ Word Recall

Match the English word in the left column with its appropriate translation in the right column.

1. *see you next time*	a. xià ge lǐbài 下个礼拜
2. *next month*	b. yī huìr 一会儿
3. *this week*	c. hòunián 后年
4. *a while*	d. xià ge yuè 下个月
5. *the year before last*	e. qùnián 去年
6. *this month*	f. shàng ge yuè 上个月
7. *this year*	g. zhège lǐbài 这个礼拜
8. *last week*	h. xià cì jiàn 下次见
9. *on time*	i. qiánnián 前年
10. *next year*	j. zhǔnshí 准时
11. *last month*	k. zhège yuè 这个月
12. *the year after next*	l. shéi 谁
13. *last year*	m. jīnnián 今年
14. *next week*	n. shàng ge lǐbài 上个礼拜
15. *who*	o. míngnián 明年

ANSWER KEY

1. h; 2. d; 3. g; 4. b; 5. i; 6. k; 7. m; 8. n; 9. j; 10. o; 11. f; 12. c; 13. e; 14. a; 15. l

Lesson 19: Sentences

In this lesson, you'll learn:

☐ More on telling time.

☐ Asking *when* with shénme shíhou 什么时候.

Sentence Builder 1

▶ 19A Sentence Builder 1 (CD 6, Track 19)

Let's look at some more time expressions having to do with the clock.

Xiànzài jǐ diǎn?

现在几点？

What time is it now?

Xiàwǔ yī diǎn.

下午一点。

It's 1:00 p.m.

Xiàwǔ sì diǎn bàn.

下午四点半。

It's 4:30 p.m.

Wǎnshang liù diǎn sìshíwǔ fēn.

晚上六点四十五分。

It's 6:45 p.m.

Chà wǔ fēn qī diǎn.

差五分七点。

It's five to seven.

Zǎoshang qī diǎn shíwǔ fēn.

早上七点十五分。

It's 7:15 a.m.

Qī diǎn yī kè.

七点一刻。

It's a quarter past seven.

Wǎnshang liù diǎn.

晚上六点。

It's 6:00 p.m.

Zhōngwǔ shí'èr diǎn.

中午十二点。

It's 12:00 p.m.

Zǎoshang jiǔ diǎn bàn.

早上九点半。

It's 9:30 a.m.

Shàngwǔ shí diǎn wǔshíwǔ fēn.

上午十点五十五分。

It's 10:55 a.m.

Wǎnshang liù diǎn líng sì fēn.

晚上六点零四分。

It's 6:04 p.m.

Qī diǎn zhěng.

七点整。

It's 7 o'clock sharp.

Chàbùduō bā diǎn.

差不多八点。

It's about 8:00.

Ⓘ

✎ Sentence Practice 1

Fill in the blanks of the conversation below.

A: Xiàn _____ jǐ _____ ?

现在几点？

(*What time is it?*)

B: Xiàwǔ _____ diǎn sìshíwǔ _____ .

下午三点四十五分。

(*It's 3:45 p.m*)

A: Wǒmen _____ diǎn chīfàn?

我们几点吃饭？

(*When are we eating?*)

B: Wǎn _____ liù dián _____ .

晚上六点半。

(*At 6:30 p.m*)

A: Nǐ de _____ jǐ diǎn lái?

你的朋友几点来？

(*What time is your friend coming?*)

B: Tā liù diǎn _____ lái.

他六点一刻来。

(*He's coming at 6:15.*)

ANSWER KEY
A: zài 在, diǎn 点; B: sān 三, fēn 分; A: jǐ 几; B: shang 上, bàn 半; A: péngyou 朋友; A: yī kè 一刻

Grammar Builder 1
MORE ON TELLING TIME

▶ 19B Grammar Builder 1 (CD 6, Track 20)

Don't forget that you can ask the time with the question Xiànzài jǐdiǎn? 现在几点？ Literally, that phrase means *How many hours is it now?* In the answer, you don't need any kind of pronoun like *it*.

Yī diǎn.
一点。
(*It's*) *1:00.*

Wǔ diǎn.
五点。
(*It's*) *5:00.*

You can also use these types of expressions as adverbs to tell what time something happens. In English, you need the preposition *at* before the time expression, but in Chinese, simply use the time expression right before the verb:

Shénme shíhou 什么时候 (*when*) | **Lái** 来 (*to come*) and **qù** 去 (*to go*)

Tā shí diǎn shuìjiào.

他十点睡觉。

He goes to sleep at 10:00. (lit., He sleeps at 10:00.)

Wǒ shíyī diǎn sānshí fēn shuìjiào.

我十一点三十分睡觉。

I go to sleep at 11:30. (lit., I sleep at 11:30.)

Wǒ xiàwǔ sān diǎn yī kè qùle yīyuàn.

我下午三点一刻去了医院。

I went to the hospital at 3:15 p.m.

Wǒ sān diǎn líng yī fēn zuò fēijī qù Shànghǎi.

我三点零一分坐飞机去上海。

I will take the plane to Shanghai at 3:01.

Ⓘ

✎ Work Out 1

Answer the following questions in Chinese with the time given in parentheses.

1. Wáng Xiānsheng jǐdiǎn shuìjiào? 王先生几点睡觉? (*10:30*) _____

_____

2. Tāmen jǐdiǎn shàngxué? 他们几点上学? (*8:05*) _____

_____

3. Nǐmen jǐdiǎn chīfàn? 你们几点吃饭? (*12:00*) _____

_____

Unit 5 Lesson 19: Sentences

4. Lǎoshī jǐdiǎn lái? 老师几点来? (2:15) _____

_____

5. Nǐ de péngyou jǐdiǎn qù gōngzuò (work)? 你的朋友几点去工作? (9:00) _____

_____

6. Māma jǐdiǎn qùle yīyuàn? 妈妈几点去了医院? (7:45) _____

_____

ANSWER KEY
1. Wáng Xiānsheng shí diǎn bàn shuìjiào. 王先生十点半睡觉。 (*Mr. Wang goes to sleep at 10:30.*)
2. Tāmen bā diǎn líng wǔ fēn shàngxué. 他们八点零五分上学。 (*They go to school at 8:05.*) 3. Wǒmen
shí'èr diǎn chīfàn. 我们十二点吃饭。 (*We eat at 12:00.*) 4. Lǎoshī liǎng diǎn shíwǔ fēn lái. 老师两点
十五分来。 (*The teacher will come at 2:15.*) 5. Wǒ de péngyou jiǔ diǎn qù gōngzuò. 我的朋友九点去
工作。 (*My friend goes to work at 9:00.*) 6. Māma qī diǎn sān kè qùle yīyuàn. 妈妈七点三刻去了医
院。 (*Mother went to the hospital at 7:45.*)

Sentence Builder 2
▶ 19C Sentence Builder 2 (CD 6, Track 21)

Nǐ jǐdiǎn qù xuéxiào?
你几点去学校?
What time are you going to school?

Wǒ sān diǎn qù xuéxiào.
我三点去学校。
I'm going to school at 3 o'clock.

Nǐmen shénme shíhou qù Zhōngguó?
你们什么时候去中国?
When are you going to China?

Wǒmen míngtiān zǎoshang zuò fēijī qù Zhōngguó.
我们明天早上坐飞机去中国。
We're taking a plane (to go) to China tomorrow morning.

Tā de lǎoshī shénme shíhou bānle jiā?

他的老师什么时候搬了家？

When did his teacher move?

Tā de lǎoshī qùnián bānle fángzi.

他的老师去年搬了房子。

His teacher moved last year.

Nàge rén shénme shíhou lái?

那个人什么时候来？

When is that person coming?

Tā dàyuē xià ge lǐbài lái.

她大约下个礼拜来。

She is coming approximately next week.

✎ Sentence Practice 2

Translate the following sentences into pīnyīn.

1. *When are you going to buy that book?* _____

   _____

2. *They will go to China next year.* _____

   _____

3. *That student bought a coat last week.* _____

   _____

4. *When did you meet your teacher?* _____

_____

5. *We saw a movie the day before yesterday.* _____

_____

ANSWER KEY

1. Nǐ shénme shíhou mǎi nà běn shū? 你什么时候买那本书？ 2. Tāmen míngnián qù Zhōngguó. 他们明年去中国。 3. Nàge xuésheng shàng ge lǐbài/xīngqī mǎile yī jiàn wàitào. 那个学生上个礼拜/星期买了一件外套。 4. Nǐ shénme shíhou rènshi le nǐ de lǎoshī? 你什么时候认识了你的老师？
5. Wǒmen qiántiān kànle diànyǐng. 我们前天看了电影。

Grammar Builder 2
SHÉNME SHÍHOU 什么时候 (*WHEN*)

▶ 19D Grammar Builder 2 (CD 6, Track 22)

The phrase shénme shíhou 什么时候 is used in Chinese to ask when something
will happen or when someone will do something. It is placed after the subject and
before the main verb in a sentence.

Nǐmen shénme shíhou lái Niǔyuē?
你们什么时候来纽约？
When will you come to New York?

Nǐ shénme shíhou shàngxué?
你什么时候上学？
When do you go to school? OR When will you go to school?

Tā shénme shíhou xiàkè?
他什么时候下课？
When does he finish class? OR When will he finish class?

Shénme shíhou 什么时候 (*when*)   **Lái** 来 (*to come*) and **qù** 去 (*to go*)

Tāmen shénme shíhou chī wǎnfàn?

他们什么时候吃晚饭?

When will they eat dinner? OR When do they eat dinner?

Ⓘ

✎ Work Out 2

Translate the following sentences into Chinese.

1. *When will you go to China?* _____

_____

2. *When/What time do you go to sleep?* _____

_____

3. *When/What time do you go to school?* _____

_____

4. *When did he buy the house?* _____

_____

5. *When did they eat (a meal)?* _____

_____

6. *When will you come?* _____

_____

7. *When will your teacher come to New York?* _____

_____

ANSWER KEY

1. Nǐ shénme shíhou qù Zhōngguó? 你什么时候去中国? 2. Nǐ shénme shíhou shuìjiào?/Nǐ jǐdiǎn shuìjiào? 你什么时候睡觉? /你几点睡觉? 3. Nǐ shénme shíhou shàngxué?/Nǐ jǐdiǎn shàngxué? 你什么时候上学? /你几点上学? 4. Tā shénme shíhou mǎile fángzi? 他什么时候买了房子? 5. Tāmen shénme shíhou chīle fàn? 他们什么时候吃了饭? 6. Nǐ shénme shíhou lái? 你什么时候来? 7. Nǐ de lǎoshī shénme shíhou lái Niǔyuē? 你的老师什么时候来纽约?

💡 Tip!

Be careful when you translate *a.m.* or *p.m.* into Chinese. While Westerners classify the hours between midnight and 11:59 in the morning as *a.m.* and the hours between 12 noon and midnight as *p.m.*, the Chinese use a more extensive and varied set of time "zones" to break down a 24-hour period.

The hours that immediately follow 12 midnight, for example, are regarded as midnight or nighttime hours in China; whereas they are considered to be morning hours in the West. So, 1:00 a.m. is therefore translated as bànyè yī diǎn 半夜一点 (*1:00 after midnight*). Here is the full set of words that are used in Chinese to specify a time period.

bànyè 半夜	*after midnight, midnight (lit., the middle of the night)*
zǎoshang 早上	*before 10 a.m.*
shàngwǔ 上午	*after 10 a.m.*
zhōngwǔ 中午	*12 p.m.(noon)*
xiàwǔ 下午	*before 6 p.m.*
wǎnshang 晚上	*after 6 p.m.*

✎ Drive It Home

Using the times provided, write out pīnyīn phrases using the words for the different parts of the 24-hour period. For example, with 2 p.m., you would write xiàwǔ liǎng diǎn 下午两点。

Shénme shíhou 什么时候 (*when*) | **Lái** 来 (*to come*) and **qù** 去 (*to go*)

1. *12 p.m.* _____

2. *7:30 p.m.* _____

3. *2:15 a.m.* _____

4. *9:45 a.m.* _____

5. *11:11 a.m.* _____

ANSWER KEY

1. zhōngwǔ 中午; 2. wǎnshang qī diǎn bàn 晚上七点半; 3. bànyè liǎng diǎn yī kè 半夜两点一刻;
4. zǎoshang jiǔ diǎn sìshíwǔ fēn 早上九点四十五分; 5. shàngwǔ shíyī diǎn shíyī fēn 上午十一点十一分

How Did You Do?

By now you should know:

☐ More on telling time.

(Still unsure? Go back to 270.)

☐ Asking *when* with shénme shíhou 什么时候.

(Still unsure? Go back to 274.)

✎ Word Recall

Let's review all the measure words we've covered so far. Match the measure word in the left column with the appropriate object(s) in the right column. Some measure words have more than one right answer.

1. ge 个   a. diànshì 电视 (*television*)

2. běn 本   b. shū 书 (*book*)

3. jiàn 件   c. zhuōzi 桌子 (*table*)

4. shuāng 双   d. wàzi 袜子 (*socks*)

5. duì 对   e. bǐ 笔 (*pen*)

6. tái 台   f. ren 人 (*person*)

7. pán 盘   g. shuǐ 水 (*water*)

8. zhī 只

h. chē 车 (*car*)

9. tiáo 条

i. chènshān 衬衫 (*shirt*)

10. píng 瓶

j. niúròu 牛肉 (*beef*)

11. bēi 杯

k. tāng 汤 (*soup*)

12. wǎn 碗

l. ěrhuán 耳环 (*earrings*)

13. zhāng 张

m. kùzi 裤子 (*pants*)

14. liàng 辆

n. jiǔ 酒 (*wine*)

ANSWER KEY

1. f; 2. b; 3. i; 4. d or l; 5. d or l; 6. a; 7. j; 8. e; 9. m; 10. n or g; 11. n or g; 12. k; 13. c; 14. h

Lesson 20: Conversations

In this lesson, you'll learn:

☐ How to talk on the phone.

☐ Use of guò 过.

🎧 Conversation 1

▶ 20A Conversation 1 (CD 6, Track 23-Chinese, Track 24-Chinese and English)

Jess is calling Wang Hai on the phone. Wang Hai isn't home, so Jess talks to his father instead.

Jiéxī: Wèi, nín hǎo. Qǐngwèn Wáng Hǎi zài ma?

洁希: 喂, 您好。 请问王海在吗?

Hǎi de bàba: Nǐ hǎo. Tā gāng chūqù le. Wǒ shì tā de bàba. Nǐ shì nǎ yī wèi zhǎo tā?

海的爸爸: 你好。 他刚出去了。 我是他的爸爸。 你是哪一位找他?

Jiéxī: Wáng xiānsheng, nín hǎo. Wǒ shì tā de tóngxué Jiéxī.

Shénme shíhou 什么时候 *(when)* | **Lái** 来 *(to come)* and **qù** 去 *(to go)*

洁希:	王先生, 您好。 我是他的同学洁希。
Hǎi de bàba:	Nǐ hǎo. Wǒ tīngguò nǐ de míngzi. Tā shuō tā yǒu yī ge wàiguó tóngxué. Nǐ shì nǎ guórén?
海的爸爸:	你好。 我听过你的名字。 他说他有一个外国同学。 你是哪国人?
Jiéxī:	Wǒ shì Měiguórén.
洁希:	我是美国人。
Hǎi de bàba:	Nǐ de Zhōngwén bùcuò. Xuéle duōjiǔ?
海的爸爸:	你的中文不错。 学了多久?
Jiéxī:	Wǒ zài Měiguó xuéle sì nián. Qùnián cái lái Zhōngguó. Wáng Hǎi jīngcháng bāng wǒ liànxí Zhōngwén.
洁希:	我在美国学了四年。 去年才来中国。 王海经常帮我练习中文。
Hǎi de bàba:	Tā zuì ài bāngzhù biérén.
海的爸爸:	他最爱帮助别人。
Jiéxī:	Qǐngwèn tā shénme shíhou huílai?
洁希:	请问他什么时候回来?
Hǎi de bàba:	Tā gēn línjū qù dǎ qiú, dàgài wǎnshang liù diǎn huílai chīfàn.
海的爸爸:	他跟邻居去打球, 大概晚上六点回来吃饭。
Jiéxī:	Máfan nín. Tā huílai de shíhou, qǐng ràng tā gěi wǒ dǎ diànhuà.
洁希:	麻烦您。 他回来的时候, 请让他给我打电话。
Hǎi de bàba:	Méi wèntí. Yǒukòng lái wǒmen jiā zuòzuo.
海的爸爸:	没问题。 有空来我们家坐坐。
Jiéxī:	Hǎo. Xièxie. Zàijiàn.
洁希:	好。 谢谢。 再见。
Hǎi de bàba:	Zàijiàn.
海的爸爸:	再见。

Jess:	*Hello. Can you please tell me if Wang Hai is at home?*
Hai's father:	*Hello. He just went out. I'm his father. Who's calling?*
Jess:	*How are you, Mr. Wang? I'm his classmate Jess.*

Hai's father:	*How are you? I've heard your name before. Wang Hai told me he has a foreign classmate. Which country are you from?*
Jess:	*I'm American.*
Hai's father:	*Your Chinese is good. How long have you been studying?*
Jess:	*I studied Chinese for four years in the U.S. and came to China last year. Wang Hai often helps me practice my Chinese.*
Hai's father:	*The thing he likes most is to help people.*
Jess:	*May I ask when he'll be back?*
Hai's father:	*He went to play ball with some neighbors. He'll probably come back at six for dinner.*
Jess:	*Could you please ask him to return my call when he comes back?*
Hai's father:	*No problem! Please come visit us when you have free time.*
Jess:	*Sure. Thanks a lot! Goodbye.*
Hai's father:	*Goodbye.*

Ⓘ

Take It Further

Wèi 喂 means *hello* and is used when you pick up the telephone. It cannot be used to mean *hello* outside of a phone conversation, however.

Gāng 刚 is an adverb that means to have *just* done something. It's placed in front of the verb that it modifies:

Tā gāng zǒu.
他刚走。
He just left./He has just left.

Nǎ yī wèi 哪一位 is a polite form of *who* (*lit., which person*). It's typically used in place of shéi 谁 (*who*) in telephone conversations where the person receiving the phone call does not know the caller.

Zhǎo 找 means *to look for something or someone*.

Cái 才 means *not until*, and it forms a link between a condition and a consequence. In the following example, tā lái 他来 (*he comes*) is the condition, and wǒ qù 我去 (*I go*) is the consequence. Notice that the conditional action comes before the consequence in Chinese, while in English the order is usually the reverse. Also notice that cái 才 is placed before the verb in the consequence.

Tā lái wǒ cái qù.
他来我才去。
I won't go until he comes.

Cái 才 can also be used after conditions that are not full sentences, as in:

Nàge xuésheng míngtiān cái lái shàngkè.
那个学生明天才来上课。
That student won't come to attend the class until tomorrow.

Another way to link two clauses is to use the expression de shíhou 的时候 (*when/while*). Note that while *when/while* is placed before the adverbial clause indicating time in English, in Chinese de shíhou 的时候 is placed after the adverbial clause.

Wǒmen dǎ qiú de shíhou, tā jìnlái hē shuǐ.
我们打球的时候，他进来喝水。
While we were playing ball, he came in to drink some water.

Gēn 跟 means *and* in the sense of *along with someone*. It's often used in conjunction with yīqǐ 一起 (*together*) when two people perform the same action:

Wǒ de māma gēn tā de māma yīqǐ qù mǎi dōngxi.
我的妈妈跟他的妈妈一起去买东西。
My mother and his mother are going together to buy things.

Yǒukòng 有空 means to *have free time*. It's a compound word that is made up of two parts: the verb yǒu 有 (*to have*) and the noun kòng 空 (*free time*). Kòng 空 literally means *empty* but in this context refers to kòngxián shíjiān 空闲时间 (*free time*). To say that someone is busy, you can use the negative form of yǒukòng 有空, which is méiyǒu kòng 没有空 or méi kòng 没空 (*not have free time*).

✏ Conversation Practice 1

1. Wáng Hǎi bù _____.

   王海不在家。

   (Wang Hai is not at home.)

2. Wáng Hǎi de bàba tīng _____ Jiéxī de _____.

   王海的爸爸听过洁希的名字。

   (Wang Hai's father has heard Jess's name before.)

3. Jiéxī shì _____.

   洁希是美国人。

   (Jess is an American.)

4. Jiéxì zài _____ xuéle sì nián _____.

   洁希在美国学了四年中文。

   (Jess studied Chinese in America for four years.)

5. Wáng Hǎi _____ línjū qù _____.

   王海跟邻居去打球。

6. Wáng Hǎi _____ huílai chīfàn.

   王海六点回来吃饭。

ANSWER KEY
1. zài jiā 在家; 2. guò 过, míngzi 名字; 3. Měiguórén 美国人; 4. Měiguó 美国, Zhōngwén 中文 5. gēn 跟, dǎqiú 打球; 6. liù diǎn 六点

Grammar Builder 1
USE OF GUÒ 过

 20B Grammar Builder 1 (CD 6, Track 25)

You've already seen how the particle le 了 is used in Chinese to indicate that an action has been completed, usually in the past. When used for this purpose, le 了 is placed immediately after the main verb in a sentence.

Tā qùle Zhōngguó.
他去了中国。
He went to China.

The word guò 过 can also be used to show that an action has been completed. However, unlike le 了 (which specifies a finite point in time when something ended), guò 过 refers to the past in broader terms and indicates a past experience rather than a past event. It implies an unspecified time frame that stretches from the distant past up until the present, and is therefore usually translated into the present perfect tense in English. Here are some examples that show the difference between le 了 and guò 过:

Wǒ xuéle liǎng nián Zhōngwén.
我学了两年中文。
I studied Chinese for two years.

Wǒ xuéguò Zhōngwén.
我学过中文。
I've studied Chinese before.

Tā de línjū qùle Zhōngguó.

他的邻居去了中国。

His neighbor went to China.

Tā de línjū qùguò Zhōngguó.

他的邻居去过中国。

His neighbor has been to China before.

Nǐ xiěle zì ma?

你写了字吗?

Did you write the characters?

Wǒ xiěle.

我写了。

I did.

Wǒ méiyǒu xiě.

我没有写。

I didn't.

Nǐ xiěguò shūfǎ ma?

你写过书法吗?

Have you ever written Chinese calligraphy before?

Wǒ xiěguò.

我写过。

Yes, I have (written it before).

Wǒ cónglái méiyǒu xiěguò.

我从来没有写过。

No, I've never written it before. OR *No, I haven't (ever written it before).*

Nǐmen kànle tā de shū méiyǒu?

你们看了他的书没有？

Did you read his book?

Wǒmen kànle.

我们看了。

Yes, we did.

Wǒmen hái méiyǒu kàn.

我们还没有看。

No, we didn't read it yet.

Nǐmen kànguò tā de shū méiyǒu?

你们看过他的书没有？

Have you (ever) read his book before?

Wǒmen kànguò.

我们看过。

Yes, we've read it already.

Wǒmen méiyǒu kànguò.

我们没有看过。

No, we haven't read it yet.

Grammatically, le 了 and guò 过 share the same structural role when forming statements and questions. As you can see from the examples above, both appear next to the verb. However, in negation with méiyǒu 没有, le 了 is dropped, while guò 过 is not.

(11)

✎ Work Out 1

Complete each sentence by determining whether the blank should be replaced with (a) guò 过, (b) le 了, or (c) *nothing at all.* Then translate the full sentences.

1. Wǒmen méiyǒu qù _____ Zhōngguó.

   我们没有去 _____ 中国。

2. Tā de tàitai zuótiān qù _____ Zhōngguó.

   他的太太昨天去 _____ 中国。

3. Nǐ qù _____ Zhōngguó méiyǒu?

   你去 _____ 中国没有？

4. Wǒ jīntiān méiyǒu _____ shàngxué.

   我今天没有 _____ 上学。

5. Duìbùqǐ, tā gāng zǒu _____ .

   对不起, 他刚走 _____ 。

6. Nà zhī māo chī _____ sān tiáo yú.

   那只猫吃 _____ 三条鱼。

7. Wáng xiānsheng qùnián mǎi _____ fángzi.

   王先生去年买 _____ 房子。

8. Wǒ de shēngrì shì _____ sān yuè sān hào.

   我的生日是 _____ 三月三号。

ANSWER KEY

1. a. Wǒmen méiyǒu qùguò Zhōngguó. 我们没有去过中国。 (*We haven't been to China before.*) 2. b. Tā de tàitai zuótiān qùle Zhōngguó. 他的太太昨天去了中国。 (*His wife went to China yesterday.*) 3. a. Nǐ qùguò Zhōngguó méiyǒu? 你去过中国没有？ (*Have you ever been to China before?*) 4. c. Wǒ jīntiān méiyǒu shàngxué. 我今天没有上学。 (*I didn't go to school today.*) 5. b. Duìbùqǐ, tā gāng zǒu le. 对不起, 他刚走

了。(*Sorry, he just left.*) 6. b. Nà zhī māo chīle sān tiáo yú. 那只猫吃了三条鱼。(*The cat ate three fish.*)
7. b. Wáng xiānsheng qùnián mǎile fángzi. 王先生去年买了房子。(*Mr. Wang bought a house last year.*)
8. c. Wǒ de shēngrì shì sān yuè sān hào. 我的生日是三月三号。(*My birthday is March 3.*)

🎧 Conversation 2

▶ 20C Conversation 2 (CD 6, Track 26-Chinese, Track 27-Chinese and English)

Wang Hai calls back and Jess asks him if he wants to go to a movie.

Jiéxī:	Wèi, nín hǎo!
洁希:	喂,您好!
Hǎi:	Wèi, Jiéxī, shì wǒ a, Wáng Hǎi. Wǒ bàba shuō nǐ gāngcái dǎ diànhuà lái. Yǒu shénme shì?
海:	喂,洁希,是我啊,王海。我爸爸说你刚才打电话来。有什么事?
Jiéxī:	Nǐ míngtiān wǎnshang yǒukòng ma? Wǒ yǒu liǎng zhāng zèngsòng de diànyǐng piào, shì Lǐ Ān de diànyǐng. Nǐ yǒu xìngqù ma?
洁希:	你明天晚上有空吗?我有两张赠送的电影票,是李安的电影。你有兴趣吗?
Hǎi:	Wǒ kàn guò tā qítā de diànyǐng. Wǒ hěn xǐhuan tā de diànyǐng.
海:	我看过他其它的电影。我很喜欢他的电影。
Jiéxī:	Nà tài hǎo le. Wǒmen kěyǐ xiān chīfàn, ránhòu qù kàn diànyǐng, zěnme yàng?
洁希:	那太好了。我们可以先吃饭,然后去看电影,怎么样?
Hǎi:	Hǎo. Dànshì wǒ míngtiān de kè hěn wǎn. Diànyǐng jǐ diǎn kāishǐ?
海:	好。但是我明天的课很晚。电影几点开始?
Jiéxī:	Liù diǎn bàn kāishǐ. Zài xuéshēng dàlóu fàngyìng.
洁希:	六点半开始。在学生大楼放映。
Hǎi:	Wǒ liù diǎn cái xiàkè. Xiàkè zhīhòu, wǒ pǎo guòlái zhǎo nǐ ba.
海:	我六点才下课。下课之后,我跑过来找你吧。
Jiéxī:	Zhēn bù hǎoyìsi. Ràng nǐ gǎn guòlái. Wǒmen kàn wán diànyǐng zhīhòu zài chīfàn, zěnme yàng?

洁希:	真不好意思。让你赶过来。我们看完电影之后再吃饭, 怎么样?
Hǎi:	Hǎo. Nà wǒmen míngtiān liù diǎn bàn jiàn.
海:	好。那我们明天六点半见。
Jiéxī:	Míngtiān jiàn.
洁希:	明天见。

Jess:	*Hello, how are you?*
Hai:	*Hi, Jess. It's me, um, Wang Hai. My mother said that you called. What's up?*
Jess:	*Are you free tomorrow night? I have two tickets that were given to me as a gift to Ang Lee's movie. Are you interested in going?*
Hai:	*I've watched his other movies before. I like them a lot.*
Jess:	*That's great! We can eat first and then go to the movie. What do you think?*
Hai:	*Okay. But my class ends very late tomorrow. What time does the movie start?*
Jess:	*6:30. It's being shown in the student center.*
Hai:	*I won't finish class until 6:00. Then I'll run over to find you.*
Jess:	*I'm really sorry to make you rush. After the movie, we'll get something to eat. How's that?*
Hai:	*Okay. See you tomorrow at 6:30.*
Jess:	*See you tomorrow.*

Ⓘ

Take It Further

Notice that when Jess answers the telephone, she uses the polite form of *you*, nín 您, even though Wang Hai is her friend. This is because she doesn't know yet who the caller is and therefore uses the formal nín hǎo 您好 rather than nǐ hǎo 你好, which is used between people who are familiar with each other.

✎ Conversation Practice 2

Fill in the blanks with the missing words in pīnyīn. Refer to the second conversation with Hai and Jess.

1. Hǎi míngtiān _____ yǒukòng.

   海明天晚上有空。

2. Hǎi _____ Lǐ Ān de diànyǐng.

   海看过李安的电影。

3. Diànyǐng _____ kāishǐ.

   电影六点半开始。

4. Hǎi liù diǎn cái _____.

   海六点才下课。

5. Jiéxī hé Hǎi kàn wán diànyǐng _____ zài chīfàn.

   洁希和海看完电影之后再吃饭。

ANSWER KEY
1. wǎnshang 晚上; 2. kànguò 看过; 3. liù diǎn bàn 六点半; 4. xiàkè 下课; 5. zhīhòu 之后

Grammar Builder 2
LÁI 来 *(TO COME)* AND QÙ 去 *(TO GO)*

▶ 20D Grammar Builder 2 (CD 6, Track 28)

Lái 来 *(to come)* and qù 去 *(to go)* are two common verbs that can be used on their own, just as in English.

Wǒmen qù kàn diànyǐng.

我们去看电影。

We're going to a movie.

Wǒ zhège zhōumò qùle bówùguǎn.

我这个周末去了博物馆。

I went to a museum this weekend.

Tāmen cóng Táiwān lái.

他们从台湾来。

They came from Taiwan.

Nǐ kěyǐ lái wǒ jiā wán ma?

你可以来我家玩吗?

Can you come and play at my home?

Both of these verbs can also be added as directional particles after another verb to indicate the direction that an action takes with regard to the physical location of the speaker. When the verb precedes lái 来, the action is shown to be towards the speaker. When the verb precedes qù 去, the action is away from the speaker.

Tā zǎoshang pǎo lái zhèlǐ, xiàwǔ pǎo qù nàli.

他早上跑来这里, 下午跑去那里。

He runs here in the morning and runs there in the afternoon.

Tāmen kāichē lái wǒ de jiā.

他们开车来我的家。

They are driving to my home.

Wǒmen kāichē qù tā de jiā.

我们开车去他的家。

We are driving to his home.

Ⅱ

✎ Work Out 2

Look over the second dialogue again and then determine whether the following sentences are true (shì 是) or false (fēi 非). Then, translate the sentence into English.

1. Wáng Hǎi méiyǒu gěi Jiéxī dǎ diànhuà. 王海没有给洁希打电话。_____

   _____

2. Wáng Hǎi méiyǒu kòng kàn diànyǐng. 王海没有空看电影。_____

   _____

3. Wáng Hǎi méiyǒu kànguò Lǐ Ān de diànyǐng. 王海没有看过李安的电影。_____

   _____

4. Wáng Hǎi hěn xǐhuan Lǐ Ān de diànyǐng. 王海很喜欢李安的电影。_____

   _____

5. Jiéxī hé Wáng Hǎi zài xuéxiào kàn diànyǐng. 洁希和王海在学校看电影。_____

   _____

6. Wáng Hǎi míngtiān xiàwǔ sì diǎn xiàkè. 王海明天下午四点下课。_____

   _____

ANSWER KEY

1. fēi 非 (*Wang Hai didn't call Jess back.*); 2. fēi 非 (*Wang Hai is not free to go to the movie.*); 3. fēi 非 (*Wang Hai hasn't watched Ang Lee's movies before.*); 4. shì 是 (*Wang Hai likes Ang Lee's movies a lot.*); 5. shì 是 (*Jess and Wang Hai will watch a movie at school.*); 6. fēi 非 (*Wang Hai will finish class at 4 p.m.*)

✎ Drive It Home

Modify each phrase using guò 过 and then le 了, and then translate each sentence accordingly. For example, with Wǒ kàn diànyǐng 我看电影, you would write: Wǒ kànguò diànyǐng. 我看过电影。(*I have seen movies before.*) Wǒ kànle diànyǐng 我看了电影。(*I saw a movie.*)

1. Nǐmen chī yú. 你们吃鱼。 _____

   _____

2. Lǎoshī qù shūdiàn. 老师去书店。 _____

   _____

3. Zhège nánháir tīng yīnyuè. 这个男孩儿听音乐。 _____

   _____

4. Tāmen chuān lán kùzi. 他们穿蓝裤子。 _____

   _____

5. Wǒ mǎi pútao. 我买葡萄。 _____

   _____

ANSWER KEY

1. Nǐmen chīguò yú. 你们吃过鱼。 (*You've eaten fish before.*) Nǐmen chīle yú. 你们吃了鱼。 (*You ate fish.*) 2. Lǎoshī qùguò shūdiàn. 老师去过书店。 (*The teacher has been to the bookstore before.*) Lǎoshī qùle shūdiàn. 老师去了书店。 (*The teacher went to the bookstore.*) 3. Zhège nánháir tīngguò yīnyuè. 这个男孩儿听过音乐。 (*This boy has listened to music before.*) Zhège nánháir tīngle yīnyuè. 这个男孩儿听了音乐。 (*This boy listened to music.*) 4. Tāmen chuānguò lán kùzi. 他们穿过蓝裤子。 (*They've worn blue pants before.*) Tāmen chuānle lán kùzi. 他们穿了蓝裤子。 (*They wore blue pants.*) 5. Wǒ mǎiguò pútao. 我买过葡萄。 (*I've bought grapes before.*) Wǒ mǎile pútao. 我买了葡萄。 (*I bought grapes.*)

How Did You Do?

By now you should know:

☐ How to talk on the phone.
(Still unsure? Go back to 278.)

☐ Use of guò 过.
(Still unsure? Go back to 283.)

✎ Word Recall

Match the English word in the left column with its appropriate translation in the right column.

1. *interest*	a. méi wèntí 没问题
2. *just now*	b. dǎ qiú 打球
3. *foreign*	c. guò 过
4. *classmate*	d. xìngqù 兴趣
5. *to help*	e. xiān 先
6. *to play ball*	f. ránhòu 然后
7. *to look for, to find*	g. wàiguó 外国
8. *suffix indicating completion of an action*	h. gāngcái 刚才
9. *then, after that*	i. zhǎo 找
10. *to say, to speak*	j. shuō 说
11. *how long*	k. tóngxué 同学
12. *goodbye*	l. máfan 麻烦
13. *no problem*	m. duōjiǔ 多久
14. *first*	n. bāngzhù 帮助
15. *to trouble*	o. zàijiàn 再见

ANSWER KEY

1. d; 2. h; 3.g; 4. k; 5. n; 6. b; 7. i; 8. c; 9. f; 10. j; 11. m; 12. o. 13. a; 14. e; 15. l

Unit 5 Essentials

Vocabulary Essentials

Test your knowledge of the key material in this unit by filling in the blanks in the following charts. Once you've completed these pages, you'll have tested your retention, and you'll have your own reference for the most essential vocabulary. This is also a great time to practice a few Chinese characters. Fill in the middle column with the characters that you remember. Or, if you only remember the pīnyīn, go back through the unit to find the character.

PĪNYĪN	CHARACTER	
		clock
		watch
		hour(s)
		minute(s) (duration)
		minute(s) (telling time)
		second(s)
		o'clock
		quarter
		half
		now
		to, before (ten minutes to/before one o'clock)

DAYS AND TIMES OF DAY

PĪNYĪN	CHARACTER	
		today
		tomorrow
		yesterday
		the day before yesterday
		the day after tomorrow
		noon
		midnight
		this morning
		this afternoon
		tonight, this evening

EXPRESSIONS WITH WEEK, YEAR AND MONTH

PĪNYĪN	CHARACTER	
		this week
		last week
		next week
		this month
		last month
		next month
		this year
		last year
		next year

If you're having a hard time remembering this vocabulary, don't forget to check out the supplemental flashcards for this unit online. Go to **www.livinglanguage.com/languagelab** for a great way to help you practice vocabulary.

Grammar Essentials

Here is a reference for the key grammar that was covered in Unit 5. Make sure you understand the summary and can use all of the grammar it covers.

ASKING FOR AND GIVING THE TIME

Xiànzài jǐdiǎn?	现在几点?	*(What time is it now?)*
jǐdiǎn	几点	*what time? when?*
Xiànzài yī diǎn.	现在一点。	*It's 1:00 now.*
Wǔ diǎn.	五点。	*(It's) 5:00.*

MORE ON TELLING TIME

sì diǎn bàn	四点半	*4:30*
wǔ diǎn sānshí fēn	五点三十分	*5:30*
liǎng diǎn yī kè	两点一刻	*2:15*
wǔ diǎn shíwǔ fēn	五点十五分	*5:15*
yī diǎn sān kè	一点三刻	*1:45*
wǔ diǎn sìshíwǔ fēn	五点四十五分	*5:45*
liù diǎn líng wǔ fēn	六点零五分	*6:05*
qī diǎn chà jiǔ fēn	七点差九分	*6:51*
chà jiǔ fēn qī diǎn	差九分七点	*6:51*

ASKING QUESTIONS WITH WHO

Nǐ shì shéi?	你是谁?	*Who are you?*
Shéi shàng ge lǐbài qùle Měiguó?	谁上个礼拜去了美国?	*Who went to the U.S. last week?*
Shéi yǒu yī kuài?	谁有一块?	*Who has one yuan?*

GUÒ 过 VS. LE 了

Use guò 过 to refer to a past experience rather than a past event, in which you would use le 了.

Wǒ xuéle liǎng nián Zhōngwén.	我学了两年中文。	*I studied Chinese for two years.*
Wǒ xuéguò Zhōngwén.	我学过中文。	*I've studied Chinese before.*
Tā de línjū qùle Zhōngguó.	他的邻居去了中国。	*His neighbor went to China.*
Tā de línjū qùguò Zhōngguó.	他的邻居去过中国。	*His neighbor has been to China before.*

Character Essentials

To practice the Chinese characters you learned in Unit 5, Conversations 1 and 2 are repeated here without pīnyīn or English translations. Translate as many characters as you can. Check your answers by listening to the conversations from your audio. Don't worry if you can't remember all of the characters. Just try to remember as many as you can.

Conversation 1

20A Conversation 1 (CD 6, Track 23-Chinese, Track 24-Chinese and English)

洁希:　　　喂, 您好。 请问王海在吗?

_____

_____

海的爸爸:　　你好。 他刚出去了。 我是他的爸爸。 你是哪一位找他?

_____

_____

洁希: 王先生, 您好。 我是他的同学洁希。

海的爸爸: 你好。 我听过你的名字。 他说他有一个外国同学。 你是
哪国人?

洁希: 我是美国人。

海的爸爸: 你的中文不错。 学了多久?

洁希: 我在美国学了四年。 去年才来中国。 王海经常帮我练习中
文。

海的爸爸: 他最爱帮助别人。

洁希:　　　　请问他什么时候回来?

海的爸爸:　　他跟邻居去打球, 大概晚上六点回来吃饭。

洁希:　　　　麻烦您。 他回来的时候, 请让他给我打电话。

海的爸爸:　　没问题。 有空来我们家坐坐。

洁希:　　　　好。 谢谢。 再见。

海的爸爸:　　再见。

Ⅱ

🗨 Conversation 2

洁希: 喂, 您好!

_____

_____

海: 喂, 洁希, 是我啊, 王海。 我妈妈说你刚才打电话来。 有什么事?

_____

_____

洁希: 你明天晚上有空吗? 我有两张赠送的电影票, 是李安的电影。 你有兴趣吗?

_____

_____

海: 我看过他其它的电影。 我很喜欢他的电影。

_____

_____

洁希: 那太好了。 我们可以先吃饭, 然后去看电影, 怎么样?

_____

_____

海:　　　好。但是我明天的课很晚。电影几点开始?

_____

_____

洁希:　　六点半开始。在学生大楼放映。

_____

_____

海:　　　我六点才下课。下课之后,我跑过来找你吧。

_____

_____

洁希:　　真不好意思。让你赶过来。我们看完电影之后再吃饭,怎
　　　　　么样?

_____

_____

海:　　　好。那我们明天六点半见。

_____

_____

洁希:　　明天见。

_____

_____

⑪

Unit 5 Quiz

A. Fill in the blanks with the words and phrases in parentheses. Then translate the complete sentences into English.

1. Wǒmen _____ *(tomorrow)* qù Zhōngguó.

   我们 _____去中国。

   _____

2. Tā de línjū jiǔ diǎn bàn _____ *(after)* bù kàn diànshì.

   他的邻居九点半 _____不看电视。

   _____

3. Tā hé lǎoshī _____ *(tomorrow afternoon)* tiàowǔ.

   他和老师 _____跳舞。

   _____

4. Nǐmen _____ *(the day before yesterday)* yǒu méiyǒu shàngxué?

   你们 _____有没有上学?

   _____

5. Nàxiē xuésheng _____ *(yesterday)* rènshi le xīn péngyou.

   那些学生 _____认识了新朋友。

   _____

B. Fill in the blanks of the conversation.

1. Nàge rén shì _____?

   那个人是谁?

   (Who is that person?)

2. Tā _____ wǒ de gēge.

   他是我的哥哥。

   (He's my brother.)

3. Tā _____ suì?

   他几岁?

   (How old is he?)

4. Tā _____ suì.

   他十六岁。

   (He is sixteen.)

5. Nǐ _____ mèimei ma?

   你有妹妹吗?

   (Do you have a younger sister?)

6. Yǒu. Wǒ _____ xǐhuan tā.

   有。 我最喜欢她。

   (I do. I like her the best.)

C. Answer the following questions in Chinese with the time in parentheses.

1. Nǐmen jǐdiǎn qù mǎi chènshān? 你们几点去买衬衫? *(12:00)* _____

    _____

2. Wáng Xiānsheng jǐdiǎn shuìjiào? 王先生几点睡觉? *(10:30)* _____

    _____

3. Lǎoshī jǐdiǎn lái? 老师几点来? *(2:15)* _____

    _____

4. Nǐ de péngyou jǐdiǎn qù shìchǎng? 你的朋友几点去市场? *(9:00)* _____

    _____

D. Complete each sentence by determining whether the blank should be replaced with (a) guò 过, (b) le 了, or (c) nothing at all. Then translate the full sentences.

1. Tā de xuésheng zuótiān qù _____ Zhōngguó.

    他的学生昨天去 _____ 中国。

    _____

2. Wǒ jīntiān méiyǒu _____ chīfàn.

    我今天没有 _____ 吃饭。

    _____

3. Wǒmen méiyǒu qù _____ xìyuàn.

    我们没有去 _____ 戏院。

    _____

4. Nǐ qù _____ Zhōngguó méiyǒu?

你去 _____ 中国没有？

_____

5. Wáng Tàitai qùnián mǎi _____ chē.

王太太去年买 _____ 车。

_____

How Did You Do?

Give yourself a point for every correct answer, then use the following key to tell whether you're ready to move on:

0-7 points: It's probably a good idea to go back through the lesson again. You may be moving too quickly, or there may be too much "down time" between your contact with Chinese. Remember that it's better to spend 30 minutes with Chinese three or four times a week than it is to spend two or three hours just once a week. Find a pace that's comfortable for you, and spread your contact hours out as much as you can.

8-12 points: You would benefit from a review before moving on. Go back and spend a little more time on the specific points that gave you trouble. Re-read the Grammar Builder sections that were difficult, and do the work out one more time. Don't forget about the online supplemental practice material, either. Go to **www.livinglanguage.com/languagelab** for games and quizzes that will reinforce the material from this unit.

13-17 points: Good job! There are just a few points that you might consider reviewing before moving on. If you haven't worked with the games and quizzes on **www.livinglanguage.com/languagelab**, please give them a try.

18-20 points: Great! You're ready to move on to the Advanced Chinese!

 **points**

Don't forget to practice and reinforce what you've learned by visiting **www.livinglanguage.com/languagelab** for flashcards, games, and quizzes.

Pronunciation and Pīnyīn Guide

The Chinese language does not have an alphabet. Each word is represented by a character, which may be composed of just one stroke (line) or as many as several dozen. To represent Chinese sounds for those who do not read characters, various systems of romanization have been devised, including pīnyīn, the standard system used in China and the one most commonly used in the United States.

Each syllable in Chinese has an initial consonant sound and a final vowel sound. There are twenty-three initial sounds (consonants) and thirty-six final sounds (vowels or combinations of vowels and consonants). Here is how each sound is written in pīnyīn, with its approximate English equivalent.

INITIAL SOUNDS

PĪNYĪN	ENGLISH
b	*b* in *bear*
p	*p* in *poor*
m	*m* in *more*
f	*f* in *fake*
d	*d* in *dare*
t	*t* in *take*
n	*n* in *now*
l	*l* in *learn*
z	*ds* in *yards*
c	*ts* in *its*
s	*s* in *sing*
zh	*j* in *judge*
ch	*ch* in *church*
sh	*hard sh* in *shhhh!*
r	*r* in *rubber*
j	*dy* in *and yet*

PĪNYĪN	ENGLISH
q	*ty* in *won't you*
x	*sh* in *shoe*
g	*g* in *get*
k	*k* in *keep*
h	*h* in *help*
y	*y* in *yes*
w	*w* in *want*

FINAL SOUNDS

a	*a* in *ma*
ai	*y* in *my*
ao	*ou* in *pout*
an	*an* in *élan*
ang	*ong* in *throng*
o	*o* in *or*
ou	*oa* in *float*
ong	*ong* in *long*
e	*e* in *nerve*
ei	*ay* in *day*
en	*un* in *under*
eng	*ung* in *mung*
i (after z, c, s, zh, ch, sh)	*r* in *thunder*
i	*ee* in *see*
ia	*yah*
iao	*eow* in *meow*
ian	*yan*
iang	*yang*
ie	*ye* in *yes*

iu	*yo-yo*
iong	*young*
in	*in* in *sin*
ing	*ing* in *sing*
u	*u* in *flu*
ua	*ua* in *suave*
uai	*wi* in *wide*
uan	*wan*
uang	*wong*
uo	*wo* in *won't*
ui	*weigh*
un	*won*
ü	*like ee in see, but with lips rounded into a pout (German hübsch, French tu.)*
üan	*like ü above with an*
üe	*like ü above with e in net*
ün	*like ü above with n in an*
er	*are*

Tone Marks

Each syllable in Mandarin Chinese must be pronounced with a tone—there are four, plus a neutral tone. Here are the tone marks as they are written in pīnyīn. They're written here over the vowel *a*, which is pronounced similarly to the vowel in *John*. Imagine saying the name *John* in the following contexts:

First Tone	ā	High and neutral, no accent. Sing "John."
Second Tone	á	From middle to high, as in asking a question. "John? Is that you?"
Third Tone	ǎ	From middle to low, and then to high, as if stretching out a question: "Jo-o-o-hn, what do you think?"
Fourth Tone	à	From high to low, as if answering a question. "Who's there?" "John."

Syllables pronounced with the neutral tone are unmarked. The tones are placed over the final vowel sound of a syllable. In the case of compound vowels, such as ai, uo, ao, etc., the tone is placed over the primary vowel.

Grammar Summary

1. NUMBERS

a. Cardinal numbers 1 to 10

yī 一	*one*	liù 六	*six*
èr 二	*two*	qī 七	*seven*
sān 三	*three*	bā 八	*eight*
sì 四	*four*	jiǔ 九	*nine*
wǔ 五	*five*	shí 十	*ten*

b. Cardinal numbers 11 to 100

shíyī *(10 + 1)* 十一	*eleven*	shíliù *(10 + 6)* 十六	*sixteen*
shí'èr *(10+ 2)* 十二	*twelve*	shíqī *(10 + 7)* 十七	*seventeen*
shísān *(10+ 3)* 十三	*thirteen*	shíbā *(10 + 8)* 十八	*eighteen*
shísì *(10 + 4)* 十四	*fourteen*	shíjiǔ *(10 + 9)* 十九	*nineteen*
shíwǔ *(10 + 5)* 十五	*fifteen*	èrshí *(2 x 10)* 二十	*twenty*
sānshí *(3 x 10)* 三十	*thirty*	qīshí *(7 x 10)* 七十	*seventy*
sìshí *(4 x 10)* 四十	*forty*	bāshí *(8 x 10)* 八十	*eighty*
wǔshí *(5x 10)* 五十	*fifty*	jiǔshí *(9 x 10)* 九十	*ninety*
liùshí *(6x 10)* 六十	*sixty*	yībǎi *(1 x 100)* 一百	*one hundred*

Note: The word yī 一 is added before shí 十 in numbers ending in the numerals 10 through 19.

èrshísān (20 + 3) 二十三	twenty-three	wǔshíliù (50+ 6) 五十六	fifty-six
sìshíjiǔ (40 + 9) 四十九	forty-nine	jiǔshíjiǔ (90 + 9) 九十九	ninety-nine

Note: The word yī 一 is added before shí 十 in numbers ending in the numerals 10 through 19.

c. Cardinal numbers from 200 to 100,000,000

yībǎi líng sì 一百零四	one hundred four	yīwàn 一万	ten thousand
èrbǎi/liǎngbǎi 二百	two hundred	yībǎiwàn 一百万	one million
yīqiān 一千	one thousand	yīqiānwàn 一千万	ten million
yīqiān líng sì 一千零四	one thousand four	yīyì 一亿	one hundred million
yīqiān líng sānshí'èr 一千零 三十二	one thousand thirty-two	shíyì 十亿	one billion
yībǎi yīshíyī 一百一十一	one hundred eleven	sānbǎi yīshí'èr 三百一十二	three hundred twelve
èrbǎi yīshí 二百一十	two hundred ten	wǔbǎi yīshíjiǔ 五百一十九	five hundred nineteen

Note: Líng 零 is used to express the zero in numbers. Also, the number two is expressed in two different ways in Chinese. Èr 二 is used for counting and numeric expressions, such as twelve (shí'èr 十二) or two hundred (èrbǎi 二百). Liǎng 两 is used in combination with nouns.

d. Ordinal numbers (dì 第 + cardinal number)

yī 一	one	dì-yī 第一	the first
jiǔ 九	nine	dì-jiǔ 第九	the ninth

Intermediate Chinese

2. NOUNS

There is no distinction in form between singular and plural nouns in Chinese. To designate a plural noun use a number or a measure word in front of the noun or the ending -men for nouns referring to human beings.

yī ge píngguǒ 一个苹果	*one apple*
liǎng ge píngguǒ 两个苹果	*two apples*
Háizimen ài chī tángguǒ. 孩子们爱吃糖果。	*The children like eating candy.*

3. PERSONAL PRONOUNS

1st person (sg.)	wǒ 我	*I/me*
2nd person (sg.)	nín (fml.) 您 nǐ (infml.) 你	*you*
3rd person (sg.)	tā 他 / 她	*he, she, it/him, her, it*
1st person (pl.)	wǒmen 我们	*we/us*
2nd person (pl.)	nǐmen 你们	*you*
3rd person (pl.)	tāmen 他们	*they/them*

Note: There is no special polite form for 2nd person plural pronoun nǐmen 你们. Instead, phrases nín liǎng wèi 您两位 (*you two/both of you*) or nín jǐ wèi 您几位 (*several of you*) can be used.

4. POSSESSIVE PRONOUNS (PERSONAL PRONOUN + DE)

1st person (sg.)	wǒ de 我的	*my/mine*
2nd person (sg.)	nín de (fml.) 您的 nǐ de (infml.) 你的	*your/yours*
3rd person (sg.)	tā de 他的 / 她的	*his, her, its/his, hers, its*
1st person (pl.)	wǒmen de 我们的	*our/ours*
2nd person (pl.)	nǐmen de 你们的	*your/yours*
3rd person (pl.)	tāmen de 他们的	*their/theirs*

5. DEMONSTRATIVE PRONOUNS (ZHÈ 这 / NÀ 那 + MEASURE WORD + NOUN)

zhè běn shū 这本书	this book
nà běn shū 那本书	that book
zhèxiē shū 这些书	these books
nàxiē shū 那些书	those books

Note: Xiē 些 both makes the noun plural and serves as a measure word. Also, in colloquial language, zhè 这 and nà 那 are pronounced as zhèi 这 and nèi 那 when combined with a measure word.

6. INDEFINITE PRONOUNS

Indefinite pronouns such as anyone, anybody, anything, or anytime consist of question words + yě 也.

Rènhé 任何 (any) + yě 也 can also be used when the indefinite is a subject.

The indefinite pronouns someone and somebody are expressed with yǒu rén 有人, while the indefinite pronoun something is expressed with diǎn dōngxi 点东西.

shéi + yě (anyone) 谁 + 也	Wǒ shéi yě bù jiàn. 我谁也不见。	I don't see anyone.
shénme dōngxi + yě (anything) 什么东西 + 也	Tā shénme dōngxi yě chī. 他什么东西也吃。	He eats anything.
nǎr + yě (anywhere) 哪儿 + 也	Nǐ nǎr yě bù zhù. 你哪儿也不住。	You don't live anywhere.
shénme shíhou + yě (anytime) 什么时候 + 也	Nǐ xǐhuan shénme shíhou lái yě kěyǐ. 你喜欢什么时候来也可以。	Come over anytime you like.

shénme rén + yě (anybody) 什么人 + 也	Shénme rén yě kěyǐ qù. 什么人也可以去。	Anybody can go.
rènhé rén + yě (anyone) 任何人 + 也	Rènhé rén yě kěyǐ qù. 任何人也可以去。	Anyone can go.
rènhé dōngxi + yě (anything) 任何东西 + 也	Rènhé dōngxi yě huì biàn. 任何东西也会变。	Anything can change.
rènhé shíhou + yě (anytime) 任何时候 + 也	Rènhé shíhou yě kěyǐ. 任何时候也可以。	Anytime is fine.
rènhé dìfang + yě (anywhere) 任何地方 + 也	Rènhé dìfang yě kěyǐ. 任何地方也可以。	Anywhere is fine. (lit., Anywhere can be.)
yǒu rén (someone/somebody) 有人	Yǒu rén zài zhèr. 有人在这儿。	Someone is here. (lit., There is person here.)
méiyǒu rén (nobody) 没有人	Gōngchēzhàn méiyǒu rén. 公车站没有人。	Nobody is at the bus stop./There are no people at the bus stop.
diǎn dōngxi (something) 点东西	Wǒ yǒu diǎn dōngxi gěi nǐ. 我有点东西给你。	I have something to give you.

The indefinites shéi yě 谁也 (anyone) and shénme dōngxi yě 什么东西也 (anything) can also be translated as everyone and everything.

Shéi yě xǐhuan wǒ. 谁也喜欢我。	Everyone loves me.
Shénme dōngxi zuìhòu yě huì sǐ. 什么东西最后也会死。	Everything eventually dies.

7. MEASURE WORDS

Nouns modified by a number word or a demonstrative pronoun require a measure word (number word or demonstrative pronoun + measure word + noun). Here are some categories of measure words:

a. Nature of the object

MEASURE WORD	CATEGORY	EXAMPLES
zhī 只	*animals*	yī zhī jī 一只鸡 (*one/a chicken*) yī zhī māo 一只猫 (*one/a cat*) yī zhī niǎo 一只鸟 (*one/a bird*)
zhī 只	*utensils*	yī zhī bēi 一只杯 (*one/a cup/glass*) yī zhī wǎn 一只碗 (*one/a bowl*) yī zhī guō 一只锅 (*one/a pot*)
tái 台	*machinery*	yī tái jīqì 一台机器 (*one/a machine*) yī tái diànnǎo 一台电脑 (*one/a computer*) yī tái diànshì 一台电视 (*one/a television*)
jiàn 件	*clothing (top)*	yī jiàn chènshān 一件衬衫 (*one/a shirt*) yī jiàn fēngyī 一件风衣 (*one/a wind break*)
tiáo 条	*clothing (bottom)*	yī tiáo qúnzi 一条裙子 (*one/a skirt*)

MEASURE WORD	CATEGORY	EXAMPLES
bǎ 把	*something with handle*	yī bǎ cháhú 一把茶壶 *(one/a teapot)* yī bǎ yǔsǎn 一把雨伞 *(one/an umbrella)* yī bǎ shànzi 一把扇子 *(one/a Chinese fan)* yī bǎ yǐzi 一把椅子 *(one/a chair)*
zuò 座	*large and imposing objects*	yī zuò sān 一座山 *(one/a mountain)* yī zuò dàlóu 一座大楼 *(one/a building)*
liàng 辆	*vehicles*	yī liàng qìchē 一辆汽车 *(one/a car)*
jiā 家	*families or enterprises*	yī jiā fànguǎn 一家饭馆 *(one/a restaurant)* liǎng jiā rénjia 两家人家 *(two families)*
ge 个	*people*	yī ge rén 一个人 *(one/a person)* liǎng ge lǎoshī 两个老师 *(two teachers)*

b. Shape of the object

MEASURE WORD	CATEGORY	EXAMPLES
zhāng 张	*flat surface*	yī zhāng zhǐ 一张纸 (*one/a piece of paper*) yī zhāng bàozhǐ 一张报纸 (*one/a newspaper*) yī zhāng zhàopiàn 一张照片 (*one/a photo*) yī zhāng chuáng 一张床 (*one/a bed*)
zhī 支	*pointed and thin or like a branch*	yī zhī bǐ 一支笔 (*one/a pen*) yī zhī qiāng 一支枪 (*one/a gun*) yī zhī jūnduì 一支军队 (*one/a troop*)
lì 粒	*granular*	yī lì mǐ 一粒米 (*one/a grain of rice*) yī lì zhǒngzi 一粒种子 (*one/a seed*)
kē 颗	*small and round*	yī kē yǎnlèi 一颗眼泪 (*one/a tear drop*) yī kē hóngdòu 一颗红豆 (*one/a red bean*)
tiáo 条	*long and thin*	yī tiáo lù 一条路 (*one/a road*) yī tiáo sījīn 一条丝巾 (*one/a silk scarf*) yī tiáo xiàn 一条线 (*one/a string*)

MEASURE WORD	CATEGORY	EXAMPLES
pán 盘	*something round and flat or shaped like a plate*	yī pán wéiqí 一盘围棋 *(one/a game of Chinese checkers)* yī pán cídài 一盘磁带 *(one/a tape)*

c. Containers that function as measure words

MEASURE WORD	CATEGORY	EXAMPLES
bēi 杯	*cup*	yī bēi shuǐ 一杯水 *(one/a cup of water)*
dài 袋	*bag*	yī dài píngguǒ 一袋苹果 *(one/a bag of apples)*
pán 盘	*plate*	yī pán cài 一盘菜 *(one/a dish)*
xiāng 箱	*box*	yī xiang lajī 一箱垃圾 *(one/a box of rubbish)*

d. Measure words denoting quantity

MEASURE WORD	CATEGORY	EXAMPLES
duì 对	*pair*	yī duì ěrhuán 一对耳环 *(a pair of earrings)*
shuāng 双	*pair*	yī shuāng wàzi 一双袜子 *(one/a pair of socks)* yī shuāng yǎnjing 一双眼睛 *(one/a pair of eyes)*
fù 副	*pair*	yī fù yǎnjìng 一副眼镜 *(one/a pair of glasses)*

MEASURE WORD	CATEGORY	EXAMPLES
qún 群	*group*	yī qún yāzi 一群鸭子 *(one/a group of ducks)* yī qún rén 一群人 *(one/a group of people)*
dá 打	*dozen*	yī dá jīdàn 一打鸡蛋 *(one/a dozen eggs)*
chuàn 串	*cluster*	yī chuàn pútáo 一串葡萄 *(one/a cluster of grapes)*

f. Amounts or portions of things

MEASURE WORD	CATEGORY	EXAMPLES
kuài 块	*piece*	yī kuài dàngāo 一块蛋糕 *(one/a piece of cake)*
dī 滴	*drop*	yī dī shuǐ 一滴水 *(one/a drop of water)*
cè 册	*volume*	yī cè shū 一册书 *(one/a volume of a set of books)*

j. Units of measurement

cùn 寸	*inch*	chǐ 尺	*foot*
yīnglǐ 英里	*mile*	gōngchǐ/mǐ 公尺 / 米	*meter*
gōnglǐ 公里	*kilometer*	gōngjīn 公斤	*kilogram*
jīn 斤	*catty*	bàng 磅	*pound*

The table below shows the different units of measure used in mainland China, Taiwan and Hong Kong.

UNITS OF MEASURE	MAINLAND CHINA	TAIWAN	HONG KONG
Length	mǐ 米 (*meter*)/ gōnglǐ 公里 (*kilometer*)	mǐ 米 (*meter*)/ gōnglǐ 公里 (*kilometer*)	chǐ 尺(*foot*)/ gōnglǐ 公里 (*kilometer*)
Weight	gōngjīn 公斤 (*kilogram*)	gōngjīn 公斤 (*kilogram*)	bàng磅(*pound*)/ gōngjīn公斤 (*kilogram*)/ jīn 斤(*catty*)

k. The measure word gè 个

Used especially with those nouns that don't have particular measure words assigned or abstract things

yī ge píngguǒ 一个苹果	*one/an apple*
yī ge zhàoxiàngjī 一个照相机	*one/a camera*
yī ge xīngqī 一个星期	*one/a week*
yī ge mèng 一个梦	*one/a dream*
yī ge zhǔyi 一个主意	*one/an idea*

l. More than one measure word may be possible.

yī tái diànnǎo 一台电脑 *or* yī bù diànnǎo 一部电脑	*one/a computer*
yī ge diànyǐng 一个电影 *or* yī bù diànyǐng 一部电影	*one/a film*

8. VERB-OBJECT VERBS VS. TWO-SYLLABLE VERBS

"Verb-object" verbs, such as chīfàn 吃饭 (lit., to eat cooked rice), consist of a verb plus an implicit (often not translated) object in that order. They differ from ordinary two syllable verbs such as míngbái 明白 (to understand) and rènshi 认识 (to know someone) in that:

Only "verb-object" verbs can be split by a particle, such as le 了.

In adverbial constructions that follow the pattern verb + object + duplicated verb + de 得, only the verb of "verb-object" verbs is repeated.

Wǒ chīfàn. 我吃饭。	I eat.
Wǒ chīle fàn. 我吃了饭。	I ate.
Wǒ jiǎnchá le. 我检查了。	I examined (someone or something).
Wǒ (de) māma zuòfàn zuò de hěn hǎo. 我(的)妈妈做饭做得很好。	My mother cooks very well.

9. EXPRESSING *TO BE*

Use hěn 很 (very) not shì 是 to connect nouns and adjectives.

Tā hěn gāo. 他很高。	He is tall. (lit., he very tall)

Use shì 是 between a subject noun and a predicate noun in an equational sentence.

Měiguó de shǒudū shì Huáshèngdùn. 美国的首都是华盛顿。	America's capital is Washington.
Jīngyú shì yī zhǒng dòngwù. 鲸鱼是一种动物。	The whale is one kind of animal.

Shì 是 is used to indicate existence or a state of being (see 19 below).

10. VERB PARTICLES

In Chinese, time expressions often fulfill the role that tense endings and auxiliaries do in English.

Míngtiān wǒ chūchāi.	明天我出差。	*Tomorrow I'm going on a business trip.*

Verbal particles are used to encode information related to verbs such as completion, duration, and future intent.

a. Completed actions: Le 了

Le 了 indicates something is different from the way it was in the past and can be used to refer to things that have not yet happened.

Tā qùle Shànghǎi. 他去上海。	*He went to Shanghai.*
Qiūtiān láile. 秋天来了。	*Now it's autumn.*
Fēijī kuài qǐfēi le. 飞机快起飞了。	*The plane is about to take off.*

b. Actions that took place from a time in the past to now: Guò 过

Wǒ qù guò Zhōngguó. 我去过中国。	*I have been to China.*
Nǐ qù guò Zhōngguó méiyǒu? 你去过中国没有?	*Have you ever been to China?*
Wǒ qù guò. 我去过。	*Yes, I have been.*
Wǒ hái méi qùguò. 我还没去过。	*No, I haven't been yet.*
Wǒ méi(yǒu) qùguò. 我没（有）去过。	*No, I have never been before.*

c. Continuous actions and states: Zài 在 and Zhe 着

Zài 在 refers to a continuous activity.

Wǒ zài kànshū. 我在看书。	*I am reading.*
Tāmen zài gōngzuò. 他们在工作。	*They are working.*
Tā zài chuān yīfu. 她在穿衣服。	*She is putting on clothes.*

Zhe 着 refers to a state of events that continues in time.

Tā zhànzhe. 他站着。	*He is standing.*
Nǐ názhe yī běn shū. 你拿着一本 书。	*You are holding a book.*
Tā chuānzhe yī jiàn hóngsè de yīfu. 她穿着一件红色的衣服。	*She is wearing a red piece of clothing.*

d. Future actions: Huì 会

One use of huì is to express that an action will (possibly) take place in the future.

Wǒ míngtiān huì qù Shànghǎi.	我明天会去上海。	*I'll (probably) go to Shanghai tomorrow.*

11. NEGATION

Bù 不 is used with the present, future or continuous tense and zài.

Méiyǒu 没有 is used with completed actions (translated into present perfect in English).

Wǒ bù xǐhuan yú. 我不喜欢鱼。	*I don't like fish.*
Wǒ de māma hái méiyǒu chīfàn. 我的妈妈还没有吃饭。	*My mother hasn't eaten yet.*

12. COMMANDS

Commands are formed by simply using a verb without any subject. You can soften the tone of a command by using the particle ba 吧 after the verb. To make a negative command add bié 别 (or bùyào 不要) in front of the verb.

Shuì! 睡!	*Sleep!*
Shuì ba. 睡吧。	*Go to sleep.*
Bié shuì. 别睡。	*Don't sleep.*

13. ADVERBIAL USE OF DE 得

verb + de 得 + adjective

| Tā chī de hěn kuài. 他吃得很快。 | He eats very fast. |
| Nǐ shuō de hěn hǎo. 你说得很好。 | You speak very well. |

verb + object + verb + de 得 + adjective

| Wǒ shuō Zhōngwén shuō de hěn bù hǎo. 我说中文说得很不好。 | I don't speak Chinese very well. (lit., I speak Chinese not very well.) |

Note that, in Chinese characters, de 得 differs from the possessive de 的, although both have the same pronunciation.

14. QUANTIFIERS (*MANY, SOME, ALL, EVERY*)

hěn duō 很多 (*many*)	Zhōngguó yǒu hěn duō ré. 中国有很多人。	There are a lot of people in China.
bù shǎo 不少 (*many*)	Wǒ yǒu bù shǎo gǒu. 我有不少狗。	I have quite a few dogs.
yīxiē 一些 (*some*)	Tā yǒu yīxiē wèntí. 他有一些问题。	He has some questions.
quánbù 全部 (*all*)	Quánbù rén dōu zǒu le. 全部人都走了。	All the people are gone.
měi 每 (*every*) + measure word	Měi ge rén dōu zǒu le. 每个人都走了。	Everyone is gone.

All and *every* can formed by duplicating a measure word and using dōu 都 before the main verb. Used with subjects that denote two things or people, dōu 都 means both.

| Měi ge rén dōu xǐhuan tā. 每个人都喜欢他。 | Everyone likes him. (lit., All the people like him.) |

Běnběn shū dōu hěn guì. 本本书都很贵。	Every book is expensive./All books are expensive.
Huáng xiānsheng hé Huáng tàitai dōu bù zài. 黄先生和黄太太都不在。	Both Mr. Huang and Mrs. Huang are not here.
Bob, Bill hé Susie dōu shì xuésheng. 鲍勃，比尔和苏西是学生。	Bob, Bill, and Susie are all students.
Wǒmen dōu shì Měiguórén. 我们都是美国人。	We are all American.

15. COMPARISON

a. Comparative adjectives: A bǐ 比 B + adjective + (exact degree of difference)

Wǒ bǐ nǐ dà. 我比你大。	I am older than you. (lit., I am bigger than you.)
Zhè běn shū bǐ nà běn shū guì. 这本书比那本书贵。	This book is more expensive than that one.
Wǒ bǐ nǐ dà sān suì. 我比你大三岁。	I am three years older than you.

b. Comparative adverbs: A + verb + de bǐ 的比 + B + adverb

Wǒ zǒu de bǐ nǐ kuài. 我走得比你快。	I walk faster than you do.

c. Expressing similarity: yǒu ... nàme 有... 那么 (as ... as) or A + hé 和 + B + yīyàng 一样 + adjective

Wǒ yǒu nǐ nàme gāo. 我有你那么高。	I am as tall as you.
Wǒ hé nǐ yīyàng gāo. 我和你一样高。	I am as tall as you. (lit., I and you are the same height.)

d. Superlative: zuì 最 + adjective

Zhè jiā lǚdiàn zuì hǎo. 这家旅店最好。	*This hotel is the best.*
Tā de chē zuì kuài. 他的车最快。	*His car is the fastest.*

16. YES/NO QUESTIONS

a. The question particle ma 吗 (declarative sentence + ma 吗)

Nǐ qù ma? 你去吗?	*Do you go?*
Wǒ qù. 我去。	*Yes, I do.*
Zhāng xiānsheng zhù zài zhèr ma? 张先生住在这儿吗?	*Does Mr. Zhang live here?*
Tā zhù zài zhèr. 他住在这儿。	*Yes, he does.*
Tā pǎo de kuài ma? 他跑得快吗?	*Does he run fast?*
Tā pǎo de kuài. 他跑得快。	*Yes, he does.*

b. verb/adverb + bù 不 + verb/adverb

Nǐ qù bù qù? 你去不去?	*Do you go or not?*
Wǒ qù. 我去。	*Yes, I do.*
Tā pǎo de kuài bù kuài? 他跑得快不快?	*Does he run fast?*
Tā pǎo de kuài. 他跑得快。	*Yes, he does.*

c. ne 呢 (*how about … ?*)

Nǐ xǐhuan hē chá ma? 你喜欢喝茶吗?	*Do you like drinking tea?*
Wǒ xǐhuan. Nǐ ne? 我喜欢，你呢?	*Yes, I do. How about you?*

d. Answering yes/no questions

Repeat the (auxliary) verb in positive or negative form.

Nǐ shì Zhāng xiǎojie ma? 你是张小姐吗？	*Are you Miss Zhang?*
Wǒ shì. 我是。	*Yes, I am.*
Wǒ bù shì. 我不是。	*No, I am not.*
Nǐ huì shuō Yīngwén ma? 你会说英文吗？	*Do you know how to speak English?*
Wǒ huì. 我会。	*Yes, I do.*
Wǒ bù huì. 我不会。	*No, I don't.*

e. Answering negative questions

Opposite of English pattern

Nǐ méiyǒu qián ma? 你没有钱吗？	*Don't you have money?*
Bù shì. Wǒ yǒu. 不是。我有。	*Yes. I have (money). (lit., No. I have money.)*
Shì. Wǒ méiyǒu. 是。我没有。	*No. I don't (have money). (lit., Yes. I don't have money.)*

17. QUESTION WORDS

shénme 什么	*what*
shénme shíhou 什么时候	*when*
nǎli/nǎr 哪里／那儿	*where*
nǎ/něi + *measure word* 哪	*which (sg.)*
nǎ/něi + xiē 哪＋些	*which (pl.)*
shéi 谁	*who/whom*
duōshǎo qián 多少钱	*how much (money)*
duōshǎo/jǐ + *measure word* 多少／几	*how many*
duōshǎo 多少	*how much*

zěnme (yàng) 怎么（样）	*how*
wèishénme 为什么	*why*

Note: Question words do not move to the front of the sentence as they do in English. The order is that of so-called "echo questions," e.g. Tā shì shéi? 他／她是谁？ *Who is he/she?* (*lit., He/she is who?*).

18. USE OF THE PREPOSITION ZÀI 在 AND OTHER LOCATION WORDS

The preposition zài 在 (*at, in, on*) is used to specify location. No form of *to be* is necessary in Chinese.

Wǒ zài xuéxiào (lǐ). 我在学校（里）。	*I am in school.*
Tā zài Měiguó. 他在美国。	*He is in the U.S.*

qiánbiān 前边	*in front of*
hòubiān 后边	*behind*
shàngbiān 上边	*above*
xiàbiān 下边	*under*
zuǒbiān 左边	*the left*
yòubiān 右边	*the right*
pángbiān 旁边	*beside*
zhōngjiān 中间	*between*
lǐ(biān) 里（边）	*inside/in*
wàibiān 外边	*outside*

zài 在 + location word + place or object name

Wǒ de shū zài zhuōzi de xiàbiān. 我的书在桌子的下边。	*My book is under the table.*

Note: The positioning of zhōngjiān 中间 is different: "A hé B de zhōngjiān A 和 B 的 中间," where A and B are separate place names or words.

19. **THERE IS/ARE**: YǑU 有 AND SHÌ 是

place word + location word + yǒu 有 + subject

Xuéxiào (lǐ) yǒu hěnduō xuésheng. 学校（里）有很多学生。	*There are a lot of students in the school. (lit., School inside there are lots of students.)*
Gōngyuán lǐ yǒu yī tiáo gǒu. 公园里有一条狗。	*There is a dog in the park. (lit., Park inside there is a dog.)*

place word + location word + shì 是 + place word

Gōngyuán de hòubiān shì xuéxiào. 公园的后边是学校。	*There is a school behind the park. (lit., The back of the park is school.)*

Note: Shì 是 can only be used to assert the existence of singular nouns.

20. HERE IS A LIST OF THE ONE HUNDRED MOST ESSENTIAL CHINESE CHARACTERS:

CHARACTER	PRONUNCIATION	MEANING
一	yī	one
二	èr	two
三	sān	three
四	sì	four
五	wǔ	five
六	liù	six
七	qī	seven
八	bā	eight
九	jiǔ	nine
十	shí	ten
百	bǎi	hundred
千	qiān	thousand
万	wàn	ten thousand
大	dà	big
中	zhōng	middle
小	xiǎo	small
车	chē	car
电	diàn	electricity
云	yún	cloud
雨	yǔ	rain
火	huǒ	fire
水	shuǐ	water
山	shān	mountain
上	shàng	on, above
下	xià	under
左	zuǒ	left

CHARACTER	PRONUNCIATION	MEANING
右	yòu	*right*
前	qián	*in front of*
后	hòu	*behind*
书	shū	*book*
菜	cài	*dish, vegetable*
鸡	jī	*chicken*
鸭	yā	*duck*
牛	niú	*cow*
羊	yáng	*sheep*
猪	zhū	*pig*
鱼	yú	*fish*
酒	jiǔ	*wine*
笔	bǐ	*pen*
字	zì	*character*
是	shì	*to be*
几	jǐ	*several*
美	měi	*beautiful*
国	guó	*country*
高	gāo	*tall, high*
低	dī	*low*
不	bù	*not*
没	méi	*not to have*
有	yǒu	*to have, there is/there are*
也	yě	*also*
了	le	*(verb suffix)*
东	dōng	*east*
南	nán	*south*
西	xī	*west*

CHARACTER	PRONUNCIATION	MEANING
北	běi	*north*
人	rén	*people*
今	jīn	*at present*
我	wǒ	*I, me*
你	nǐ	*you*
他	tā	*he*
她	tā	*she*
来	lái	*come*
去	qù	*go*
们	men	*(plural particle)*
做	zuò	*do*
元	yuán	*dollar*
两	liǎng	*two*
再	zài	*again*
见	jiàn	*see*
刀	dāo	*knife*
分	fēn	*separate, minute, cent*
到	dào	*until, reach*
力	lì	*strength*
加	jiā	*plus*
又	yòu	*also*
口	kǒu	*mouth*
门	mén	*door*
叫	jiào	*call*
名	míng	*first name*
和	hé	*and*
茶	chá	*tea*
在	zài	*in, on, at*

CHARACTER	PRONUNCIATION	MEANING
坐	zuò	*sit*
报	bào	*report, newspaper*
外	wài	*outside*
内	nèi	*inside*
天	tiān	*sky*
太	tài	*too (excessive), very*
好	hǎo	*good, well*
姓	xìng	*last name*
学	xué	*learn*
文	wén	*written language*
家	jiā	*home, family*
写	xiě	*write*
对	duì	*correct*
老	lǎo	*old*
年	nián	*year*
月	yuè	*month, moon*
日	rì	*day, sun*
从	cóng	*from*

21. IMPORTANT SIGNS IN CHINESE CHARACTERS:

CHARACTER	MEANING
男	*Men*
女	*Women*
卫生间 *or* 厕所 *or* 洗手间	*Lavatory, Toilet, Restroom*
有人	*Occupied (lit., there is person)*
无人	*Vacant (lit., there is no person)*
不准抽烟	*No Smoking*
不准进入	*No Admittance*

CHARACTER	MEANING
敲	*Knock*
铃	*Ring, Bell*
私人	*Private*
查询	*Inquire Within*
停! / 止步!	*Stop!*
去!	*Go!*
小心!	*Look out!*
危险!	*Danger!*
慢走	*Go slowly!*
绕道	*Detour*
警告	*Caution*
保持右走	*Keep to the Right*
桥	*Bridge*
不准停车	*No Parking*
衣帽间	*Check Room*
兑换	*Money Exchange*
资料	*Information*
等候室	*Waiting Room*
不要伸出窗外	*Don't Lean Out (of the Window)*
飞机场	*Airport*
铁路	*Railroad*
快车	*Express (lit., fast car)*
慢车	*Local (lit., slow car)*
站	*Stop (bus, train, etc.)*
不可张贴	*Post No Bills*
修理中	*Under Repair*
入口	*Entrance*
出口	*Exit*

CHARACTER	MEANING
配家具房子	*Furnished Rooms*
房子	*House*
油漆未干	*Wet Paint*
十字路口	*Crossroads*
肉店	*Butcher*
饼店	*Bakery*
牛奶	*Milk*
裁缝店	*Tailor Shop*
鞋店	*Shoe Store*
理发店	*Barber Shop*
菜市场 / 市场	*Grocer, Market*
药房 / 药店	*Pharmacy, Drugstore*
糖果店	*Confectioner, Candy Store*
文具店	*Stationery Store*
信箱	*Mail Box*
酒吧	*Bar, Tavern*
公安局	*Police Station*
酒	*Wines*
油站	*Gas Station*
书店	*Book Store*
市政府	*City Hall*
点心 / 小吃	*Refreshments, Snacks*
(冷) 水	*(Cold) Water*
(热) 水	*(Hot) Water*

Glossary

English - Chinese

A

a few/a little yī diǎndiǎn 一点点
a little more of ... zài lái yìdiǎn ... 再来一点 ...
a long time hěn jiǔ 很久
a lot hěn duō 很多
a while yī huìr 一会儿
abdominal pain (to have) dùzi tòng 肚子痛
able (to be) kěyǐ 可以 (in terms of permission), néng(gòu) 能(够) (in terms of proficiency)
about dàgài 大概, dàyuē 大约
academic performance chéngjì 成绩
accounting kuàijì 会计
 accountant kuàijìshī 会计师
across the street duìmiàn 对面
address dìzhǐ 地址
adjectival particle de 的
adverbial particle de 得
after zhīhòu 之后
after that ránhòu 然后
afternoon xiàwǔ 下午
afterwards ránhòu 然后
again zài 再
ago yǐqián 以前
airport jīchǎng 机场
 airplane fēijī 飞机, fēijī chǎng 飞机场
alcoholic drink jiǔ 酒
all dōu 都
all gone guāng 光
allow (to) ràng 让
 allowed (to be) kěyǐ 可以
almost chàbùduō 差不多
 almost time to do something (lit. quickly ... as of now) Kuài ... le. 快. ... 了。
alright hǎo ba 好吧
also yě 也, háiyǒu 还有
always zǒngshì 总是
America Měiguó 美国
 American (people) Měiguórén 美国人
and hé 和
and (for connecting two adjectives or adverbs) yòu ... yòu ... 又 ... 又 ...
another zài lái ... 再来 ...
anyone shénme rén yě, shéi yě 什么人也, 谁也
anything shénme dōngxi yě 什么东西也
anywhere nǎr, nǎli yě 哪儿, 哪里也

apartment gōngyù 公寓
appear to be kàn qǐlái 看起来
apple píngguǒ 苹果
apply (to) shēnqǐng 申请
approximately dàgài 大概
April sì yuè 四月
around zuǒyòu 左右
as ... adjective/adverb as ... (used for people and things nearby) yǒu ... zhème 有 ... 这么
 as ... adjective/adverb as ... (used for people and things far away) yǒu ... nàme 有 ... 那么
ask (to) wèn 问
 ask directions (to) (lit., to ask the road) wènlù 问路
at zài 在
attend (a) class (to) shàngkè 上课
attend university (to) shàng dàxué 上大学
audit a class (to) pángtīng 旁听
August bā yuè 八月
aunt
 aunt (father's older brother's wife) bómǔ 伯母
 aunt (father's sister) gūgu 姑姑
 aunt (father's younger brother's wife) shěnshen 婶婶
 aunt (mother's brother's wife) jiùmǔ/jiùmā 舅母/舅妈
 aunt (mother's sister) yímǔ/yímā 姨母/姨妈
Australia Àozhōu 澳洲
 Australian Àozhōurén 澳洲人
autumn qiūtiān 秋天

B

back (body) bèibù 背部
bad huài 坏
badminton yǔmáoqiú 羽毛球
bag bāo 包
ball qiú 球
banana xiāngjiāo 香蕉
bandage to a wound (to) bāozā shāngkǒu 包扎伤口
baseball bàngqiú 棒球
basketball lánqiú 篮球
bathroom wèishēngjiān 卫生间
be (to) shì 是
 be (located) at (to) zài 在
beautiful piàoliang 漂亮
because yīnwèi 因为
bed chuáng 床

bedroom wòfáng 卧房
beef niúròu 牛肉
beer píjiǔ 啤酒
before zhīqián 之前
behind hòubiān 后边
belly dùzi 肚子
belt pídài 皮带
between zhōngjiān 中间
between … and … zài … hé … zhōngjiān 在 … 和 … 中间
bicycle zìxíngchē 自行车
big dà 大
biology shēngwù 生物
birthday shēngrì 生日
bitter kǔ 苦
black hēi 黑
black pepper hēi hújiāo 黑胡椒
bleed (to) liúxiě 流血
block lùkǒu 路口
blow (to) chuī 吹
blue lán 蓝
book shū 书
bookstore shūdiàn 书店
bookshelf shūjià 书架
boots xuēzi 靴子
boss lǎobǎn 老板
bottle píng 瓶
box hé 盒
boy nánháir 男孩儿, nánhái 男孩
bowl wǎn 碗
bread miànbāo 面包
breakfast zǎocān 早餐
bridge qiáo 桥
bring (to) gěi 给
bring me … Gěi wǒ … 给我
Britain Yīngguó 英国
British (people) Yīngguórén 英国人
brother (older) gēge 哥哥
brother (younger) dìdi 弟弟
brown zōngsè 棕色
building dàlóu 大楼
bunch (as in cluster) chuàn 串
bus gōngchē 公车
bus stop gōngchē zhàn 公车站
butter huángyóu 黄油
buy (to) mǎi 买

C

cabbage bāoxīncài 包心菜
cafeteria shítáng 食堂
cake dàngāo 蛋糕
calf xiǎotuǐ 小腿
call (to) jiào 叫
called (to be) (full name) jiào 叫
called (to be) (surname) xìng 姓
campus xiàoyuán 校园
can (noun) guàn 罐
Canada Jiānádà 加拿大
Cantonese Guǎngdōngrén 广东人
car chē, qìchē 车, 汽车
careful (to be) xiǎoxīn 小心
carp lǐyú 鲤鱼
carrot húluóbo 胡萝卜
carton hé 盒
cash xiànjīn 现金
cat māo 猫
catch a cold (to) zháoliáng 着凉
CD jīguāng chàngpiàn 激光唱片
celery qíncài 芹菜
cereal màipiàn 麦片
chair yǐzi 椅子
change (monetary) língqián 零钱
change trains/subways/buses (to) huàn chē 换车
check (payment) zhīpiào 支票
Check please! Qǐng nǐ jiézhàng! 请你结帐!
check (to) jiǎnchá 检查
check (someone's) pulse (to) bǎmài 把脉
cheek liǎnjiá 脸颊
chemistry huàxué 化学
chest xiōngbù 胸部
chest pain (to have) xiōngbù tòng 胸部痛
chicken jī 鸡
chicken meat (boneless) jīròu 鸡肉
China Zhōngguó 中国
Chinese (language) Zhōngwén 中文
Chinese (people) Zhōngguórén 中国人
Chinese cuisine Zhōngcài 中菜
chocolate qiǎokèlì 巧克力
chopsticks kuàizi 筷子
church jiàotáng 教堂
cinema diànyǐngyuàn 电影院
city chéngshì 城市
class kè 课

classmate tóngxué 同学

classroom jiàoshì 教室

classical music gǔdiǎn yīnyuè 古典音乐

clean gānjìng 干净

clean (to) qīnglǐ 清理

clock shízhōng 时钟

close (to) guān 关

clothes, clothing yīfu 衣服

clothing store fúzhuāng diàn 服装店

coat wàitào 外套

coffee kāfēi 咖啡

cold lěng 冷

cold (sickness) gǎnmào 感冒

colleague tóngshì 同事

color sè 色, yánsè 颜色

come (to) lái 来

come over (to) guòlái 过来

come in jìnlái 进来

company gōngsī 公司

comparatively bǐjiào 比较

computer diànnǎo 电脑

concentrate (to) jízhōng jīngshén 集中精神

Congratulations! Gōngxǐ nǐ! 恭喜你!

cook (to) shāocài 烧菜, shāofàn 烧饭, zuòfàn 做饭

cooked rice fàn 饭

cooking pēngrèn 烹饪

corner lùkǒu 路口

cost of living shēnghuófèi 生活费

cough késou 咳嗽

Could you ... ? (lit., bother you) máfan nǐ 麻烦你

Could I trouble you for ... Máfan nǐ gěi wǒmen ... 麻烦你给我们 ...

cousin

cousin (father's brother's daughter, older than you) tángjiě 堂姐

cousin (father's brother's daughter, younger than you) tángmèi 堂妹

cousin (father's brother's son, older than you) tánggē 堂哥

cousin (father's brother's son, younger than you) tángdì 堂弟

cross the street (to) guò mǎlù 过马路

crowded yōngjǐ 拥挤

cucumber huángguā 黄瓜

culottes qúnkù 裙裤

cup bēizi 杯子

currency unit, equivalent to the dollar unit yuán 元

colloquial word for yuán kuài 块

one one-hundredth of a yuán, equivalent to the cent fēn 分

one tenth of a yuán, equivalent to the dime jiǎo 角

colloquial word for jiǎo máo 毛

cycling qí zìxíngchē 骑自行车

D

dance (to) tiàowǔ 跳舞

dark shēn 深

daughter nǚ'ér 女儿

day tiān 天

deadline zuìhòu qīxiàn 最后期限

December shí'èr yuè 十二月

degree (temperature) dù 度

delicious hǎochī 好吃

department (college level) xì 系

department store bǎihuò gōngsī 百货公司

dessert tiándiǎn 甜点

diarrhea (to have) lā dùzi 拉肚子

dictionary zìdiǎn 字典

different bùtóng 不同

difficult nán 难

dim sum diǎnxīn 点心

dining room fàntīng 饭厅

dinner wǎncān 晚餐

dirty zāng 脏

discount (to give a) dǎzhé 打折

discuss (to) tántan 谈谈

dish of food cài 菜

dislike (to) bù xǐhuan 不喜欢

do (to) zuò 做

doctor yīshēng 医生

document wénjiàn 文件

dog gǒu 狗

Don't worry. Méi shì. 没事。

dormitory sùshè 宿舍

dress liányīqún 连衣裙

drink (to) hē 喝

drive (a car) (to) kāichē 开车

duck yā 鸭

E

each měi 每

ear ěrduo 耳朵

east dōng 东

eat (to) chī 吃
economize (to) shěng 省
egg(s) jīdàn 鸡蛋
eight bā 八
either … or … huòzhě 或者
elbow zhǒu 肘
electronics store (lit., home appliances
　store) jiāyòng diànqì diàn 家用电器店
elephant xiàng 象
eleven shíyī 十一
employee gùyuán 雇员
engineering gōngchéng 工程
　engineer gōngchéngshī 工程师
English (language) Yīngwén 英文
enlightened kāimíng 开明
even more gèng 更
evening wǎn 晚, wǎnshang 晚上
every měi 每
　every day měi tiān 每天
　everyone měi ge rén 每个人
　everything yīqiè 一切
examination kǎoshì 考试
examine (to) jiǎnchá 检查
exchange (to) huàn 换
Excuse me. Láojià. 劳驾。
Excuse me. (apologizing) Duìbùqǐ. 对不起。
　(asking for a favor), guì 费expensive
extracurricular activities kèwài huódòng
　课外活动
eye yǎnjing 眼睛

F

face liǎn 脸
familiar with (to be) shúxī 熟悉
family jiā 家
far yuǎn 远
fashionable shímáo 时髦
fast kuài 快
father fùqin 父亲
　dad bàba 爸爸
fax machine chuánzhēnjī 传真机
fear (to) pà 怕
February èr yuè 二月
feel (to) gǎndào 感到
　feel dizzy (to) tóuyūn 头晕
　feel nauseous (to) ěxin 恶心
　feel unwell(to) bù shūfu 不舒服
female nǚ 女

fever (to have a) fāshāo 发烧
fewer than (lit. not enough) bù gòu 不够
file dǎng'àn 档案, wénjiàn 文件
　filing cabinet dǎng'àn guì 档案柜
film diànyǐng 电影
finally zhōngyú 终于
find (to) zhǎo 找
fine hǎo 好
finger shǒuzhǐ 手指
　fingernail zhǐjia 指甲
finish class (to) fàngxué 放学
first xiān 先
fish yú 鱼
　fishing diàoyú 钓鱼
five wǔ 五
food fàn 饭, shíwù 食物
　food market càishìchǎng 菜市场
foot jiǎo 脚
football (American) gǎnlǎnqiú 橄榄球
for example bǐrú 比如
forehead étóu 额头
foreign wàiguó 外国
　foreign language wàiyǔ 外语
forget (to) wàng 忘
fork chāzi 叉子
forty sìshí 四十
four sì 四
France Fǎguó 法国
　French (people) Fǎguórén 法国人
　French (language) Fǎwén 法文
frequently jīngcháng 经常
Friday xīngqī wǔ 星期五
friend péngyou 朋友
from cóng 从
　from … to … cóng … dào … 从 … 到 …
fruit shuǐguǒ 水果

G

garlic suàntóu 蒜头
Germany Déguó 德国
　German (people) Déguórén 德国人
　German (language) Déwén 德文
get off (to) (a vehicle) xià chē 下车
get on (to) (a vehicle) shàng chē 上车
get out chùqù 出去
girl nǚháir 女孩儿, nǚhái 女孩, nǚháizi 女孩子
give (to) gěi 给
　Give me another … Zài gěi wǒ … 再给我 …

Give me … Gěi wǒ … 给我

give/get an injection (to) dǎ zhēn 打针

glass bēizi 杯子

glass (measure word) bēi 杯

go (to) qù 去

go to the hospital (to) qù yīyuàn 去医院

go abroad (to) chūguó 出国

Go ahead. Hǎo ba. 好吧。

go ahead (to) wǎng qián 往前, zǒu ba 走吧

go online (to) shàngwǎng 上网

go straight ahead (to) yīzhí wǎng qián zǒu 一直往前走

go to a clinic (to) qù zhěnsuǒ 去诊所

go to a movie/the movies (to) kàn diànyǐng 看电影

go to a stadium (to) qù tǐyùguǎn 去体育馆

go to class (to), to start class shàngkè 上课

go to school (to), to attend school shàngxué 上学

go to the beach (to) qù hǎitān 去海滩

go to work (to), be at work (to) shàngbān 上班

gold jīnsè 金色

good hǎo 好

goodbye zàijiàn 再见。

graduate (to) bìyè 毕业

graduate student yánjiūshēng 研究生

graduate school yánjiūyuàn, yánjiūsuǒ 研究院, 研究所

grandfather

grandfather (maternal side) wàigōng 外公

grandfather (paternal side) yéye 爷爷

grandmother

grandmother (maternal side) wàipó 外婆

grandmother (paternal side) nǎinai 奶奶

grape pútao 葡萄

grasp (to) bǎ 把

green lǜ 绿, lǜsè 绿色

grey huīsè 灰色

H

half bàn 半

ham huǒtuǐ 火腿

hand shǒu 手

happy kuàilè 快乐

hat màozi 帽子

have (to) yǒu 有

Do (you) have … ? … yǒu méiyǒu … ? … 有没有 … ?

Do you have … ? Nǐmen yǒu … ma? 你们有 … 吗?

don't/doesn't have méiyǒu 没有

have a chat (to) tántan 谈谈

Have a seat. Qǐng zuò. 请坐。

have fun (to) wán de kāixīn 玩得开心

have to (to) bìxū 必须

he tā 他

headache (to have a) tóu tòng 头痛

hear (to) tīngdào 听到

heel zúgēn 足跟

hello Nǐ hǎo. 你好。

help (to) bāngzhù 帮助

her (object pronoun) tā 她

her (possessive pronoun) tā de 她的

here zhèlǐ 这里

hers tā de 她的

hiking yuǎnzú 远足

him tā 他

his tā de 他的

history lìshǐ 历史

hit (to) dǎ 打

hobbies àihào 爱好

hockey qūgùnqiú 曲棍球

hold (to) ná 拿

holiday jiàqī 假期

home jiā 家

homework gōngkè 功课

Hongkongese Xiānggǎngrén 香港人

hospital yīyuàn 医院

hot là 辣, tàng 烫

hotel lǚguǎn 旅馆, lǚdiàn 旅店, jiǔdiàn 酒店

hour (amount of time) xiǎoshí 小时, zhōngtóu 钟头

hour (o'clock) diǎn, diǎn zhōng 点, 点钟

house fángzi 房子

how zěnme yang? 怎么样, zěnyàng 怎样

how far? yǒu duō yuǎn? 有多远?

how long? duōjiǔ 多久

how many? jǐ 几?

How much?/ How many? duōshǎo 多少

how to get to … ? zěnme zǒu 怎么走

hungry è 饿

husband xiānsheng 先生

I

I wǒ 我

I don't want to … Wǒ bù xiǎng … 我不想 …

I need … Wǒ yào … 我要 …

I would like to have ... Wǒ xiǎng yào ... 我想要 ...

I'm sorry Duìbùqǐ. 对不起。

I'm sorry. (lit., to find it embarrassing (to do something)) Bù hǎoyìsi. 不好意思。

ice cream bīngjílíng 冰激凌

if rúguǒ 如果

if ... (then) rǔguǒ ... jiù 如果 ... 就

illness bìng 病

in lǐ 里, zài 在

in a hurry, in a rush cōngmáng 匆忙

in addition háiyǒu 还有

in front of qiánbiān 前边, ménkǒu 门口

in style shímáo 时髦

in this/that case ... nà ... 那 ...

inexpensive piányi 便宜

inflammation fāyán 发炎

inside lǐbiān 里边

instant noodles fāngbiànmiàn 方便面

intelligent cōngmíng 聪明

interest xìngqù 兴趣

intersection lùkǒu 路口, shízì lùkǒu 十字路口

interview miànshì 面试

It's nothing. (Don't worry. No problem.) Méi shì. 没事。

it's only ... zhǐshì 只是

Italy Yìdàlì 意大利

Italian (people) Yìdàlìrén 意大利人

Italian (language) Yìdàlìwén 意大利文

its tā de 它的

J

jacket jiákè 夹克

January yī yuè 一月

Japan Rìběn 日本

Japanese (people) Rìběnrén 日本人

Japanese (language) Rìwén 日文

job gōngzuò 工作

jogging huǎnbùpǎo 缓步跑, mànpǎo 慢跑

jot something down (to) jì xiàlái 记下来

juice guǒzhī 果汁

July qī yuè 七月

June liù yuè 六月

just now gāngcái 刚才

K

keep (to) liú 留

kick (to) tī 踢

kilogram gōngjīn 公斤

kilometers gōnglǐ 公里

kind (noun) zhǒng 种

kitchen chúfáng 厨房

knife dāo 刀

knitting biānzhī 编织

know a fact (to), know something (to) zhīdào 知道

know (to) (someone) rènshi 认识

know how to (to) huì 会

L

laboratory shíyànshì 实验室

laborer gōngrén 工人

large dà 大

large (size) dàhào 大号

last month shàng ge yuè 上个月

last week shàng ge lǐbài 上个礼拜

last year qùnián 去年

late night snack yèxiāo 夜宵, xiāoyè 宵夜

law fǎlǜ 法律

lawyer lǜshī 律师

learn (to) xué 学

leave zǒu 走

Leave. (polite) Zǒu ba. 走吧。

leave a message (to) liúyán 留言

leave one's own country (to) chūguó 出国

left zuǒ 左

left side (of) (the) zuǒbiān 左边

leg tuǐ 腿

less and less or more and more yuè lái yuè 越来越

let (to) ràng 让

let me ràng wǒ 让我

let ... ràng ... ba 让 ... 吧

library túshūguǎn 图书馆

library card túshūzhèng 图书证

lie down (to) tǎng 躺

light qiǎn 浅

light green qiǎn lǜsè 浅绿色

like (to) xǐhuan 喜欢

lips zuǐchún 嘴唇

listen (to) tīng 听

live in (to) zhù zài 住在

lively, busy, bustling rènào 热闹

living room kètīng 客厅

lobster lóngxiā 龙虾

look (to) kàn 看

look for (to) zhǎo 找
love (to) ài 爱
lunch wǔcān 午餐

M

Mahjong Májiàng 麻将
major zhuānyè, zhǔxiū 专业, 主修
make (to) zuò 做
make a date (to) yuē 约
make a medical house call (a doctor) (to) chū
  zhěn 出诊
make a phone call (to) dǎ diànhuà 打电话
make an appointment (to) yuē 约, yùyuē 预约
male nán 男
man nánrén 男人
many, much hěn duō 很多
many times hěn duō cì 很多次
March sān yuè 三月
market shìchǎng 市场
May wǔ yuè 五月
May I . . . qǐng nǐ/nín 请你/您
May I ask . . . ? qǐng wèn 请问
May I have . . . ? (lit., Could you give me . . . ?)
  Nǐ kěyǐ gěi wǒ . . . ma? 你可以给我 . . . 吗?
maybe kěnéng 可能
me wǒ 我
meal fàn 饭
measure word for books, photo albums,
  magazines běn 本
measure word for cars, taxis, bicycles liǎng 两
measure word for plants kē 棵
measure word for bottled drinks píng 瓶
measure word for automobiles, bicycles,
  carts liàng 辆
measure word for garments worn over the
  lower half of the body, or for objects that
  are long and thin (scarves), also for animals
  (dogs, fish, bulls...) tiáo 条
measure word for garments worn over the upper part or full length of the body jiàn 件
measure word for knives bǎ 把
measure word for machines tái 台
measure word for meal dùn 顿
measure word for number of family members
  kǒu 口
measure word for objects that are pointed
  and thin, utensils, and some animals zhī 只
measure word for objects that are small and

round chuàn 串
measure word for objects that have a flat surface (tables, desks, chairs . . .) zhāng 张
measure word for people, cities, groups, and
  nations gè 个
measure word for small plants and
  vegetables kē 颗
measure word for soup, rice (bowl) wǎn 碗
measure word for tables, desks, chairs zhāng
  张
measure word for tile, tablets, other thin and
  flat objects piàn 片
measure word for water, coffee, tea, wine
  (cup, glass) bēi 杯
measure word of general unit for ordering
  food (dish, plate) pán 盘
meat ròu 肉
(medication) taken after a meal fàn hòu fú 饭
  后服
(medication) taken before a meal fàn qián fú
  饭前服
medium (size) zhōnghào 中号
meet (to) rènshi 认识
meeting huìyì 会议
have a meeting (to) kāihuì 开会
in a meeting (to be) kāihuì 开会
menu càidān 菜单
meters mǐ 米
midnight bànyè 半夜
milk niúnǎi 牛奶
milk tea nǎichá 奶茶
mine wǒ de 我的
minute fēn 分
minute(s) fēnzhōng 分钟, fēn 分
Miss xiǎojie 小姐
Monday xīngqī yī 星期一
money qián 钱
more and more yuè lái yuè 越来越
moreover érqiě 而且
morning zǎoshang 早上
mother mǔqīn 母亲
mom māma 妈妈
motorcycle mótuōchē 摩托车
mouth zuǐba 嘴巴, kǒu 口
movie diànyǐng 电影
movie theater diànyǐngyuàn 电影院
Mr. xiānsheng 先生
Mrs. tàitai 太太

museum bówùguǎn 博物馆
mushrooms mógu 蘑菇
music yīnyuè 音乐
must bìxū 必须
mustard jièmo 芥末
my wǒ de 我的

N

Nanjingese Nánjīngrén 南京人
napa cabbage báicài 白菜
napkin cānjīn 餐巾
near jìn 近
 nearby fùjìn 附近
neck bózi 脖子
neighbor línjū 邻居
never cónglái méiyǒu... 从来没有...
new xīn 新
newspaper bàozhǐ 报纸
next week xià ge lǐbài 下个礼拜
next month xià ge yuè 下个月
next year míngnián 明年
next to pángbiān 旁边
night wǎnshang 晚上
nine jiǔ 九
nineteen shíjiǔ 十九
Ninety jiǔshí 九十
no, not bù 不
 negative particle used for commands bié 别,
  bùyào 不要
 no need to bùyòng 不用
 No problem. Méi shì. 没事。Méiyǒu wèntí.
  没有问题。
 Not bad. Bùcuò. 不错
noisy chǎo 吵
noodles miàntiáo 面条
noon zhōngwǔ 中午
north běi 北
nose bízi 鼻子
novel xiǎoshuō 小说
November shíyī yuè 十一月
now xiànzài 现在
nurse hùshi 护士

O

o'clock diǎn, diǎn zhōng 点, 点钟
October shí yuè 十月
of course dāngrán 当然
office bàngōngshì 办公室

official Chinese currency Rénmínbì 人民币
often jīngcháng 经常
ok hǎo ba 好吧
 ... is it alright? ... hǎo bù hǎo? ... 好不好?
old (things) jiù 旧
on zài 在
 on (top of) shàngbiān 上边, shàng, 上
 on foot zǒulù 走路
 on the corner zài lùkǒu 在路口
 on/to the left zài zuǒbiān 在左边
 on the phone jiǎng diànhuà 讲电话
 on/to the right zài yòubiān 在右边
 on time zhǔnshí 准时
 on vacation fàngjià 放假
one yī 一
 one dozen yī dǎ 一打
 one hundred yībǎi 一百
 one million yībǎiwàn 一百万
 one more zài lái ... 再来 ...
 one thousand yīqiān 一千
onion yángcōng 洋葱
open (to) chǎngkāi 敞开
 open (the mouth) (to) zhāngkāi 张开
 open-minded kāimíng 开明
or (suggesting a preference) háishì 还是
orange (color) júsè 橘色
orange (fruit) júzi 橘子
order (to) (food) diǎn 点
 order a dish (to) diǎn cài 点菜
ought to yīnggāi 应该
our wǒmen de 我们的
ours wǒmen de 我们的
out of style guòshí 过时
outside wàibiān 外边
over there zài nàli 在那里

P

painting túhuà 图画
pair shuāng 双
pants kùzi 裤子
paper zhǐ 纸
parent jiāzhǎng 家长
park gōngyuán 公园
particle for softening commands ba 吧
particle indicating completion of an
 action guò 过
particle indicating an ongoing action zài 在
particle indicating an ongoing state of

being zhe 着
particle indicating that an action has been completed le 了
particle used for comparison (than) bǐ 比
part-time job jiānzhí 兼职
pay (to) fù 付
  pay by check (to) yòng zhīpiào fùqián 用支票付钱
  pay by credit card (to) shuākǎ 刷卡
  pay in cash (to) fù xiànjīn 付现金
Peking duck Běijīng (kǎo) yā 北京烤鸭
Pekingese Běijīngrén 北京人
pen bǐ 笔
pepper hújiāo 胡椒
perhaps kěnéng 可能
person, people rén 人
pharmacy yàofáng 药房
philosophy zhéxué 哲学
photograph zhàopiàn 照片
physics wùlǐ 物理
pink fěnhóngsè 粉红色
place lǐ 里
  placed first (to be) pái dì yī míng 排第一名
plan (to) dǎsuan 打算
plaster cast (to have a) dǎ shígāo 打石膏
plate pánzi 盘子
play (ball games with hands, bridge or drums) (to) dǎ 打
  play (piano) (to), to pluck tán 弹
  play a game (to) wán yóuxì 玩游戏
  play a sport (to) zuò yùndòng 做运动
  play ball (to) dǎ qiú 打球
  play drums (to) dǎ gǔ 打鼓
  play piano (to) tán gāngqín 弹钢琴
  play soccer (to) tī zúqiú 踢足球
  play the flute (to) chuī dízi 吹笛子
  play violin (to) lā xiǎotíqín 拉小提琴
please (used to make an invitation or ask a favor) qǐng 请
  Please say that again. Qǐng zài shuō yī cì. 请再说一次。
  Please sit. Qǐng zuò. 请坐。
  please … (lit., please you …) qǐng nǐ/nín 请你/您
poetry shī 诗
police officer jǐngchá 警察
  police station jǐngchá jú 警察局
polite kèqi 客气

popular liúxíng 流行
  pop music liúxíng yīnyuè 流行音乐
pork zhūròu 猪肉
  pork chop(s) zhūpái 猪排
  twice-cooked pork huíguōròu 回锅肉
possessive particle de 的
post office yóujú 邮局
potatoe(s) mǎlíngshǔ 马铃薯, tǔdòu 土豆
pound bàng 磅
practice (to) liànxí 练习
prefix for ordinal numbers dì 第
prepare (to) zhǔnbèi 准备
  prepare for a lesson (to) yùxí 预习
pretty piàoliang 漂亮
pretty good bùcuò 不错
principal xiàozhǎng 校长
printer dǎyìnjī 打印机, yìnbiǎojī 印表机
private tutoring sīrén bǔxí 私人补习
profession gōngzuò 工作
program, show jiémù 节目
pull (to) lā 拉
purple zǐsè 紫色
put (to) fàng 放

Q

quarter of an hour kè 刻
question particle ma 吗
quick kuài 快
quite tǐng 挺

R

radio shōuyīnjī 收音机
rainbow cǎihóng 彩虹
raincoat yǔyī 雨衣
read (to) kàn 看
  read a map (to) kàn dìtú 看地图
  read a book kàn shū 看书
red hóng 红, hóngsè 红色
  red wine hóngjiǔ 红酒
reference book cānkǎoshū 参考书
refrigerator bīngxiāng 冰箱
relatively bǐjiào 比较
remind (to) tíxǐng 提醒
rest (to) xiūxi 休息
restaurant cānguǎn 餐馆, fànguǎn 饭馆
restroom cèsuǒ 厕所, xǐshǒujiān 洗手间
review (to) wēnxí 温习
  review a lesson (to) fùxí 复习

ride (to) qí 骑

right yòu 右

  right side (of) (the) yòubiān 右边

ring jièzhi 戒指

road lù 路

roast kǎo 烤

  roast chicken kǎo jī 烤鸡

room fángjiān 房间

rose méiguì 玫瑰

Russian (language) Éwén 俄文

S

salad shālā 沙拉

salary xīnshuǐ 薪水

salty xián 咸

same yīyàng 一样

Saturday xīngqī liù 星期六

save (to) (as in to store up) chǔ 储, cún 存

say (to) shuō 说

scalding tàng 烫

scared of (to be) pà 怕

school xuéxiào 学校

season jìjié 季节

second(s) miǎo 秒

see (to) kànjiàn 看见, jiàn 见, kàn 看

  see a play (to) kàn xìjù 看戏剧

See you later! Děng huìr jiàn! 等会见!

  See you next time! Xià cì jiàn! 下次见!

  See you soon! Huítóu jiàn! 回头见!

self zìjǐ 自己

send a fax (to) fā chuánzhēn 发传真

September jiǔ yuè 九月

seven qī 七

several jǐ ge 几个

  several days jǐ tiān 几天

  several times jǐ cì 几次

Shanghaiese Shànghǎirén 上海人

she tā 她

ship chuán 船

shirt chènshān 衬衫

sister

  sister (older) jiějie 姐姐

  sister (younger) mèimei 妹妹

sore throat (to have a) sǎngzi tòng 嗓子痛

stomachache (to have a) wèi tòng 胃痛

shiver (to) fādǒu 发抖

shoes xiézi 鞋子

  shoestore xiédiàn 鞋店

shop shāngdiàn 商店

should yīnggāi 应该

shoulder jiānbǎng 肩膀

shrimp xiā 虾

shut (to) guān 关

sibling xiōngdìjiěmèi 兄弟姐妹

sick (to be) bìngle 病了

sidewalk rénxíngdào 人行道

silver yínsè 银色

sing (to) chànggē 唱歌

sit (to) zuò 坐

six liù 六

ski (to) huáxuě 滑雪

skirt qúnzi 裙子

skort qúnkù 裙裤

sleep (to) shuì 睡

  sleep (to) shuìjiào 睡, 睡觉

slice (measure word) piàn 片

slow, slowly màn 慢

small xiǎo 小, xiǎohào 小号

  small town xiǎo zhèn 小镇

sneakers yùndòngxié 运动鞋

soccer (football) zúqiú 足球

socks wàzi 袜子

soda sūdǎ shuǐ 苏打水

sofa shāfā 沙发

some yīxiē 一些

  someone yǒu rén 有人

  something (yī)diǎn dōngxi, (yī)xiē dōngxi
    (一) 点东西, (一) 些东西

  something to drink hē de 喝的

son érzi 儿子

soup tāng 汤

sour suān 酸

south nán 南

soy sauce jiàngyóu 酱油

Spain Xībānyá 西班牙

  Spanish (people) Xībānyárén 西班牙人

  Spanish (language) Xībānyáwén 西班牙文

spare ribs páigǔ 排骨

speak (to) shuō 说

spicy là 辣

spoon tāngchí 汤匙, sháozi 勺子

sport tǐyù 体育

spring chūntiān 春天

  spring rolls chūnjuǎn 春卷

staff yuángōng 员工, gōngzuò rényuán 工作人员

stand (to) zhàn 站

start (to) kāishǐ 开始
stay (to) dāi 待 (呆), liú 留
steak niúpái 牛排
steamed qīng zhēng 清蒸
  steamed fish qīng zhēng yú 清蒸鱼
still haí 还
stir-fried chǎo 炒
stir-fried dish chǎocài 炒菜
stitch up (to) (a wound) féngxiàn 缝线
store shāngdiàn 商店
  store clerk shòuhuòyuán 售货员
straight yīzhí 一直
street jiē 街
string beans sìjìdòu 四季豆
strong qiángzhuàng 强壮
student xuésheng 学生
study (to) xué 学
style kuǎnshì 款式
submit homework (to) jiāo gōngkè 交功课
subway dìtiě 地铁
  subway station dìtiě zhàn 地铁站
such as bǐrú 比如
sugar táng 糖
summer xiàtiān 夏天
Sunday xīngqī tiān 星期天
supper wǎncān 晚餐
supplement (to) (money) bāngbǔ 帮补
surname xìng 姓
sweater máoyī 毛衣
sweet tián 甜
swim (to) yóuyǒng 游泳

T

table zhuōzi 桌子
Taiji / Tai Chi Tàijíquán 太极拳
take (to) ná 拿
  take (to) (a form of transportation) zuò 坐, dā 搭
  take a business trip (to) chūchāi 出差
  take a cardiogram (to) zuò xīndiàntú 做心电图
  take medicine (to) chī yào 吃药
  take personal leave (to) qǐng (shì)jià 请事假
  take sick leave (to) qǐng bìngjià 请病假
  take (someone's) temperature (to) liáng tǐwēn 量体温
tall gāo 高
taste (to) cháng 尝
taxi chūzūchē 出租车
tea chá 茶

teach (to) jiāo 教
teacher lǎoshī 老师
telephone diànhuà 电话
  telephone booth diànhuàtíng 电话亭
television diànshì 电视
temperature (body) tǐwēn 体温
ten shí 十
ten thousand yīwàn 一万
tender nèn 嫩
tennis wǎngqiú 网球
test (to) kǎo 考
  test, to take an exam kǎoshì 考试
textbook kèběn 课本
Thank you. Xièxie. 谢谢。
that nà 那
the best zuì hǎo de 最好的
the most zuì 最
the year after next hòunián 后年
the year before last qiánnián 前年
theater xìyuàn 戏院
their/theirs tāmen de 他们的
them tāmen 他们
then ránhòu 然后
there nàli 那里
there is/there are yǒu 有
therefore suǒyǐ 所以
these zhèxiē 这些
they tāmen 他们
thigh dàtuǐ 大腿
think (to) xiǎng 想
thirteen shísān 十三
thirty sānshí 三十
this zhè 这
  this afternoon jīntiān xiàwǔ 今天下午
  this month zhège yuè 这个月
  this morning jīntiān zǎoshang 今天早上
  this way zhèbiān 这边
  this week zhège lǐbài 这个礼拜
  this year jīnnián 今年
those nàxiē 那些
three sān 三
throat sǎngzi 嗓子
Thursday xīng qī sì 星期四
ticket piào 票
tidy (to) qīnglǐ 清理
tie the score (to) dǎ chéng píngshǒu 打成平手
tight jǐn 紧
time (in broad terms) shíhou 时候

time (in hours and minutes) shíjiān 时间
time off fàngjià 放假
time(s) biàn 遍, cì 次
to, before (ten minutes to/before one o'clock) chà (chà shí fēn yī diǎn), 差 (差十分一点)
today jīntiān 今天
together yīqǐ 一起
tomato fānqié 番茄
tomorrow míngtiān 明天
the day after tomorrow hòutiān 后天
tongue shétou 舌头
tonight jīntiān wǎnshang 今天晚上
too tài 太
tooth yáchǐ 牙齿
traditional Chinese dress qípáo 旗袍
traffic light hónglǜdēng 红绿灯
train station huǒchēzhàn 火车站
travel lǚxíng 旅行
trendy liúxíng 流行
trouble (to) máfan 麻烦
trunk bízi 鼻子
T-shirt T-xùshān/hànshān T-恤衫/汗衫
Tuesday xīngqī èr 星期二
turn
turn around the corner guǎi ge wān 拐个弯
turn left wǎng zuǒ zhuǎn 往左转
turn right wǎng yòu zhuǎn 往右转
twelve shí'èr 十二
twenty èrshí 二十
two èr 二
two (used to describe amount) liǎng 两

U

uncle
uncle (father's older brother) bóbo 伯伯
uncle (father's sister's husband) gūfu 姑夫
uncle (father's younger brother) shūshu 叔叔
uncle (mother's brother) jiùjiu 舅舅
uncle (mother's sister's husband) yífu 姨夫
under xiàbiān, xià 下边, 下
underpants nèikù 内裤
underpass rénxíng dìdào 人行地道
understand (to) míngbái 明白
university dàxué 大学
us wǒmen 我们
usually tōngcháng 通常

V

vacation jiàqī 假期
vanilla xiāngcǎo 香草
vegetables shūcài 蔬菜
vegetarian chīsù 吃素
very fēicháng 非常, tǐng挺, hěn很
volleyball páiqiú 排球
vomit (to) tùle吐了

W

wait (to) děng 等
walk (to) zǒu 走
want (to) yào 要
Do you want … ? Nǐ yào…ma? 你要 … 吗?
want (to), would like … xiǎng 想
wash (to) xǐ 洗
watch shǒubiǎo 手表
watch (to) kàn 看
watch TV (to) kàn diànshì 看电视
water shuǐ 水
we wǒmen 我们
wear (to) chuān 穿
Wednesday xīngqī sān 星期三
week xīngqī 星期
week lǐbài 礼拜
weekday (lit., workday) gōngzuòrì 工作日
weekend zhōumò 周末
well hǎo 好
well … nà 那
west xī 西
western cuisine xī càn 西餐
what shénme 什么
What nationality? Nǎ guórén? 哪国人?
what time shénme shíhou 什么时候
What time is it now? Xiànzài jǐdiǎn? 现在几点?
what time? jǐdiǎn 几点
what's more … érqiě 而且
when jǐdiǎn 几点, shénme shíhou 什么时候
where nǎli 哪里
Where (at)? Where is … ? zài nǎli? 在哪里?
which nǎ 哪
which day nǎ tiān 哪天
which place nǎli 哪里
which station nǎge zhàn 哪个站
white bái, báisè 白, 白色
who, whom shéi 谁
whole body quánshēn 全身

why wèishénme 为什么
wife tàitai 太太
will huì 会
wine hóngjiǔ 红酒, jiǔ 酒
winter dōngtiān 冬天
woman nǚrén 女人
work gōngzuò 工作
   work overtime (to) jiābān 加班
   worker gōngrén 工人
wrist shǒuwàn 手腕
writing xiězuò 写作

Y

year nián 年
yellow huáng 黄, huángsè 黄色
yesterday zuótiān 昨天
   the day before yesterday qiántiān 前天
yoga yújiā 瑜伽
you nǐ 你
you (plural) nǐmen 你们
You're welcome. Bù kèqi. 不客气。
young lady xiǎojie 小姐
young, youthful niánqīng 年轻
your (plural) nǐmen de 你们的
your (singular) nǐ de 你的
your (fml.) nín de (fml.) 您的 (fml.)
yours (fml., plural) nǐmen de 你们的

Z

zero líng 零

Chinese - English

A

ài 爱 to love
àihào 爱好 hobbies
Àozhōu 澳洲 Australia
Àozhōurén 澳洲人 Australian

B

bā yuè 八月 August
bā 八 eight
ba 吧 particle for softening commands
bǎ 把 to grasp, measure word for knives
bàba 爸爸 dad
bái 白 white
báicài 白菜 napa cabbage
bǎihuò gōngsī 百货公司 department store
báisè 白色 white
bǎmài 把脉 to check (someone's) pulse
bàngōngshì 办公室 office
bàn 半 half
bàngqiú 棒球 baseball
bàng 磅 pound
bāngbǔ 帮补 to supplement (money)
bāngzhù 帮助 to help
bànyè 半夜 midnight
bāo 包 bag
bāoxīncài 包心菜 cabbage
bāozā shāngkǒu 包扎伤口 to bandage to a wound
bàozhǐ 报纸 newspaper
bēi 杯 measure word for water, coffee, tea, wine; cup, glass
běi 北 north
bèibù 背部 back
Běijīng (kǎo) yā 北京烤鸭 Peking duck
Běijīngrén 北京人 Pekingese
bēizi 杯子 cup, glass
běn 本 measure word for books, photo albums, magazines
bǐ 比 particle used for comparison (than)
bǐ 笔 pen
biàn 遍 times
biānzhī 编织 knitting
biǎodì 表弟 cousin (mother's sibling's or father's sister's son, younger than you)
biǎogē 表哥 cousin (mother's sibling's or father's

sister's son, older than you)

biǎojiě 表姐 cousin (mother's sibling's or father's sister's daughter, older than you)

biǎomèi 表妹 cousin (mother's sibling's or father's sister's daughter, younger than you)

bié 别 negative particle used for commands

bǐjiào 比较 relatively, comparatively

bìng 病 illness

bīngjílíng 冰激凌 ice cream

bìngle 病了 be sick

bīngxiāng 冰箱 refrigerator

bǐrú 比如 such as, for example

bìxū 必须 to have to, must

bìyè 毕业 to graduate

bízi 鼻子 nose, trunk

bóbo 伯伯 uncle (father's older brother)

bómǔ 伯母 aunt (father's older brother's wife)

bówùguǎn 博物馆 museum

bózi 脖子 neck

bù 不 no, not

bùcuò 不错 pretty good, not bad

bù gòu 不够 fewer than (lit. not enough)

Bù hǎoyìsi. 不好意思。 I'm sorry. (lit., to find it embarrassing (to do something))

Bù kèqi. 不客气。 You're welcome.

bù shūfu 不舒服 to feel unwell

bù xǐhuan 不喜欢 to dislike

bùtóng 不同 different

bùyào 不要 negative particle used for commands

bùyòng 不用 no need to

C

cài 菜 dish of food

càidān 菜单 menu

cǎihóng 彩虹 rainbow

càishìchǎng 菜市场 food market

cānguǎn 餐馆 restaurant

cānjīn 餐巾 napkin

cānkǎoshū 参考书 reference book

cèsuǒ 厕所 restroom

chá 茶 tea

chà (chà shí fēn yī diǎn) 差 (差十分一点) to, before (ten minutes to/before one o'clock)

chàbùduō 差不多 almost

cháng 尝 to taste

chǎng 敞 to open

chànggē 唱歌 to sing

chǎo 吵 noisy

chǎo 炒 stir-fried

chǎocài 炒菜 stir-fried dish

chāzi 叉子 fork

chē 车 car

chéngjì 成绩 academic performance

chéngshì 城市 city

chènshān 衬衫 shirt

chī yào 吃药 to take medicine

chī 吃 to eat

chīsù 吃素 vegetarian

chū zhěn 出诊 to make a medical house call (a doctor)

chǔ 储 to save

chuàn 串 measure word for objects that are small and round, bunch, cluster

chuān 穿 to wear

chuán 船 ship

chuáng 床 bed

chuánzhēnjī 传真机 fax machine

chūchāi 出差 to take a business trip

chúfáng 厨房 kitchen

chūguó 出国 to leave one's own country, to go abroad

chuī dízi 吹笛子 to play the flute

chuī 吹 to blow

chūnjuǎn 春卷 spring rolls

chūntiān 春天 spring

chūzūchē 出租车 taxi

cì 次 time(s)

cóng 从 from

cóng … dào … 从 … 到 … from … to …

cónglái méiyǒu 从来没有 never

cōngmáng 匆忙 in a hurry, in a rush

cōngmíng 聪明 intelligent

cún存:: to store up

D

dǎ chéng píngshǒu 打成平手 to tie the score

dǎ diànhuà 打电话 to make a phone call

dǎ gǔ 打鼓 to play drums

dǎ qiú 打球 to play ball

dǎ shígāo 打石膏 to have a plaster cast

dǎ zhēn 打针 to give/get an injection

dà 大 large, big

dǎ 打 to hit, to play (ball games with hands, bridge, and drums)

dā 搭 take (a form of transportation)

dàgài 大概 approximately, about

dàhào 大号 large (size)
dāi 待 (呆) to stay
dàlóu 大楼 building
dàngāo 蛋糕 cake
dǎng'àn 档案 file
dǎng'àn guì 档案柜 filing cabinet
dāngrán 当然 of course
dāo 刀 knife
dǎsuan 打算 to plan
dàtuǐ 大腿 thigh
dǎyìnjī 打印机 printer
dàxué 大学 university
dàyuē 大约 about
dǎzhé 打折 to give a discount
de 得 adverbial particle
de 的 adjectival particle, possessive particle
Déguó 德国 Germany
Déguórén 德国人 German (people)
Děng huìr jiàn! 等会见! See you later!
děng 等 to wait
Déwén德文 German (language)
dì 第 prefix for ordinal numbers
diǎn cài 点菜 to order a dish
diǎn 点 to order (food); o'clock
diǎn zhōng点钟 o'clock, hour
diànhuà 电话 telephone
diànhuàtíng 电话亭 telephone booth
diànnǎo 电脑 computer
diànshì 电视 television
diǎnxīn 点心 dim sum
diànyǐng 电影 film, movie
diànyǐngyuàn 电影院 cinema, movie theater
diàoyú 钓鱼 fishing
dìdi 弟弟 younger brother
dìtiě 地铁 subway
dìtiě zhàn 地铁站 subway station
dìzhǐ 地址 address
dōng 东 east
dōngtiān 冬天 winter
dōu 都 all
dù 度 degree (temperature)
Duìbùqǐ. 对不起。 Excuse me. (apologizing)
duìmiàn 对面 across the street
dùn 顿 measure word for meal
duōjiǔ 多久 how long?
duōshǎo 多少 how much
dùzi tòng 肚子痛 to have abdominal pain
dùzi 肚子 belly

E

è 饿 hungry
èr yuè 二月 February
èr 二 two
ěrduo 耳朵 ear
érqiě 而且 moreover, what's more …
èrshí 二十 twenty
érzi 儿子 son
étóu 额头 forehead
Éwén俄文 Russian (language)
ěxin 恶心 to feel nauseous

F

fā chuánzhēn 发传真 to send a fax
fādǒu 发抖 to shiver
Fǎguó 法国 France
Fǎguórén 法国人 French (people)
fǎlǜ 法律 law
fàn hòu fú 饭后服 (medication) taken after a meal
fàn qián fú 饭前服 (medication) taken before a meal
fàn 饭 meal, food (lit., cooked rice)
fàndiàn 饭店 hotel
fàng 放 to put
fāngbiànmiàn 方便面 instant noodles
fàngjià 放假 on vacation, time off
fángjiān 房间 room
fànguǎn 饭馆 restaurant
fàngxué 放学 to finish class
fángzi 房子 house
fānqié 番茄 tomato
fàntīng 饭厅 dining room
fāshāo 发烧 to have a fever
Fǎwén法文 French (language)
fāyán 发炎 inflammation
fēicháng 非常 very
fēijī 飞机 airplane
fēijī chǎng 飞机场 airport
fēn 分 minute
fēn 分 one one-hundredth of a yuán, equivalent to the cent; minute(s)
féngxiàn 缝线 to stitch up (a wound)
fěnhóngsè 粉红色 pink
fēnzhōng 分钟 minute(s)
fù xiànjīn 付现金 to pay in cash
fù 付 to pay
fùjìn 附近 nearby

fùqin 父亲 father
fùxí 复习 to review a lesson
fúzhuāng diàn 服装店 clothing store

G

gǎndào 感到 to feel
gāngcái 刚才 just now
gānjìng 干净 clean
gǎnlǎnqiú 橄榄球 football (American)
gǎnmào 感冒 a cold
gāo 高 tall
gè 个 measure word for people, cities, groups, and nations
gēge 哥哥 older brother
Gěi wǒ … 给我 bring me … , give me …
gěi 给 to bring, to give
gèng 更 even more
Gōng xǐ nǐ! 恭喜你! Congratulations!
gōngchē 公车 bus
gōngchē zhàn 公车站 bus stop
gōngchéng shī 工程师 engineer
gōngchéng 工程 engineering
gōngjīn 公斤 kilogram
gōngkè 功课 homework
gōnglǐ 公里 kilometers
gōngrén 工人 laborer, worker
gōngsī 公司 company
gōngyù 公寓 apartment
gōngyuán 公园 park
gōngzuò rényuán 工作人员 staff
gōngzuò 工作 work, job, profession
gōngzuòrì 工作日 weekday (lit., workday)
gǒu 狗 dog
guǎi ge wān 拐个弯 turn around the corner
guān 关 shut, close
guàn 罐 can (noun)
guāng 光 all gone
Guǎngdōngrén 广东人 Cantonese
gǔdiǎn yīnyuè 古典音乐 classical music
gūfu 姑夫 uncle (father's sister's husband)
gūgu 姑姑 aunt (father's sister)
guì 贵 expensive
guò mǎlù 过马路 to cross the street
guò 过 particle indicating completion of an action
guòlái 过来 to come over
guòshí 过时 out of style
guǒzhī 果汁 juice
gùyuán 雇员 employee

H

hái 还 still
háishì 还是 or (suggesting a preference)
háiyǒu 还有 also, in addition
hànshān 汗衫 T-shirt
hǎo ba 好吧 ok, alright, go ahead
… hǎo bù hǎo? … 好不好? … is it alright?
hǎo 好 good, fine,well
hǎochī 好吃 delicious
hē de 喝的 something to drink
hé 和 and
hē 喝 to drink
hé 盒 box, carton
hēi hújiāo 黑胡椒 black pepper
hēi 黑 black
hēisè 黑色 black
hěn duō cì 很多次 many times
hěn duō 很多 a lot, many, much
hěn jiǔ 很久 a long time
hěn, tǐng 很, 挺 very
hóng shāo zhūròu, hóng shāo ròu 红烧猪肉, 红烧肉 braised pork
hóng shāo 红烧 braised (in soy sauce)
hóng 红 red
hóngjiǔ 红酒 red wine
hónglǜdēng 红绿灯 traffic light
hóngsè 红色 red
hòubiān 后边 behind
hòunián 后年 the year after next
hòutiān 后天 the day after tomorrow
huáxuě 滑雪 to ski
huài 坏 bad
huàn chē 换车 to change trains/subways/buses
huàn 换 to exchange
huǎnbùpǎo 缓步跑 jogging
huáng 黄 yellow
huángguā 黄瓜 cucumber
huángsè 黄色 yellow
huángyóu 黄油 butter
huàxué 化学 chemistry
huì 会 to know how to, will
huíguōròu 回锅肉 twice-cooked pork
huīsè 灰色 grey
Huítóu jiàn! 回头见! See you soon!
huìyì 会议 meeting
hújiāo 胡椒 pepper
húluóbo 胡萝卜 carrot

huǒchēzhàn 火车站 train station
huǒtuǐ 火腿 ham
huòzhě 或者 either … or …
hùshi 护士 nurse

J

jī 鸡 chicken
jǐ cì 几次 several times
jǐ ge 几个 several
jǐ tiān 几天 several days
jì xiàlái 记下来 to jot something down
jǐ 几 how many
jiā 家 family, home
jiābān 加班 to work overtime
jiákè 夹克 jacket
jiàn 件 measure word for garments worn over the upper part or full length of the body
jiàn 见 to see
Jiānádà 加拿大 Canada
jiānbǎng 肩膀 shoulder
jiǎnchá 检查 to examine, to check
jiǎng diànhuà 讲电话 on the phone
jiàngyóu 酱油 soy sauce
jiānzhí 兼职 part-time job
jiāo gōngkè 交功课 to submit homework
jiào 叫 to call, to be called
jiāo 教 to teach
jiǎo 脚 foot
jiǎo 角 one tenth of a yuán,
jiàoshì 教室 classroom
jiàotáng 教堂 church
jiàqī 假期 holiday, vacation
jiāyòng diànqì diàn 家用电器店 electronics store (lit., home appliances store)
jiāzhǎng 家长 parent
jīchǎng 机场 airport
jīdàn 鸡蛋 egg(s)
jǐdiǎn 几点 what time?, when?
jiē 街 street
jiémù 节目 program, show
jiějie 姐姐 older sister
jièmo 芥末 mustard
jièzhi 戒指 ring
jīguāng chàngpiàn 激光唱片 CD
jìjié 季节 season
jǐn 紧 tight
jìn 近 near
jǐngchá jú 警察局 police station

jǐngchá 警察 police officer
jīngcháng 经常 often, frequently
jìnlái 进来 come in
jīnnián 今年 this year
jīnsè 金色 gold
jīntiān wǎnshang 今天晚上 tonight
jīntiān xiàwǔ 今天下午 this afternoon
jīntiān zǎoshang 今天早上 this morning
jīntiān 今天 today
jīròu 鸡肉 chicken meat (boneless)
jiǔ yuè 九月 September
jiǔ 九 nine
jiù 旧 old (things)
jiǔ 酒 wine, alcoholic drink
jiùjiu 舅舅 uncle (mother's brother)
jiùmǔ/jiùmā 舅母, 舅妈 aunt (mother's brother's wife)
jiǔshí 九十 ninety
jízhōng jīngshén 集中精神 to concentrate
júsè 橘色 orange (color)
júzi 橘子 orange (fruit)

K

kāfēi 咖啡 coffee
kāichē 开车 to drive (a car)
kāihuì 开会 in a meeting, to have a meeting
kāimíng 开明 open-minded, enlightened
kāishǐ 开始 to start
kàn 看 to see, to look, to read
kàn diànyǐng 看电影 to go to a movie/the movies
kàn dìtú 看地图 to read a map
kàn qǐlái 看起来 appear(s) to be
kàn shū 看书 read a book
kàn xìjù 看戏剧 to see a play
kànjiàn 看见 to see
kǎo jī 烤鸡 roast chicken
kǎo 烤 roast
kǎo 考 to test
kǎoshì 考试 test, examination, to take an exam
kěnéng 可能 maybe, perhaps
kè 课 class
kè 刻 quarter of an hour
kē 棵 measure word for plants and grass
kē 颗 measure word for small plants and vegetables
kèběn 课本 textbook
kèqi 客气 polite
késou 咳嗽 cough

kètīng 客厅 living room

kèwài huódòng 课外活动 extracurricular activities

kěyǐ 可以 to be able (in terms of permission), to be allowed

kǒu 口 mouth; measure word for number of family members

kǔ 苦 bitter

Kuài … le 快　了 almost time to do something (lit. quickly … as of now)

kuài 块 colloquial word for yuán

kuài 快 fast, quick

kuàijìshī 会计师 accountant

kuàijì 会计 accounting

kuàilè 快乐 happy

kuàizi 筷子 chopsticks

kuǎnshì 款式 style

kùzi 裤子 pants

L

lā dùzi 拉肚子 to have diarrhea

lā xiǎotíqín 拉小提琴 to play violin

lā 拉 to pull

là 辣 hot, spicy

lái 来 to come

lánqiú 篮球 basketball

lán 蓝 blue

lánsè 蓝色 blue

lǎobǎn 老板 boss

Láojià. 劳驾。 Excuse me. (asking for a favor)

lǎoshī 老师 teacher

le 了 particle indicating that an action has been completed

lěng 冷 cold

lǐ 里 place, in

liǎn 脸 face

liáng tǐwēn 量体温 to take (someone's) temperature

liǎng 两 two (used to describe amount), measure word for cars, taxis, bicycles

liǎnjiá 脸颊 cheek

liànxí 练习 to practice

liányīqún 连衣裙 dress

lǐbài 礼拜 week

lǐbiān 里边 in, inside

lìjiāoqiáo 立交桥 overpass

líng 零 zero

língqián 零钱 change (monetary)

línjū 邻居 neighbor

lìshǐ 历史 history

liù yuè 六月 June

liù 六 six

liú 留 to stay, to keep

liúxiě 流血 to bleed

liúxíng yīnyuè 流行音乐 pop music

liúxíng 流行 popular, trendy

liúyán 留言 to leave a message

lǐyú 鲤鱼 carp

lóngxiā 龙虾 lobster

lǜ 绿 green

lù 路 road

lǚguǎn 旅馆 hotel

lùkǒu 路口 corner, intersection, block

lǜsè 绿色 green

lǜshī 律师 lawyer

lǚxíng 旅行 travel

M

ma 吗 question particle

máfan 麻烦 to trouble

　máfan nǐ 麻烦你 Could you…? (lit., bother you)

　Máfan nǐ gěi wǒmen … 麻烦你给我们 …
　　Could I trouble you for …

mǎi 买 to buy

màipiàn 麦片 cereal

Májiàng 麻将 Mahjong

mǎlíngshǔ 马铃薯 potatoes

māma 妈妈 mom

màn 慢 slow, slowly

mànpǎo 慢跑 jogging

māo 猫 cat

máo 毛 equivalent to the dime; colloquial word for jiāo

máoyī 毛衣 sweater

màozi 帽子 hat

měi ge rén 每个人 everyone

Méi shì. 没事。 It's nothing., Don't worry., No problem.

měi tiān 每天 every day

měi 每 every, each

méiguì 玫瑰 rose

Měiguó 美国 America

Měiguórén 美国人 American (people)

mèimei 妹妹 younger sister

Méiyǒu wèntí. 没有问题。 No problem.

méiyǒu 没有 don't/doesn't have

ménkǒu 门口 in front of (lit. at the door)
mǐ 米 meters
miànbāo 面包 bread
miànshì 面试 interview
miàntiáo 面条 noodles
miǎo 秒 second(s)
míngbai 明白 to understand
míngnián 明年 next year
míngtiān 明天 tomorrow
mógu 蘑菇 mushrooms
mótuōchē 摩托车 motorcycle
mǔqīn 母亲 mother

N

nǎge zhàn 哪个站 which station
Nǎ guórén? 哪国人? What nationality?
nǎ tiān 哪天 which day
nàxiē 那些 those
nǎ 哪 which
ná 拿 to hold, to take
nà 那 that
nà ... 那 ... that, well ..., in this/that case ...
nǎichá 奶茶 milk tea
nǎinai 奶奶 grandmother (paternal side)
nàli 那里 there
nǎli 哪里 where, which place
nǎli yě 哪里也 anywhere
nán 南 south
nán 男 male
nán 难 difficult
nánhái 男孩 boy
nánháir 男孩儿 boy
Nánjīngrén 南京人 Nanjingese
nánrén 男人 man
nǎr yě 哪儿也 anywhere
nèikù 内裤 underpants
nèn 嫩 tender
néng(gòu) 能够 to be able (in terms of proficiency)
nǐ 你 you
nǐ de 你的 your, yours (singular)
nǐ hǎo 你好 hello
Nǐ hǎo ma? 你好吗? How are you?
Nǐ kěyǐ gěi wǒ ... ma? 你可以给我 ... 吗?
   May I have... ? (lit., Could you give me ... ?)
Nǐ ne? 你呢? And you?
Nǐ yào...ma? 你要 ... 吗? Do you want ... ?
nián 年 year
niánqīng 年轻 young, youthful

nǐmen de 你们的 your, yours (plural)
Nǐmen yǒu ... ma? 你们有 ... 吗? Do you have
   ... ?
nǐmen 你们 you (plural)
nín de 您的 your/yours (fml.)
niúnǎi 牛奶 milk
niúpái 牛排 steak
niúròu 牛肉 beef
nǔ 女 female
nǔ'ér 女儿 daughter
nǔháir 女孩儿 girl
nǔháizi 女孩子 girl
nǔhái 女孩 girl
nǔrén 女人 woman

P

pà 怕 to be scared of, to fear
pái dì yī míng 排第一名 to be placed first
páigǔ 排骨 spare ribs
páiqiú 排球 volleyball
pán 盘 measure word of general unit of ordering
   food; dish, plate
pángbiān 旁边 next to
pángtīng 旁听 to audit a class
pánzi 盘子 plate
pēngrèn 烹饪 cooking
péngyou 朋友 friend
piào 票 ticket
piàn 片 measure word for tile, tablets, other thin
   and flat objects; slice
piányi 便宜 inexpensive
piàoliang 漂亮 beautiful, pretty
pídài 皮带 belt
píjiǔ 啤酒 beer
píng 瓶 measure word for bottled drinks; bottle
píngguǒ 苹果 apple
pútao 葡萄 grape

Q

qī 七 seven
qī yuè 七月 July
qí zìxíngchē 骑自行车 cycling
qí 骑 to ride
qiǎn lǜsè 浅绿色 light green
qiǎn 浅 light
qián 钱 money
qiánbiān 前边 in front of
qiángzhuàng 强壮 strong

qiánnián 前年 the year before last
qiántiān 前天 the day before yesterday
qiáo 桥 bridge
qiǎokèlì 巧克力 chocolate
qìchē 汽车 car
qíncài 芹菜 celery
qǐng 请 please (used to make an invitation or ask a favor)
qǐng (shì)jià 请（事）假 to take personal leave
qǐng bìngjià 请病假 to take sick leave
Qǐng nǐ jiézhàng! 请你结帐! Check please!
qǐng nǐ/nín 请你/您 please … (lit., please you …), may I …
qǐng wèn 请问 May I ask … ?
Qǐng zài shuō yī cì. 请再说一次。 Please say that again.
qīng zhēng yú 清蒸鱼 steamed fish
qīng zhēng 清蒸 steamed
Qǐng zuò. 请坐。 Have a seat., Please sit.
qīnglǐ 清理 to clean, to tidy
qípáo 旗袍 traditional Chinese dress
qiú 球 ball
qiūtiān 秋天 autumn
qù 去 to go
qù hǎitān 去海滩 to go to the beach
qù tǐyùguǎn 去体育馆 to go to a stadium
qù yīyuàn 去医院 to go the hospital
qù zhěnsuǒ 去诊所 to go to a clinic
quánshēn 全身 whole body
qūgùnqiú 曲棍球 hockey
qùnián 去年 last year
qúnkù 裙裤 culottes, skort
qúnzi 裙子 skirt

R

ràng … ba 让 … 吧 let …
ràng 让 to allow, to let
ràng wǒ 让我 let me
ránhòu 然后 after that, afterwards, then
rén 人 person, people
rènào 热闹 lively, busy, bustling
Rénmínbì 人民币 official Chinese currency
rènshi 认识 to know (someone), to meet
rénxíng dìdào 人行地道 underpass
rénxíngdào 人行道 sidewalk
Rìběn 日本 Japan
Rìběnrén 日本人 Japanese (people)
Rìwén 日文 Japanese (language)
ròu 肉 meat

rǔguǒ … jiù 如果 … 就 if … (then)
rúguǒ 如果 if

S

sān yuè 三月 March
sān 三 three
sǎngzi tòng 嗓子痛 to have a sore throat
sǎngzi 嗓子 throat
sānshí 三十 thirty
sè 色 color
shāfā 沙发 sofa
shālā 沙拉 salad
shàngbān 上班 to go to work, to be at work
shàng chē 上车 to get on (a vehicle)
shàng dàxué 上大学 to attend university
shàng ge lǐbài 上个礼拜 last week
shàng ge yuè 上个月 last month
shàngxué 上学 to go to school, to attend school
shàngbiān, shàng 上边, 上 on (top of)
shāngdiàn 商店 shop/store
Shànghǎirén 上海人 Shanghaiese
shàngkè 上课 to attend (a) class, to go to class
shàngwǎng 上网 to go online
shāocài 烧菜 to cook
shāofàn 烧饭 to cook
sháozi 勺子 spoon
shéi 谁 who, whom
shēn 深 dark (colors)
shěng 省 to economize
shēnghuófèi 生活费 cost of living
shēngrì 生日 birthday
shēngwù 生物 biology
shénme dōngxi yě 什么东西也 anything
shénme rén yě, shéi yě 什么人也, 谁也 anyone
shénme shíhou 什么时候 what time, when
shénme 什么 what
shēnqǐng 申请 to apply
shěnshen 婶婶 aunt (father's younger brother's wife)
shétou 舌头 tongue
shī 诗 poetry
shí'èr yuè 十二月 December
shíyī yuè 十一月 November
shí yuè 十月 October
shí 十 ten
shì 是 to be
shìchǎng 市场 market
shí'er 十二 twelve

shíhou 时候 time (in broad terms)

shíjiān 时间 time (in hour and minutes)

shímáo 时髦 fashionable, in style

shíwù 食物 food

shíyànshì 实验室 laboratory

shíyī 十一 eleven

shízhōng 时钟 clock

shízi lùkǒu 十字路口 intersection

shòuhuòyuán 售货员 store clerk

shǒu 手 hand

shǒubiǎo 手表 watch

shǒuwàn 手腕 wrist

shǒuyīnjī 收音机 radio

shǒuzhǐ 手指 finger

shū 书 book

shuākǎ 刷卡 to pay by credit card

shuāng 双 pair

shūcài 蔬菜 vegetables

shūdiàn 书店 bookstore

shuì 睡 to sleep

shuìjiào 睡，睡觉 to sleep

shuǐ 水 water

shuǐguǒ 水果 fruit

shūjià 书架 bookshelf

shuō 说 to say, to speak

shūshu 叔叔 uncle (father's younger brother)

shúxī 熟悉 to be familiar with

sì yuè 四月 April

sì 四 four

sìjìdòu 四季豆 string beans

sīrén bǔxí 私人补习 private tutoring

sìshí 四十 forty

suān 酸 sour

suàntóu 蒜头 garlic

sūdǎ shuǐ 苏打水 soda

suǒyǐ 所以 therefore

T

tā de 他的 his

tā de 她的 her (possessive pronoun), hers

tā 他 he, him

tā 她 she, her

tái 台 measure word for machines

tài 太 too

Tàijíquán 太极拳 Taiji / Tai Chi

tàitai 太太 Mrs., wife

tāmen de 他们的 their, theirs

tāmen 他们 they, them

tán gāngqín 弹钢琴 to play piano

tán 弹 to play (piano), to pluck

tāng 汤 soup

tàng 烫 hot, scalding

táng 糖 sugar, candy

tǎng 躺 to lie down

tāngchí 汤匙 spoon

tángdì 堂弟 cousin (father's brother's son, younger than you)

tánggē 堂哥 cousin (father's brother's son, older than you)

tángjiě 堂姐 cousin (father's brother's daughter, older than you)

tángmèi 堂妹 cousin (father's brother's daughter, younger than you)

tántan 谈谈 to have a chat, to discuss

tǐyù 体育 sports

tī zúqiú 踢足球 to play soccer

tī 踢 to kick

tiān 天 day

tián 甜 sweet

tiándiǎn 甜点 dessert

tiáo 条 measure word for garments worn over the lower half of the body, or for the objects that are long and thin, also for animals (dogs, fish, bulls...)

tiàowǔ 跳舞 to dance

tīng 听 to listen

tǐng 挺 quite, very

tīngdào 听到 to hear

tǐwēn 体温 temperature (body)

tíxǐng 提醒 to remind

tǐyù 体育 sport

tōngcháng 通常 usually

tóngshì 同事 colleague

tóngxué 同学 classmate

tóu tòng 头痛 to have a headache

tóuyūn 头晕 to feel dizzy

tǔdòu 土豆 potato

túhuà 图画 painting

tuǐ 腿 leg

tùle 吐了 to vomit

túshūguǎn 图书馆 library

túshūzhèng 图书证 library card

T-xùshān T-恤衫 T-shirt

W

wàibiān 外边 outside

wàigōng 外公 grandfather (maternal side)

wàiguó 外国 foreign

wàipó 外婆 grandmother (maternal side)

wàitào 外套 coat

wàiyǔ 外语 foreign language

wán de kāixīn 玩得开心 to have fun

wán yóuxì 玩游戏 to play a game

wǎn 碗 measure word for soup, rice; bowl

wǎn晚 evening

wǎncān 晚餐 dinner, supper

wǎng qián 往前 to go ahead

wǎng yòu zhuǎn 往右转 turn right

wǎng zuǒ zhuǎn 往左传 turn left

wàng 忘 to forget

wǎngqiú 网球 tennis

wǎnshang 晚上 evening, night

wàzi 袜子 socks

wèi tòng 胃痛 to have a stomachache

wèishēngjiān 卫生间 bathroom

wèishénme 为什么 why

wèn 问 to ask

wénjiàn 文件 document, file

wènlù 问路 to ask directions (lit., to ask the road)

wēnxí 温习 to review

wǒ bù xiǎng … 我不想 … I don't want to …

wǒ de 我的 my, mine

Wǒ xiǎng yào … 我想要 … I would like to have …

Wǒ yào … 我要 … I need …

wǒ 我 I, me

wòfáng 卧房 bedroom

wǒmen de 我们的 our, ours

wǒmen 我们 we, us

wǔ yuè 五月 May

wǔ 五 five

wǔcān 午餐 lunch

wùlǐ 物理 physics

X

xì 系 department (college level)

xī cān 西餐 western cuisine

xǐ 洗 to wash

xī 西 west

xiā 虾 shrimp

xià chē 下车 to get off (a vehicle)

Xià cì jiàn! 下次见! See you next time!

xià ge lǐbài 下个礼拜 next week

xià ge yuè 下个月 next month

xiàbiān, xià 下边, 下 under

xiān 先 first

xián 咸 salty

xiǎng 想 to want, think, would like …

xiàng 象 elephant

xiāngcǎo 香草 vanilla

Xiānggǎngrén 香港人 Hongkongese

xiāngjiāo 香蕉 banana

xiànjīn 现金 cash

xiānsheng 先生 Mr., husband

Xiànzài jǐdiǎn? 现在几点? What time is it now?

xiànzài 现在 now

xiǎo zhèn 小镇 small town

xiǎo 小 small

xiǎojie 小姐 Miss., young lady

xiǎoshí 小时 hour (amount of time)

xiǎoshuō 小说 novel

xiǎotuǐ 小腿 calf

xiǎoxīn 小心 to be careful

xiǎoyè 宵夜 late night snack

xiàoyuán 校园 campus

xiàozhǎng 校长 principal

xiàtiān 夏天 summer

xiàwǔ 下午 afternoon

Xībānyá 西班牙 Spain

Xībānyárén 西班牙人 Spanish (people)

Xībānyáwén西班牙文 Spanish (language)

Xièxie. 谢谢。 Thank you.

xiédiàn 鞋店 shoe store

xiézi 鞋子 shoes

xiězuò 写作 writing

xǐhuan 喜欢 to like

xīn 新 new

xīngqī èr 星期二 Tuesday

xīngqī liù 星期六 Saturday

xīngqī sān 星期三 Wednesday

xīngqī sì 星期四 Thursday

xīngqī tiān 星期天 Sunday

xīngqī wǔ 星期五 Friday

xīngqī yī 星期一 Monday

xīngqī 星期 week

xìng 姓 surname, to be called

xìngqù 兴趣 interest

xīnshuǐ 薪水 salary

xiōngbù tòng 胸部痛 to have chest pain

xiōngbù 胸部 chest

xiōngdìjiěmèi 兄弟姐妹 sibling

xǐshǒujiān 洗手间 restroom

xiūxi 休息 to rest

xìyuàn 戏院 theater
xué 学 to study, to learn
xuésheng 学生 student
xuéxiào 学校 school
xuēzi 靴子 boots

Y

yā 鸭 duck
yáchǐ 牙齿 tooth
yángcōng 洋葱 onion
yǎnjing 眼睛 eye
yánjiūshēng 研究生 graduate student
yánsè 颜色 color
yánjiūyuàn, yánjiūsuǒ 研究院, 研究所 graduate school
yàofáng 药房 pharmacy
yào 要 to want
yě 也 also
yèxiāo 夜宵 late night snack
yéye 爷爷 grandfather (paternal side)
yībǎiwàn 一百万 one million
yībǎi 一百 one hundred
yī bēi jiǔ 一杯酒 a glass of wine
yī dǎ 一打 one dozen
yī diǎndiǎn 一点点 a few/a little
yī huìr 一会儿 a while
yīqiān 一千 one thousand
yīwàn 一万 ten thousand
yī yuè 一月 January
yī 一 one
Yìdàlì 意大利 Italy
Yìdàlìrén 意大利人 Italian (people)
Yìdàlìwén 意大利文 Italian (language)
yífu 姨夫 uncle (mother's sister's husband)
yīfu 衣服 clothes, clothing
yímǔ/yímā 姨母/姨妈 aunt (mother's sister)
yìnbiǎojī 印表机 printer
yīnggāi 应该 should, ought to
Yīngguó 英国 Britain
Yīngguórén 英国人 British (people)
Yīngwén 英文 English (language)
yínháng 银行 bank
yínsè 银色 silver
yīnwèi 因为 because
yīnyuè 音乐 music
yīqǐ 一起 together
yīqián 以前 ago
yīqiè 一切 everything

yīshēng 医生 doctor
yīxiē 一些 some
yīyàng 一样 same
yīyuàn 医院 hospital
yīzhí wǎng qián zǒu 一直往前走 go straight ahead
yīzhí 一直 straight
yǐzi 椅子 chair
yòng zhīpiào fùqián 用支票付钱 to pay by check
yōngjǐ 拥挤 crowded
yǒu duō yuǎn? 有多远? how far?
yǒu rén 有人 someone
yóuyǒng 游泳 to swim
yòu 右 right
yǒu 有 to have, there is/are
yòu … yòu … 又 … 又 … and (for connecting two adjectives or adverbs)
yǒu … nàme 有 … 那么 as … adjective/adverb as … (used for people and things far away)
yǒu … zhème 有 … 这么 as … adjective/adverb as … (used for people and things nearby)
… yǒu méiyǒu … ? … 有没有 … ? Do (you) have … ?
yòubiān 右边 the right side of
yóujú 邮局 post office
yú 鱼 fish
yuán 元 currency unit, equivalent to the dollar unit
yuǎn 远 far
yuángōng 员工 staff
yuǎnzú 远足 hiking
yuè lái yuè 越来越 more and more, less and less
yuè 月 month
yuē 约 to make an appointment, to make a date
yújiā 瑜伽 yoga
yǔmáoqiú 羽毛球 badminton
yùndòngxié 运动鞋 sneakers
yùxí 预习 to prepare for a lesson
yǔyī 雨衣 raincoat
yùyuē 预约 to make an appointment

Z

zài … hé … zhōngjiān 在 … 和 … 中间 between … and …
Zài gěi wǒ … 再给我 … Give me another …
zài jiā 在家 at home
Zàijiàn. 再见。 Goodbye.
zài lái … 再来 … one more, another
zài lái yīdiǎn … 再来一点 … a little more of …

zài lùkǒu 在路口 on the corner

zài nàli 在那里 over there

zài nǎli? 在哪里? (At) where? Where is … ?

zài nǎli? 在哪里? Where is … ?

zài 再 again

zài 在 at, in, on; particle indicating an ongoing action, to be (located) at

zāng 脏 dirty

zǎocān 早餐 breakfast

zǎoshang 早上 morning

zěnme yàng? 怎么样 how … ?

zěnme zǒu 怎么走 how to get to … ?

zěnyàng 怎样 what, how

zhàn 站 to stand

zhāng 张 measure word for objects that have a flat surface (tables, desks, chairs…)

zhāngkāi 张开 to open (the mouth)

zhǎo 找 to look for, to find

zháoliáng 着凉 to catch a cold

zhàopiàn 照片 photograph

zhàoxiàngjī 照相机 camera

zhèbiān 这边 this way

zhège lǐbài 这个礼拜 this week

zhège yuè 这个月 this month

zhèxiē 这些 these

zhe 着 particle indicating an ongoing state of being

zhè 这 this

zhèlǐ 这里 here

zhéxué 哲学 philosophy

zhī 只 measure word for objects that are pointed and thin, utensils, and some animals

zhǐ 纸 paper

zhīdào 知道 to know a fact, to know something

zhīhòu 之后 after

zhǐjia 指甲 fingernail

zhīpiào 支票 check (payment)

zhīqián 之前 before

zhǐshì 只是 it's only …

zhǒng 种 kind (noun)

Zhōngcài 中菜 Chinese cuisine

Zhōngguó 中国 China

Zhōngguórén 中国人 Chinese (people)

zhōnghào 中号 medium (size)

zhōngjiān 中间 between

zhōngtóu 钟头 hour (amount of time)

Zhōngwén 中文 Chinese (language)

zhōngwǔ 中午 noon

zhōngyú 终于 finally

zhǒu 肘 elbow

zhōumò 周末 weekend

zhù zài 住在 to live in

zhuānyè, zhǔxiū 专业, 主修 major

zhǔnbèi 准备 to prepare

zhǔnshí 准时 on time

zhuōzi 桌子 table

zhūpái 猪排 pork chop(s)

zhūròu 猪肉 pork

zìdiǎn 字典 dictionary

zìjǐ 自己 self

zǐsè 紫色 purple

zìxíngchē 自行车 bicycle

zōngsè 棕色 brown

zǒngshì 总是 always

Zǒu ba. 走吧。 Leave. (polite)

zǒulù 走路 on foot

zǒu 走 to leave, to walk

zǒu 走 to leave, to get out

zúgēn 足跟 heel

zuì hǎo de 最好的 the best

zuì 最 the most

zuǐba 嘴巴 mouth

zuǐchún 嘴唇 lips

zuìhòu qīxiàn 最后期限 deadline

zuò xīndiàntú 做心电图 to take a cardiogram

zuò yùndòng 做运动 to play a sport

zuò 做 to do, to make

zuò 坐 sit, to take (a form of transportation)

zuǒ 左 left

zuǒbiān 左边 the left side of

zuòfàn 做饭 to cook

zuótiān 昨天 yesterday

zuǒyòu 左右 around

zúqiú 足球 soccer (football)